# FIDDLER'S
# MOLL

LIFE WITH YEHUDI

# FIDDLER'S MOLL

## DIANA MENUHIN

### WITH A FORWORD
### BY YEHUDI MENUHIN

St. Martin's Press
New York

Library of Congress Cataloging in Publication Data

Menuhin, Diana.
  Fiddler's moll.

  1. Menuhin, Yehudi, 1916–    2. Violinists,
violoncellists, etc.—Biography.    I. Title.
ML418.M27M45   1985        787.1′092′4   [B]        85-2665
ISBN 0-312-28819-0

First published in Great Britain by George Weidenfeld & Nicolson Ltd.

First U.S. Edition

10 9 8 7 6 5 4 3 2 1

195638

To my beloved Yehudi with gratitude
for letting me share his life

## MAREOTIS
### (For Diana Gould)

Now everywhere Spring opens
Like an eyelid still unfocused,
Unsharpened in expression yet or depth,
But smiling and entire, stirring from sleep.

Birds begin, swindlers of the morning.
Flowers and the wild ways begin;
And the body's navigation in its love
Through wings, messages, telegrams
Loose and unbodied roam the world.

Only we are held here on the
Rationed love – a landscape like an eye,
Where the wind gnashes by Mareotis,
Stiffens the reeds and glistening salt,
And in the ancient roads the wind,
Not subtle, not confiding, touches once again
The melancholy elbow cheek and paper.

Lawrence Durrell

# Contents

# *Illustrations*

# *Acknowledgements*

My deepest thanks to John Moorehead, who shaped my unwieldy manuscript with such sensitive comprehension. My gratitude to John Curtis, whose warm encouragement enabled me to keep my nose to the grindstone. My admiration to Jane Price, whose sharp eye translated my baroque hand into legible typescript; and last but not least my affectionate praise to Linden Lawson, for so deftly adding her bright touch to tidy up the whole. And to all those close and valued friends who because of the necessity of cramming these fifteen years into a book have not been mentioned despite their significance, I offer my apologies.

# *Foreword*
## by Yehudi Menuhin

At last Diana has been persuaded to write down something of our years together. I say 'something' advisedly – for although one must indeed travel a certain distance before one can look back, we have covered a lot of ground to put it mildly, both literally and figuratively, much more than might fill five volumes. In fact these pages only cover our first fifteen years together, not even half of our married life. Every day together has been both as wonderfully new and exciting as it was tried and trusted.

As the reader can imagine, Diana's great creative gifts have often caused me to feel a certain guilt – for justice should have dictated that I serve *her* self-expression as she has always served mine.

Diana comprises in her character and keeps in equilibrium a wider range of temperament and seemingly opposing gifts than any other person I know: frugal yet generous, controlled yet full of abandon, critical yet forgiving, authoritative yet humble, independent yet not arrogant, apparently invulnerable yet easily hurt – with a ready dry wit which is never cruel, and combining a most fertile imagination with a most efficient and practical attitude, especially under pressure of crisis. This creation of extraordinary organic complexity is contained in a being of supreme aesthetic nature and presence. I always say that Diana's code is aesthetic rather than moral. What is unbelievable is that an irrepressible vitality accompanies a total lack of egocentric initiative and even of self-confidence, therefore it has taken all this time for her to agree to share with you the impressions contained in these pages. Thus the reader and I will share something of those qualities which have been the inspiration of my life.

# FIDDLER'S MOLL

## 1

# Beginnings

19 OCTOBER 1947. CHELSEA REGISTRY OFFICE. 9 a.m.
Eight people gathered together in No Man's Land rather like a handful of strangers stranded on a wayside platform awaiting with varying degrees of emotion the eventual arrival of a belated train. I felt suspended from all reality, all significance on this chilly October morning, distanced from the whole core of its reason, Yehudi: Yehudi as my world; all things meant him, his life that I would share, all endless toil but a radiant one. And this grey reduction blurred and distorted any vision, creating a weird hiatus that had nothing whatsoever to do with either of us.

It was the archetypal registry office, smelling of stale cigarettes, peeling linoleum and faint disinfectant, furnished with chairs, a desk and shelves of books, doubtless full of the requisite rules, acceptances, refusals, permissions and rejections appertaining to the act of making one flesh twain. And try though I might to listen to the edicts droned by nice Mr Marsh and good Mr Stream, the two improbably and aqueously named officials in charge of the dismal ceremony, my outraged heart was torn by the disparity between emotional meaning and legal desert and sought to escape into an inner dialogue which I hoped would protect my dream against the mildew of this appalling black comedy.

The dusty litany tolled on and I suppose we made the right responses, but my mind's eye was taking over. Against the walls was ranged an incongruous human frescoe: Mama the relieved female parent, my lovely sister Griselda obviously making witty copy in her head, Louis Kentner, her husband, the wonderful pianist, with his best detached Hungarian air, dear old hung-over Harold Holt's red cabbage face, Yehudi's sweet 'Aunt Edie', very happy, and my step-grandmother in her best black looking pure Galsworthy, the only one not out of place.

Yehudi himself looked embarrassed and grumpy as though he had been dragged into the whole setting against his better judgement and would have escaped had he been able to summon sufficient courage. The process of sealing us together continued its ink-smelling way while I tried to recapture a rapture that seemed to have been soaked up by the blotting paper on Messrs Marsh's and Stream's desk as I recalled that first meeting at my mother's house some three years back when Yehudi had shared a very rationed lunch with Mama, Griselda, myself, Anthony Asquith and Michael Redgrave. All of us were grey and thin as stale wafers after five years of bombs and spam, while he strode into the drawing-room looking an insultingly pink-cheeked, fair-haired happy young man, the very image of health and well-being. It was one of those Victorian conversation pictures, 'Virtuous Joy bringing Light to Cynical Souls'.

Yehudi had at that time still been married to his first wife Nola and that day happened to be his little daughter Zamira's fifth birthday. And it was then, so he told me afterwards, that seeing me sitting on the low stool in front of the fireplace, he had decided he would add me to his life. I was later to learn that what Y wants is usually what he gets or, to be more precise, it comes his way without any apparent noticeable effort on his part (Y being our pseudonym to escape the formality of 'Yehudi').

Whether summoned by a nudge from Messrs Marsh and Stream or a rapturous sigh of relief from my mother I don't exactly recall, but I returned from my reverie to find our cue had arrived. Y fumbled a ring (Cartier) from the last of the pockets to be fished in, we signed the book and shook hands with the beaming officials ('I promise you, Miss Gould', Mr Stream had said, 'I'll keep it a dead secret: 9 a.m. on a Sunday. Like when I got Lord Jumper's sixth marriage through without so much as the *Daily Shocker* popping up the coal-hole').

And so, bless him, he did, and we all scooted down the King's Road, past that Dickensian graveyard where as a child my reluctant eyes would be drawn to the sad and withered wraiths of the workhouse women wandering among the headstones aimlessly as though waiting for the Last Bus Heavenwards, to Griselda and Louis's ravishing house. There Griselda, always adding style to the grimmest occasion, cracked open a magnum of Mumm, Mama appraised the ring, glasses were raised, dispelling the last wisps of fog from the gloomy morning, and just as I was beginning to smell a faint whiff of orange blossom, Y put down his untouched glass, took me soberly by the elbow, kissed everyone a hasty farewell, propelled me into the car and off we went hell-bent for the

Albert Hall just in time for the rehearsal of the Paganini B minor Violin Concerto.

And so it has been ever since.

Later we went to Claridges for the first of a few thousand meals eaten in hotel suites at top speed followed by Y's Napoleonic gift of falling asleep as he pulls the last fishbone from his back teeth; then up again scrambling into his afternoon concert suit in which, I remarked (without effecting any noticeable leavening of his mood) that he looked the spitting image of the assistant-manager at the desk below, and off back to the Albert Hall. Puffin Asquith sat with me at the concert and, cocking his head on one side, whispered, 'Darling, what lovely harmonics, no wonder the French call them *flageolets*!'. I, thinking of the beans of the same name, whispered back, 'Yes, the same gastric sound', and got an admonitory tilt of the head to the other side. It all went hummingly and that friendly devoted family that is the Albert Hall audience gave Y a honeymoon of a reception. Of course it was the nearest approach to a honeymoon I was to get so far except for the one delightful spin that evening in Y's new Jaguar. Y drove à l'américaine, ignoring all four gears to the fury of the sophisticated engine which shook, trembled, stalled and hiccoughed through the lovely autumnal twilight, browning leaves dangling like little damp flags from the thinning trees, green banks afire with pyracantha berries and that woollen blue of an English October sky that is like an overwashed baby's blanket, past Knole and up Egg Pie Lane to have dinner and spend the night at the cottage of my great friends, those fine actors, Cyril Ritchard and Madge Elliott.

Next morning after breakfast with the dew barely dried from the lawn we left that haven and drove off to London and from there by train to Derby, or was it Leicester, where the station master staggered me by greeting us in resplendent top hat and tails. William Walton accompanied me to Yehudi's recital during which he hissed in his most Sitwellian manner 'Oh God, *not* the D minor Partita? Let's skip this one and come back at the interval'. 'Willie,' said the new bride, 'I must stay', and with a grim grin he did so.

There followed Glasgow and Edinburgh on which programmes Y first treated me to a piece called *La Capricieuse* by Elgar, so reminiscent of the tinkle of bone china teacups held by crooked fingers that I conceived there and then a book to be called *Grounds for Divorce* in which, should he ever torture me again with that musical pâtisserie, or otherwise upset me, I should inscribe such outrages. Y looked mystified and rather hurt. The book is by now of monumental proportions.

Finally we went off across the Atlantic, in those days of propeller planes which gasped their way in four or five movements, like a Bach sonata, only less harmoniously, until they made New York. If I remember correctly, this one's radio gave out and a steward with a very yellow smile woke us up to announce that we were trying to reach Iceland. Of that stopover all I recall is the wet black rocks in the wet black night and unwelcome gelatinous poached eggs. Also that we did reach New York finally – New York where in those days one could walk safely in the streets, a city which was a tonic with its electric air, its mood of unquenchable exuberance, its tingling nerve. Hardly were we installed and Y had given a recital at Carnegie Hall than we took off again, this time to his house Alma, sitting in the Santa Cruz mountains on the peninsula south of San Francisco in a setting of scrub and wild lilac, live oak (ilex) and madrones, while across the wide valley were stands of huge redwoods and in the little river between, bay trees and eucalyptus, pepper and persimmon.

To an English eye the garden around the house presented a sad prospect with precisely two flowerbeds, one front one back, like parlour carpets laid down to impress casual callers. Inside the somewhat box-shaped white house my spirits sank lower: a suite of 'Heppledale' oak for the glass-walled dining room and one of 'Chippenwhite' covered in extremely expensive clay-coloured linen with a pattern of dull green Chinese dragons in the living room. Pictures? A reproduction of *Le Pont à Arles* and over the chimney-piece one of those oils competently done by a member of the Association of Oil and Water-colour Artists of a white villa draped in very violet wisteria. To my dismay there was added a sudden sense of personal superfluousness when I entered the bedroom (this as in all American houses magnificently equipped with a walk-in cupboard as big as a small room and a glass-lined boudoir masking some six dozen shelves, drawers and shoeracks); superfluousness because although Y's First Mistake (I may well be his Second, but so far I've been too machiavellian for him to discover) had not lived in the house for over two years, every drawer was stuffed full, every hanger dripping with clothes such as I had not seen in a decade, to say nothing of eighty pairs of shoes and a bathroom closet bursting, as were the dressing-table shelves with quarts and pints of scent, eau-de-cologne,

4

lavender water and other more practical and less savoury adjuncts to the art of living as a luxurious female. Dear Y was so happy to show me his home that I covered my sense of rejection as best I could, exclaiming at the lovely huge green-tinted glass windows and the grass-cloth walls that still smelt faintly of hay. And turning my back on the abandoned luxuriousness of all those accoutrements sticking their tongues out at me, I asked him to show me the rest.

The music-room, thank God, was his: wood-panelled with lovely simple couches and a magnificent Bösendorfer piano, with a view to a rock garden (then as bare as a set of dentures) above which was a grey-green slope of feathery olive trees. His study also was his own with a desk, a vitrine full of exquisite ivory pieces, ceiling-high shelves of tattered music bulging out of threadbare folders and – at last – books! Being Yehudi they all of course bore titles such as *Die Gegenwart des Menschen* or *Mann, wohin gehst Du?* or *How to maintain Synovial Fluid in the Articulations* cheek by jowl with *One Hundred and Seventy Easy Exercises Before Breakfast* with, as light reading, Nekrassov's *How to be Happy and Free in Russia.* Up in the penthouse, which had been specially built as a den for his spouse, I found no desk but a divan, the easier on which no doubt to read the set of Kipling and *Forever Amber* which comprised its library. Down again to the charming sun room – all glass – looking out over a stretch of green lawn studded with Chinese Elms to the big swimming-pool; and there at last I found two paintings, one squeezed in a corner, a wonderful green and black and white *Scarecrow* by Portinari, the great Brazilian painter; and the other, also by Portinari, which had been banished to a cupboard, a haunting half-finished portrait of Yehudi painted when Y's plane had once been delayed leaving Rio till the small hours. Y must have been about twenty and, as I recalled him then, rather plump, golden and serene, dreamy and benevolent. But Portinari had caught another inner side, eagle-headed, fierce and far-seeing, a touch uncompromising and aloof, a young man impatient with small views and weak impulses. One, in fact, I was to learn early on to recognize and watch out for. I hauled it out with delight, framed it and hung it opposite *The Scarecrow.* Excellent taunt for all Philistines, I felt.

I also dragged out no fewer than fourteen empty trunks and cases and, folding these lovely clothes with envious care and masses of tissue paper, despatched the lot to New York. In their place I hung my two coats, three dresses and one pair of trousers, filled about half a row of shelves with my sparse jerseys and shirts and lingerie and shamefacedly hooked four pairs of battered shoes on the racks. They looked very lost and forlorn but they spoke of the war and the Blitz and of an extraordinary epoch when values became basic, priorities were gloriously clear and simple and finding oneself alive an everyday gift. Gradually I began to feel less of a stranger.

The following day Yehudi took me down to see his inimitable parents 'Aba' and 'Mammina' in their ranch-house some seven miles away at the far end of the local village of Los Gatos. This house, set in a few acres of orchard and vegetable patches and shaded by large trees, was devotedly tended by my father-in-law. To him it was the heart of all he had longed for when, like so many other young Orthodox Jews bent on poring over the Talmud and the Torah in a dark room, forbidden to fly a kite on the Sabbath, he had dreamed of working the earth, of growing fruit and flowers in the sun, of raising chickens and escaping the intellectual claustrophobia to which he seemed eternally chained. Y's mother, Mammina, had been born in the Crimea. She was very emancipated and Russian with a neat small figure (5 foot nothing and a 21-inch waistline) and long blue eyes set above a pair of prominent Slavic cheekbones, which challenged appraisal of every person, place or thing they encountered. Meeting her for the first time, I realized with a familiar shock that I was back in my old profession of the ballet, with my teacher firmly watching and guiding my every movement, a uniquely Russian characteristic of authority, devotion and high-mindedness that brooked nothing lower than the best and had little patience with either the weak or the second-rate.

Aba was equally small in stature, alive with nervous energy and at this moment of seeing his adored son after months of absence, sending forth sparks of electricity and joy, like some gadget invented to give out light and warmth at the same time. Together they made a strangely disparate couple in temperament, and yet their very differences combined to give an extraordinary sense of vivid life and colour, of two very definite and alive human-beings with not a fuzzy, smudged edge between them – nothing bland nor pabulous – a challenge if ever there were one.

Aba, to judge by contemporary photographs of that period *circa* 1910, had been a noble-looking young man with a slightly fanatic blue eye, straight fair hair and a firm aquiline nose that already betrayed a deter-

mination to battle with whatever and whomever opposed him ideolog-
ically.

Mammina still had traces of the beauty that, according to Aba, had
set all Palestine agog when she arrived there from the Crimea with her
adored mother. At the time her wavy golden hair had been long enough
for her to sit on comfortably and she possessed that peculiar teasing
coquettishness that is essentially the Russian girl's chief weapon. (Yehudi's younger sister, Yaltah, who was an excellent pianist, had the same
long, golden hair as her mother.) Years later I was told by her cousin –
Aunt Edie – that Mammina had turned up in London unescorted at the
age of seventeen, already speaking at least four languages, and had surveyed the city with a cool eye, gone to bed in her corsets and generally
left everyone astounded at her savoir-faire and total independence.

It was some years after that the two attractive young people were to
meet again in New York and teach Hebrew in a New Jersey school.
Here their avante-garde ideas of taking the wretched encased children
out of the fuggy classroom and into the yard to give them air as well as
learning eventually earned them their dismissal. But, having fallen in
love, they finally married and Mammina, typically self-reliant and aloof,
saved enough of her tiny salary to afford to give birth to Yehudi in a
private room of the Mount Sinai Hospital in New York on 22 April
1916. Four years later, when they had moved to California, Yehudi's
elder sister, Hephzibah, was born, whose blonde beauty and splendid
pianism need no introduction. Yaltah was born two years later. Hephzibah was to marry Lindsay Nicholas (Nola's brother) in 1938 and have
two splendid sons, Kronrod and Marston; and later on, by her second
husband, a charming daughter, Clara. And Yaltah had two sons, Lionel
and Robert Rolfe.

Now, as I beheld Aba and Mammina in California some thirty years
after in their comfortable late middle age, set amongst Aba's beloved
orange and avocado trees, his precious apricots, his vegetables and flowers, I couldn't help thinking here was a couple who had miraculously
been spared what most of the rest of us, Jew or Gentile, had endured of
horror, anguish, pain, fear and loss.

My own family's experience had been very different.

# ❧2❧

# Foundations

My mother, Evelyn Suart, had been born in India of an officer in the Royal Horse Artillery and of my enchanting grandmother, 'Goggo', who, abandoning him after five years to his beloved polo ponies, returned to Europe, where for no known reason she put her little girl into a divine school in Brussels. Divine because, finding there that Evelyn was totally incapable of maths, they wasted no further time teaching her beyond the simplicities of addition and subtraction, so that to the day of her death she could neither multiply nor divide. Detecting musicality in her, Goggo took her promptly to the great Belgian violinist Eugène Ysaÿe, who told her to study both the piano and the violin, under two of his assistants, and to return after a year when he would decide which instrument she should play. She did return and duly played the first movement of the Bach Double Violin Concerto with another pupil. 'What was it like, Mummy?' I asked in later years. 'Cats on the roof, darling.' Ysaÿe had said, 'Fais une omelette de ton violon, chère petite, tu seras pianiste.' After studying in Vienna and Berlin, she became one of the leading young women pianists in England, pioneering the then almost unknown Debussy.

My father, Gerard Gould, came from an Irish family who had been mayors and landowners in Cork since the fourteenth century, leaving there at the end of the eighteenth when the local peasantry had burnt down Knockraha, the family house, in one of those idle passionate moments so representative of that unpredictable people. My family had then taken themselves off to Spain and Portugal to restore their fortunes in booze and, having achieved that high-minded aim, left there in about 1800 to settle in Paris where they had lived ever since.

My mother was left a widow after five years of marriage when my father, carrying despatches for the Foreign Office between France and England, contracted typhoid and died at thirty, leaving her penalized by death duties with three tiny children to bring up.

8

Mama, Harkie-Pom or Dame Trample-Pleasure, as she was severally called, was never more than a parent in the strict, late Edwardian sense, doing the conventional thing by her children. Where sympathy, tenderness, warmth, psychological watching were concerned, she was twice over zero. A woman of invincible charm and great musical talent, I early reckoned that she was an arrested prodigy of fourteen years, and philosophically decided that that was the only way to accept her without being irredeemably hurt. Our Chelsea home, Mulberry House, to which my father had moved us all after my younger sister Griselda's birth, was run for my mother and by her. It hummed with life and her musical Sundays brought into our lives a wonderful assortment of European musicians, writers, painters, actors and poets. Nonetheless, the terrible sorrow that enveloped my early childhood was palpable. The shock of my father's death must have been to my mother like having her right arm amputated, leaving her to walk around in the wavering circles which that disbalance leaves, together, I imagine, with the utter disbelief, the childlike anger that she should have been so arbitrarily and senselessly deprived. When I was seven she married again, this time to Cecil Harcourt, then a lieutenant commander in the Royal Navy, and later to become Commander-in-Chief Nore, one position below First Sea Lord.

For much of the time we children were left to the care of nannies and governesses. I can remember vividly my very first recognition of boredom as a solid horror. I was five; Griselda, in the pram, three; and the group of gossiping nannies, with their mouths opening and shutting way above my head like ageing macaws, seemed nailed into the path at the corner of Rotten Row. They, their hapless little charges and their alien chatter came to me like a sudden flash of eternity – of all that life held or ever would hold – ghastly immobility, helplessness, incomprehension; that power of grey serge and flannel around and above me, the bitter wind that hurt my ears and to which all nurses seem impervious. No, it *couldn't* be, it musn't be. I could just reach Nanny's skirt where her corset-end stuck through the thick material, like the buttress holding up the cathedral majesty of her behind, and I tugged at it desperately, unable to bear for one moment longer this intolerable vision of the *néant*, the void that had suddenly appeared. 'Nanny, please, please can we go home, *please?*' I cried up into that dour red Scottish face from Inverness. 'You're a verra rude little girl,' said Nanny, who had never forgiven me for not having the glorious golden curls of my brother Gerard and sister Griselda, added to which she had probably reached a particularly salacious moment in the Kensington Gardens' Nurses' eddas, runes and sagas which I irredeemably, unfortunate child that I was, had managed to ruin.

The posse broke up, I did my childhood act of 'retiring into the wood', my mother's apt description of my withdrawing into my huge mop of woolly dark brown hair when in disgrace with fortune and everyone else's eyes – and trotted home in disapproving silence, holding on to the perambulator. Then and there, deep in my wood, I decided I would fill my life with work, with movement, with anything that would deflect that dreadful grey vision of utter nothingness. The London of the twenties *was* very grey; very rigid, very dutiful and very wetly dull for most small children. Governesses, walks, discipline, Sunday school repeating itself like a pulse – an irrevocable force in one's dominated life.

But there was music; with three Bechsteins in the house and any amount of visiting string-players we children would stay awake half the night, to Nanny's fury and frustration, listening to chamber music in the long room below the nurseries. Alas! although music was in my bloodstream, it was early declared by my impatient mother not to be in my fingers and, after a couple of years of struggling with one of the Bechsteins, I was abandoned with disgust and Griselda took my place with soothing success for Mama.

School followed, adding more grinding effort it seemed, for although Mama never dreamt of helping *any* of us, it was firmly understood that we were always to be top of the class, and the strain was like having a dustbin lid held over my throbbing head ready to close as soon as any inexpertness on my part dropped me into the darkness of the bin. Griselda sailed through school with the minimum of effort. I worked like a desperate little navvy and held my own till advanced maths defeated me and I fell from grace into second place in class, my essentially wandering, romantic mind totally paralyzed before the abstractions of logarithms, isosceles triangles and the mystifying terrors of trigonometry. I could find no poetry in numbers, no feeling, and, above all, no words – words were my symbols, however inadequate – numbers, symbols deprived of feeling – therefore I was no good.

So life got greyer despite four proposals of marriage from Gerard's

FOUNDATIONS

school pals before I was nine; one of whom I knocked out cold on the lawn of Elm Park Gardens when he taunted my cowardly but ravishing, golden-curled Gerard, polishing him off with a good sharp upper-cut which caused a feud between our nurses and a quick end to the tea party. Incidentally, he had not been among my aspirants.

But it was at that very school of Gerard's, Mr Gibbs' of Sloane Street, where the young gentlemen's sisters joined them once a week for foxtrot and waltz, that the dancing mistress advised my mother to have me trained as a ballet dancer. My mother, too preoccupied to take me herself, sent me along the King's Road with my dour Scottish nurse to Phoenix House, to comment upon the classes taken by the retired Diaghilev ballerina Serafina Astafieva. A less likely pair of judges it would have been beyond the wildest imagination to choose, an eight-year-old girl and a caustic, dry inhabitant of Inverness, whose only artistic attribute, as far as I can recall, was that of a pretty fair rendering of 'The Campbells are coming' by means of putting a stout finger up one nostril in imitation of the bagpipes. Be that as it may, this ill-assorted couple climbed the staircase of the lovely old house and entered the first-floor classroom. Someone was banging away at a piano and the air was full of flying legs – we were gestured to a bench by what I can only described as one of the most beautiful ruins I have ever seen – before or since.

Attired in an ancient chiffon evening dress, grey-white tights and frayed satin evening shoes, Madame Astafieva's hair (varied in colour) escaped from a kind of voile bandage which, because of the elegance of her head, assumed the look of a turban. Her skin was very white, her bones very fine, her eyes riveting and the whole fudged by a mixture of what seemed to a small girl to be flour and charcoal, but which I suppose were the cosmetics of those days.

I remember a cigarette in a long holder and a great deal of gesticulation backed by some incomprehensible orders rapped out to the flying limbs. In the front row was a sprite made of the thinnest wire, black and white as a pencil drawing and with the same unerring line – probably just in her first teens – and beside her, slim-limbed and slender with feet like swans' necks and a long, narrow, well-bred face, a youth with a sense of rhythm and direction that also remained in my child's memory. Judging by a fine outcropping of acne, he must have been about sixteen or seventeen. They were Alicia Markova and Frederick Ashton.

Class finished, Madame Astafieva beckoned Nanny and me into her *sanctum sanctorum*, a kind of Tamburlaine tent stretched across the entry to the room, acrid with smoke; a huge table occupied most of it, covered with a thick carpet, a dozen ashtrays piled with pyramids of red-stained stubs, and a welter of books, papers, periodicals, an odd point-shoe or two and some more of those gauzy scarves. She poked around the compost for a time and finally extracted what I suppose was a prospectus, stared at the speechless small child, glared at Nanny, and dismissed us with a wave of her freshly lit cigarette. 'Och! Horrible,' snorted Nanny in her best Inverness, and so reported no doubt to my mother on return. Alas and alack!

One night, it must have been on the return of Diaghilev to England in the twenties, my mother flew ecstatically into the night nursery, tore me out of bed and bid a protesting Nanny dress me at once, as she was going straight back to the Coliseum, where she had just spent the afternoon, to take me to see the ballet. I can remember little now except an atmosphere of pure fairy tale, that heavenly other-worldliness with which most of us are born and which gradually fades from the awakening mind before the rationalization of growing up, as will colour before too crude and naked a light. Everyone and everything was beautiful and it belonged to the world of Once Upon a Time ... I never forgot that dream of sound and colour and smell. For the ballet has its own peculiar smell, of tarlatan and sweat, rosin and benzine; of size and seccotine and of dust, layer upon layer of dust from countless stages stirred and blown about by the legs and arms of a thousand dancers, and by the draughts of a hundred 'flys', stamped into cloth and canvas and ironed in, painted over, sealed, forever imprisoned in costume and décor, and so carrying with it the musty history of each and every one. Once I could have told the *Carnaval* from the *Schéhérazade* backdrop in the pitch dark, merely from the smell alone.

The lady dancing-teacher at Mr Gibbs' eventually returned to the attack, and this time my mother roused herself sufficiently to take me on the No. 19 bus to Cambridge Circus, there to enter, in Shaftesbury Avenue, one of those dread Victorian buildings that would make a prison look like a brothel by comparison. Again we found ourselves in a large studio, one wall a sheet of glass, *barres* on each side, and no sign of a soul. No sign, maybe, but *sound* enough; emanating from a neighbouring room was the yell of an elderly voice in a mixture of Italian,

Russian and English: 'I raz, i dwa, i tri ...'. I sat in frozen terror waiting for some fiend to emerge. About ten minutes later – and the same amount of trilingual abuse – a darling old man tripped out in a black alpaca jacket, with a round head powdered with what looked like rock-salt, merry black eyes and that kind of all-embracing smile that Italians alone can bestow. My mother said something apposite, I suppose, as to my wanting to dance and he ordered me to take off my coat and shoes and get going. I daren't think what idiotic gyrations I offered in an attempt to convince him, but Enrico Cecchetti, the Diaghilev Ballet's great teacher, after turning me this way and that and pinching my legs and feet, for all the world like a farmer judging a heifer at a country fair, pronounced me excellent material and told my mother that I was to come to his class every morning.

Again, alas and alack! She told him that, as it would be a good six years or more before I could prove his trust, she did not intend being landed with an illiterate nitwit of a daughter and I was starting day-school next week. Cecchetti, sensing my disappointment, gave me a hug and told my mother that he had an excellent disciple, Marie Rambert, who had opened a school in Notting Hill Gate. So, at just nine years old, I started ballet classes with her every Saturday morning. My mother promised that if I proved any good, I could go to the weekly afternoon classes and if and when I reached the top class in school, I could attend the grown-up morning classes as well. And so my appalling energy was at last harnessed and the foundations of every gastric agony from which I have ever suffered well and truly and eternally laid. Day-school was from 9 a.m. until 1 p.m.; up to the heights of Notting Hill on the No. 31 bus, hungrily chewing sandwiches while I tried to concentrate on my 'prep'; then the class, which in the main consisted of one long abrasive shout – we were like vegetables to be cleaned and scraped on a nutmeg-grater; a run for the bus, a long rattle home to Chelsea; gobbled nursery tea, followed by at least four subjects for prep; supper and bed, worn out. This was from the age of nine to fifteen, when I at last passed out of school and was to win my right to morning classes as well as afternoon ones.

At that time, the early 1930s, Rambert's was undeniably the best ballet school in England, and from it were to come Frederick Ashton, Walter Gore, Anthony Tudor, Andrée Howard – who, from a host of others, became great choreographers – and if I did cry into my pillow most nights and cringe through a hailstorm of criticisms every day, was it not worth being Freddie's first partner at fourteen, creating his first ballet, *Leda and the Swan*, and dancing the title role in Anthony Tudor's *Lysistrata* some years later? One day I plucked up the courage (by then not yet totally doused) to ask Madame who had been the victim of the trilingual exhortations I had heard two or three years earlier through the wall in Cecchetti's studio – 'Oh,' said she, 'that would have been Anna Pavlova having a private class'. I shuddered.

After all, those of us born in the early part of this century felt that we were born for the dance alone, with little thought of such buffers as films and publicity that shelter today's dancers. We were fated to become a lost generation in the annals of the ballet. And had it not been for Rambert, her energy and her vision, we who did belong to her school would never have been carried on to our later careers.

It was the trough of the wave into which we were thrown and in which we struggled; its crest had been the great Diaghilev seasons behind us, and we were destined but to maintain the motion against the next crest, the one that was to carry the ballet to its present popularity. Diaghilev was still alive and was a god – indeed, the God of my childhood prayers was always inextricably mixed up with the Magician of the *Petrushka* curtain, reposing with a faintly canny benevolence in a beautiful blue bath robe upon a fluffy cloud, and therefore he was also somehow Serge Diaghilev.

Thus we bore patiently the cold, damp studios, the constant and vituperative correction, the long, exhausting hours spent steaming in the depressing penumbra of the inadequate electric light. We were taught that everything must come second to the dance. We were not to skate, to ride, to ski; never were we to smoke or to drink; and was not the great Karsavina the very embodiment of Stanislavsky's dictum: 'You must love Art in yourself and not yourself in Art'?

And so we grew up, slogging our way through *cabriole* and *entrechat*, battling with *batteries* and all the hideous muscular agonies which lay between us and our elusive goal, and every year the Diaghilev Ballet arrived to perform in London and refresh our faith, to lift us from physical despair to airy regions, to a phantasmagoria wherein the stubborn flesh was magically subdued and where the limbs of the dancers made poetry of problems. And we were blessed, for were we not growing up in a world in which the fairy-tale need never desert us, where it would be forever tangible, a thing of magic and yet of flesh and blood, transcendental though actual, at once a legend and a fact? Small wonder I sometimes put my clothes on back to front and didn't know Chelsea from Fulham. . . .

Gradually we came to know the great names: Léonide Massine, Lydia Sokolova, Lubov Tchernicheva, Alexandra Danilova, Anton Dolin, George Balanchine, Bronislava Nijinska, and a score of others, and if my style has suddenly become reminiscent of a telephone directory, then the reader must just bear with me, for those names were as magic – as an incantation to us – and were the very essence of our lives.

Just as in these days schoolgirls and boys follow their favourite film star, or pop idol, pinning his or her image on the wall, so we would cull from those few magazines which published them pictures of Danilova in *Bal*, of Nemchinova in *Biches*, or Lopokova in *The Good-humoured Ladies*. And how much more satisfactory were our pin-ups, what sound and movement they evoked; how inspiring it was to enjoy a world outside this one of bus tickets and banana skins, to grow up knowing that there really are Elysian fields to dance in, that one need never entirely abandon those illusions which are so swiftly shattered by the ink bottle and the blackboard; the exquisite dream, then, was ours of escaping into a planet hung with the heaven's embroidered cloths and where the people trod so softly that they never harmed our dreams. . . . This was the fabric of our lives, the background against which we worked, the inspiration which drove us to emulate that which we yet knew to be unattainable.

Then one day, when I was at my most elated (for was not the Ballet in London, and had not my mother already taken me *en matinée* to see *Aurora*, *Sylphides*, and *Petrushka*?), Marie Rambert rang early and asked my mother not to let me go to school that morning, but to pack me off to class and, above all, to see that I was furnished with a clean tunic. I was evidently well on my way to earning the title bestowed on me some years later by Freddie Ashton – that of the 'Safety-Pin Queen' – and my sartorial condition could obviously not be left to chance.

That was all: class and a clean tunic.

Nor can I remember now, looking back with envy upon that intolerable sense of security and exaltation that is the happy prerogative of youth, whether I half guessed who was thus to be honoured with a clean tunic on my behalf, albeit I do recall a feeling of extreme desire to do well, coupled with the simple pleasure of being given the opportunity to do so. Oh! the lovely, unentangled nerves of the young and dedicated, so soon to become threadbare with the advent of anxiety and first misgivings. . . .

The bus drive to Notting Hill Gate, engraved upon my heart with a tattooing needle, seemed endless, lurching and swaying through the stucco jungle of Earls Court, past the great open bazaars of Messrs Pontings, Barkers and Derry and Toms, to attack with a grind of gears and in a protesting baritone the antique-encrusted slopes of Kensington Church Street, and finally to eject one upon the pavement, from which point could already be discerned the Gothic fastness of Madame Rambert's Ballet School. And over a dozen times I looked into my little case to see whether my clean tunic were still there and as pristine as when I had set out.

At last, however, I reached the studio, ran up that narrow passage, bounded by the disapproving church on the one hand and the gentlemen's toilet on the other, and rushed to the dressing room ... then nearly catapulted from it, so thick was the atmosphere of terrified tension within. The girls, all of them older than myself by several years, looked for all the world as gay as pigs in a slaughterhouse. I changed quickly in a strange silence and we all trooped out to the *barre*. I, beastly child, was as happy as a cricket. No name had been mentioned; the exalted visitor was but a symbol of terror, as yet unmaterialized. Maybe Madame had forbidden those who knew to reveal their dread knowledge? However it was, the *barre* began with leaden legs (and which were in no way lightened by the grimly determined accompaniment of the piano where, in the tradition of the time, a long-suffering and half-frozen effigy thumped out scraps of dog-eared operas and the less happy efforts of those nineteenth-century composers whose music unfortunately had not decomposed as quickly as they). The *barre* over, we continued the routine torture in the centre.

And it was then that the door opened and Diaghilev came in.

He looked as my god should look – imposing, aristocratic, omnipotent. He was the benevolent despot of the blue bathrobe, only he was dressed in black, very elegant and discreet, and, instead of the pointed beard and necromantic hat, there was the magnificent leonine head of dark hair with that single white animal streak through it.

I do not know what the others felt, nor did I ask them afterwards; all

*I* remember was a feeling of electric shock, as though my whole body were galvanized. And I remember class continuing, all of us sweating like bulls; and then Diaghilev calling me out to do a variation from *Aurora's Wedding*. I danced the Carnation Fairy on ancient shoes. Then he asked for more. I distinctly remember (with that perverse and triumphant negativeness that is one of my most salient attributes) doing an *enchaînement en diagonale* which included turns *en attitude*, and which I executed with all the grace of a broken umbrella. ... However, he was very kind about this and I was allowed to recover such laurels as I had gained, by dancing the variation Freddie Ashton had written for me in *Leda and the Swan* (in which I was Leda and Freddie a resplendent swan in a beautiful white feather toque from Messrs Barkers of Kensington High Street).

Class had long since finished and I was alone as I made my *révérence* and retired, somewhat blown, to the dressing room, feeling a trifle flat, as though I had only half explained myself.

I was removing one of the antique wrappings, which in those days I considered adequate point shoes, when there came a knock at the door. I hopped to it, opened it, and there, smiling with devastating charm, was *god*! 'Alors, ma petite fille,' he said, with a lovely Slav accent, 'tu vas venir à mon ballet.' And I, anxious to reveal to my god that I was, however unknown to him, in no need of being proselytized, but already a devoted follower and disciple, answered: 'Mais oui, Monsieur Diaghilev, je viens avec Maman, ce soir!' To which he replied, laughing: 'Non, mon enfant, je voulais dire que tu viendras *danser* chez moi, comme l'a fait la petite Markova avant toi!' That I should think he was inviting me to attend a performance, when he intended that I should join the Company, struck him as very droll and he laughed again and led me out to where Madame was waiting in the studio.

All this had happened in the half-open door of the dressing room, and when the full realization of what he meant dawned upon me I let out some kind of sound, an ecstatic gasp that I had hoped yet held the respect due to a god from his humblest vestal virgin. There followed a discussion between him and Rambert about next year and governesses, and that I would certainly be tall because of the length of my legs (I was then, oh happy days!, not the Eiffel Tower I was destined to become), and that I wasn't to overwork and get too much muscle (Rambert, stoutly: 'But Diana is an EEL!'), but I was drunk on honeydew and took in little. And I was to go at *night* to performances (not just to matinées) as much as possible to absorb as many ballets as I could before the close of the season.

Afterwards Diaghilev would always take me backstage and introduce me to the Company as 'la seule jeune fille que j'aimerais épouser', and to receive such a proposal of marriage, even couched in vague and general terms, completed the heaven in which I had so suddenly found myself.

And so I was to see some of my idols face to face; Danilova and Lifar, and thence to the lovely Tchernicheva, whom he delegated to look after me when the following year I was to join his ballet company.

The months passed, ten classes a week, and then the summer, spent hanging on to the ends of brass bedsteads in small hotels in Brittany and on the Côte d'Argent, doing my *barre* – always that benighted *barre* – slipping on linoleum, the bed skidding away from my grim grip, now on splintering wood with hard knots to bruise the instep, but always slogging, pulling, twisting, sweating, hoping, despairing, and always before me, now so near, the vision of my gods and goddesses within focus, so that I would forget the weariness of the grind, the tempting sound of tennis balls on the courts outside, the noise of other children splashing in the sea.

And then it was August and one stifling morning I was working early, hanging on to the washbasin in the room in the annexe of a little hotel in Guéthary, which smelled of yeast from the bakery below. The door to the adjoining room opened and Mummy came in, a newspaper dangling from her hand. 'Darling,' she said, 'I am so sorry; Diaghilev is dead!'; and there was no cry of 'The King is dead: long live the King!', for there was only the one Diaghilev and no other to follow.

Nothing that has ever happened since then has quite lightened the heavens which for me the dark had suddenly invaded.

And history or destiny was to repeat itself. Still with Rambert and about a year or more after that first shattering blow, in the middle of class the door opened and the most extraordinary figure stood framed in its Gothic arch; half-bird and half Egyptian Mummy, a small erect dead-white-faced woman with enormous obsidian eyes, black silk hair and wrapped, I realized, in clothes of very chic but very individualist style. She was greeted as the goddess she indubitably was, led to a chair in front of the big mirrors and proceeded to watch the class with a totally expressionless and quite terrifying face – it was as though a spiritual effigy of the Dance had suddenly materialized in protoplasm and I, at least, felt both bewildered and bewitched. By this time I was the string bean Diaghilev had said I would become, therefore impracticable to the Company already forming itself from the School, and thoroughly wretched, demoted and unwanted. It seemed to me that when I was dancing on the right of the front line Anna Pavlova was looking to the left and vice-versa. Heavy-hearted, I made my curtsy with the rest and retired to the changing room. Imagine my ecstatic surprise when two weeks later my mother received a letter from Rambert reporting that Pavlova wished to engage Diana Gould as soloist, that she could be partnered by Aubrey Hitchens, a tall dancer in her company, and that, as she was returning from a holiday to rejoin her company in Holland and from there to London, would I please call on her at Ivy House to settle my joining the Company? The cloud was dispelled, my Olympus was in view once more and soon I would be on the slopes again.

But it was not to be: on the journey from the Midi there was an accident on the line and all the passengers were made to leave the train; in a cold damp dawn Anna Pavlova contracted pneumonia and died within two weeks on 23 January 1931.

I was beginning to believe that there had been a Black Fairy at my christening, and indeed for a great deal of my life I have heard the beating of her wings.

I remained with Rambert until Charles Cochran engaged me for *The Miracle* which was to be produced by Max Reinhardt with dances by Léonide Massine. Beside my understudying the two chief roles, the Madonna (Lady Diana Cooper) and the Nun (Tilly Losch), I and my dearest pal, Wendy Toye, were to act with four lesser dancers as religious novices and fill in the occasional dances with which Massine adorned that wonderful production, which opened on 9 April 1932.

Another and a different wonderland, if you like, but imagine watching and working for the greatest German theatre director of his era and one of the two last great choreographers of Diaghilev – I was still only in my teens; and the tremendous hard work of learning two unwritten mime roles as well as the extra bits Wendy and I were given as the young novices, added to the various dance sequences, entailed a seventeen-hour day.

It was Massine who picked me up by the scruff of the neck and took me to Egorova in Paris – one of Diaghilev's stars in *The Sleeping Princess* and amongst the many great Russian teachers established in Paris since the Revolution. She was stoutish, neat with a handsome narrow head, perfect manners and the most expressive hands I have ever seen in any dancer. Her classes were a revelation and a joy. Cecchetti's method, informed by his own spirit, did undeniably furnish a dancer with a very strong technique, but the latter, lacking the spirit, tended to knock all spontaneous dance out of one, while the lyrical improvizations of Egorova made of every class a performance, cleared the gymnastics from one's movements and related arms, head, wrists, neck, hands and legs into one co-ordinated body that responded to the music. Slowly under that calm but severe guidance I not only regained a little self-confidence but also recaptured dancing.

Soon I was offered a chance by Massine to join the Russian company (Col. de Basil's Ballets Russes) gathered together from the remnants of the Diaghilev Ballet but, foolish virgin that I was, I shrank from accepting and returned to London. However, there my ever-flagging fortune rose again. George Balanchine, Diaghilev's other great choreographer, had formed his own company in Paris and would need two English soloists in order eventually to bring it to London. From Paris where his company was already rehearsing, Balanchine appealed to Rambert and she accordingly sent Prudence Hyman – a lovely natural dancer – and me as the soloists.

Filled with quaking apprehension and wonder, Pru and I arrived at class on a boiling hot June day in a rather small studio with a nasty linoleum floor and were greeted with glares that would have made Medusa's seem like Mae West's in warmth of welcome. But that wasn't all: seated at the piano, very compact and expressionless, with a head resembling the boiled egg of a very rare bird, was George Balanchine himself. We curtsied, he pointed to the *barre* and class began – began, believe it or not, with the Master himself improvising at the piano – an amazing mixture of Cole Porter jazz, Kurt Weill opera and odd Russian melodies, but all wedded in such a way as to create a strong, steady beat and an underlying, if somewhat bewildering, rhythm.

He was determined to torture the British; to wear them down till (if they lasted as long as a week) they would crawl to him on shattered legs and, with tears streaming down their scarlet, ravaged faces, beg for home and country. The *barre* was doubled, the 'allegro' tripled, the 'adagio' quadrupled with nice little invented agonies of his own to defeat any attempt to catch one's heaving breath or even waggle a cramped foot. The remaining drill was made as complicated as possible: all improvised and accompanied by this inspired and extraordinary musical mêlée tattooed on the old upright piano in a kind of secret session with something going on inside his head. Occasionally he would rap out a correction, and would leave the piano stool only to demonstrate the next agony he and his musical *alter ego* had contrived to destroy us utterly once and for all and forever amen.

But we won through – wonder of wonders; one day at the end of that nightmare week, George smiled and nodded, mischievously and admiringly, and we moved into the top-floor rehearsal room at the Théâtre des Champs-Elysées and were appointed our roles. Tilly Losch, Tamara Toumanova's co-star, joined us, most of the company were resigned to accept us by then, and anyway Tilly and I were old friends from *The Miracle* of only a year ago. Balanchine's method was as clear and prepared as Massine's – but intellectually he was of so much higher a calibre that he would always change, risk, challenge himself and his dancers. Therefore one was not only literally but also figuratively on one's toes and slightly fearful of what difficulties and intricacies might be cooking in that still head, behind those enigmatic eyes. For him, it soon became clear to me, the dancer was an instrument through which to crystallize, to materialize his deep musical sense. He was incapable of breaking a musical phrase, unable to compose a single cliché – this was after all 1933 and most ballets were still things of romantic expression or visual beauty – indeed the most modern and innovative had been those Nijinsky, his sister Nijinska and Balanchine himself, had written for Diaghilev. There followed a highly successful season in Paris and what is politely known as a *succès d'estime* at the Savoy Theatre in London, where I had the great good fortune to dance *L'Après-midi d'un Faune* with Serge Lifar.

Three years later when I joined the Markova-Dolin company as soloist, Nijinska herself was to coach me in her old role of The Hostess in *Les Biches*. This was one of the greatest of ballet challenges. More onerous still was that she chose me to be her chief liaison officer between herself and the other dancers.

I would sit all day on the edge of my chair watching for that small beckoning sign from the white-gloved finger, jump to my numbed feet and, straining every nerve, try and understand the mixture of Russian and French delivered in the toneless whisper of the almost totally deaf:

'Mademoiselle Diana,' she would mouth, 'you will tell Miss ... that she is a sylphide from the air and not an elephant with a sore foot.' 'Oui, Madame.' Pause 'Madame says would you dance with more lightness and grace, please.' Swallow and return to chair. And more of the same all day.

She was probably the most directly inspiring of all the Russians with whom I worked. For me she was the epitome of all that had signified the ballet – the dance – and which, given the period in which I was born, meant that wonderful Byzantine fairy tale full of wizards and disembodied spirits and oriental fantasy. And, despite the fact that it mainly contained witches and warlocks and intrigues that would have made the court of Byzantium look like a kindergarten, nothing in all the anguish and betrayal, the endlessly enjoined battles that were particularly the lot of the foreign dancer trying to make her way in the closely guarded territory of the Russian enclave – nothing ever quite tore the fabric of that dream to tatters – not even the splinters of glass in my powder-bowl, the shoe-ribbons snipped just far enough to give way onstage; not even having a revolver pointed at me in the dressing room I shared with her by one of Massine's current mistresses – not the costumes ripped to bits by lascivious fingers for which I was made to pay the fines – above all, not being driven for four hours on end by Nijinska through my role in *Biches* till I fell at her feet with froth on my lips and blood oozing through one shoe where a blister had burst on my big toe. None of it counted when one was within that magic circle, feeling in one's bloodstream the utter commitment, the almost savage passion, the slavish devotion to the one and only reason to live and move and have one's being – the dance. 'The way to perfection', said Walter Pater, 'is through a series of disgusts', and this in a way was what it was – a primeval struggle – but it was electrifying in every sense, for it galvanized even as it shocked and burnt one, and although I only caught the last glimpse, so powerful was the essence that those older than myself, who had known more of that magic ambience, were so impregnated with it that they carried it on as though lighted once and forever by some eternal flame.

I may have only lived and danced in the afterglow but, looking back, I realize I had known and been a tiny part of something very valuable and infinitely precious.

One of my last glimpses of that fantasy world happened in the glamorous interior of the Paris District Metro, rattling alongside Nijinska who had called me to her sad little villa on the outskirts of Paris, and in true Russian fashion was so late that we had to continue our conversation on the way back to Paris, bumping together past that ghastly landscape of pinched, mean, brick houses, fringed with scruffy grass and mangy shrubs, guarded by rusted railings and where every sad street seems to be called either Rue Gambetta or Avenue Jean Jaurès; there she revealed to me her new inspiration for an already half-formed company with Baronova as Assoluta, Dolin as primo, myself as leading dramatic dancer and so on, and would I please gather everyone of those inimitable corps-de-ballet dancers from the Markova-Dolin company for her? The squalid landscape dissolved before my eyes into décors by Marie Laurencin, Matisse, Picasso even, as I listened intently to that beloved low drone, and having arrived at the Gare St Lazare, we hugged each other, arranging to meet within a month in London – September 1939. But Hitler had other ideas and war soon shattered our dream.

## ❧3❧

# Two Kinds of War

Back in London I settled into Mulberry House and it wasn't long before the realities of war appeared right on our doorstep. In the very first week of the Blitz the back of the house was blown out by a bomb, carrying away half the lower staircase and cynically killing the poor parlour maid who had taken refuge under it. The force of the bomb also knocked the dotty Irish cook, eponymously named Mrs Batty, head-downwards into the flour-bin, from which she'd been rescued by the air-raid wardens looking like Whimsical Walker, the King of Clowns and shaking a furious fist skywards yelling 'Bogger the Germans; bogger the lot'.

Despite these irritations I continued to find work on the stage in London all through the War, later on, acting in Barrie's *What Every Woman Knows* at the Apollo Theatre, playing Lady Sybil Tenterden with a cast including Irene Vanbrugh, Nicholas Hannen and Barbara Mullen. It was a hugely enjoyable experience except for the fact that the leading lady took against me because *Picture Post* showed three pictures of my face and one of her behind.

After shooting a few poison-tipped arrows in my direction, she bought herself a second quiverful when she overheard my saying she had a laugh like faulty plumbing. Nor did it help when the reviews claimed the play 'was the wrong way round because Maggie was supposed to have all the charm and Lady Sybil none and the opposite was the unhappy fact'. One cannot win – either one is a popular flop and loved by one's colleagues or a success and loathed. It took me most of my rocky career to learn that sad truth.

When the notice went up for the Barrie play, Cyril Ritchard, rang and asked me to supper, said he'd seen me dance since I was seventeen and would I like to go with them to Cairo and Alexandria to do Frou Frou in *The Merry Widow?* Would I indeed? I leapt at the idea, knocking over my wine glass as was my wont (my encouraging mother used to call me Clumsina) and then, sobering, tentatively asked if I might see the script. Cyril dug it out; there was one long talking scene and song, the rest was a *pas-de-deux* in the last act. Perhaps it was the fault of the translation from the German, but it was quite the feeblest, coyest and most drivelling set of lines I'd ever set eyes on.

Looking at Cyril and thinking here goes one of the best chances I've ever had, I asked whether he would allow me to rewrite the scene in French and English, pointing out that Frou Frou was a French dancer in Vienna and would probably have spoken a mixture of French and German in the original version. Cyril, being Cyril, agreed and I wrote gutter French à la Toulouse-Lautrec and slightly cleaner English.

Be that as it may, when we opened at the Cairo Opera House in 1944 I realized that I had forgotten that French was the educated Egyptian's language, so I had to deal with a roaring audience who understood every dirty phrase, and winkle my way backwards out of King Farouk's box where I had been summoned after the first act, refusing all sorts of lovely and unlovely things and bolting back to my dressing room at the double.

The bliss of Cairo and Alexandria after four years of the Blitz and queueing for two ounces of suspicious cooking fat, of bits of cheese and soap that looked and tasted identical; the bliss of grand young Englishmen queueing up humbly in the hall at Shepheard's while one picked one's fancy and paid the rest back for years of cold arrogance; the utter bliss of finding a whole confrère of poets and writers: Robin Fedden, Bernard Spencer, Gwyn Williams, Lawrence Durrell, Patrick Balfour (later Lord Kinross), of 'tiring the sun with talking and sending him down the sky' – bliss it was at that hour to be young, and to be in Egypt was very heaven. Even the young secretaries at the Embassy wrote poetry and I was treated like Zuleika Dobson by one and all.

Of course there was a darker side: the sickening poverty and disease that crawled around one, clung to one, climbed up one like a plague of insects, infesting one's mind, one's dreams at night, arousing frustrated fury that everyone of the Felahin was born with at least three diseases and was likely to acquire five; that the incredibly bright little eight-year-old boy who could memorize nine orders for food and bring them to the dressing rooms without a single error would be a somnolent sack, soaked with bilharzia within ten years; that those swarms of beggars, whole families with perhaps only one full set of eyes between them, were doomed to opthalmia from birth, to syphilis, tuberculosis and God knows what rotting limbs? Did all this form a kind of deadly compost upon which flourished that magically beautiful quality that was Egypt, the scent, shape and feel of which was intangible?

And yet once one had escaped the modern urban dirt, there was always the desert with its smell of sand cooling after a hot day, of unnameable spices, of the dung of camel and donkey and human being; of the feel of the dawn wind bringing in cleaner air from the empty south; of the vibrations of a vast past great civilization lying above and in and under the sand. Durrell was British Information Officer in Alexandria at the time and he used to drive me out into the desert past Pompey's Pillar to Lake Mareotis, pale cyclamen under an empty sky. 'I've never seen so much room in a sky before', I said. And he answered, 'I'll write you a poem for that', and such was the origin of his poem 'Mareotis', written after I was gone.

For leave I did eventually, with the Company in a ghastly small P & O tub crammed with female Polish soldiers who may have been models of courage and military valour, but who brought up every meal with dreadful regularity at twice-daily boat-drill as we assembled shoulder-to-shoulder on the narrow deck, dodging the Nazi submarines and taking a week to reach Brindisi on the Adriatic coast at 4 a.m. in the sleet of the Bora, a vindictive wind that howls down the narrow sea every winter.

I howled too for the lovers I had left behind, for the bewitchment of Egypt, for the hopelessness of a war that could still be heard thudding and banging away up the coast at Campobasso. And as we crowded into two of those buses, so battered and rusty and scarred that only an Italian driver could revive them from their imminent demise and shake a last journey out of them, I felt that odd release from life that total misery alone can bring – a kind of drifting, anchorless from all beliefs, all responsibilities, floating in a spiritual vacuum, part soothing, part frightening, totally dark in its wretchedness.

At 9 p.m. we arrived at Bari, as dismal a town as you could hope to see, built entirely on copulation (Mussolini having promised a huge financial grant to whichever city would offer the highest birthrate within the year). It looked to my jaded eye like the best advertisement for a chastity belt anyone could invent. I accompanied the chorus to their dwelling – obviously a disused brothel. When we opened the doors the cockroaches ran with the rustle of dried leaves behind the doors. Dust, must, stale sweat and freezing cold. They all, as should a well-trained chorus, burst into a unison of tears and said they wanted to go home.

And so did I, but, though younger than nearly all of them, I had been put in charge by Cyril. So I charged, ending up most unexpectedly in the office of Colonel Henry Croom-Johnson, a friend of my girlhood, who was doing his accounts surrounded by shelves of Just What I Wanted. 'Diana, by all that's extraordinary, what *are* you doing here?' he asked. 'I'll tell you later,' I said, 'meanwhile I need three dozen thick blankets, six bottles of brandy, three dozen pillows, a dozen bottles of disinfectant, loo-paper and insecticide.'

Eventually I got them all and brought them back to the poor boys and girls whom I found sitting on the filthy beds, eyes swollen with weeping, desultorily kicking at the odd cockroach with a dainty Egyptian shoe and resigned to remain in that state, I suppose, all night. After distributing the various booty and keeping back one bottle of brandy and a sample of other essentials, I and my companion, the sweet young singer Georgina, made our way to our assigned star-status dwelling: clearly, at one glance, the smaller and probably grander of the ex-brothels. Together we contemplated with fatigued dismay the two rusty iron cots, the sheets covered with the dried blood spots of crushed lice, rolled ourselves up in our army blankets, took off our shoes and lying on the stone floor, drank ourselves into a stupor of sleep.

The following day we rehearsed in the vast opera house, having discovered that the Nazis, making a great swoop on Bari on New Year's dawn, had blown up every Liberty ship in the harbour carrying all the food supplies and blasted the glass out of every window and skylight in the town as well as having forced the locks off all the doors, and most of the theatre's timbers. So we danced and sang with a light snow falling on our shoulders from the fretwork roof over the stage, while my dressing room window had a large thin paper poster drawing-pinned across it which filtered the icy Bora through in gusts of Banshee fervour. Heating there was none. Madge Elliott, lucky creature, was able to sing her rôle with her mink coat slung across her shoulders. I had to make do with a wilting tu-tu, and a stiff upper lip.

Italy never fails in the dramatic – that is why she is the mother and fatherland of opera. Thus despite the cold, the glassless windows, the doors permanently ajar and the dehydrated potatoes and meat which comprised our twice-daily diet, she lifted us from a low octave to a high pitch of discomfort, from an operatic basso-profundo to alto falsetto by encouraging Vesuvius on that very first day to blow her top. Had we been in Naples, this would at least have brightened our miseries both figuratively and literally, but finding ourselves on the opposite coast, it merely meant that we were subjected to twenty-four hours of raining soot pouring down as though Kafka had rewritten Judgment Day. Cascades of jet-black rain descended in a steady stream on the already hideous carton-shaped buildings and those of us unable to beg an umbrella arrived at the opera house looking as though we were offering the troops a nigger minstrel show rather than the whipped cream delights of Lehar's *Merry Widow*. Hungry, dirty, cold and tired, we thrashed our way through eight performances a week, I, for one, ashamed of my self-pity as soon as I got on stage and beheld those 3,000 soldiers on twenty-four hour leave, and glad to offer a little respite for them in what life they had left.

Over the next few months we took *The Merry Widow* to several other war zones in Europe and our experiences were seldom less extraordinary than those first performances in Bari. In Naples, where we used to be regularly bombed, the Americans in charge of the city would insist on turning off all the lights often leaving us on stage in the middle of a song ('Velia, Oh Velia'), or while I was taking a running leap at a partner, suddenly to become totally invisible. On one occasion Cyril Ritchard was so irritated by the length of a raid that he went out onto the stage, asked the poor marooned soldiers whether they had torches, told them to shine them on us, and somehow we got on with the show and finished amid cheers.

Later on when we were in Brussels we visited the hospitals where the airforce men were undergoing operation after operation to mend their poor shattered faces, some still noseless, some with part of a cheek restored or half a chin; and there one soon discovered how easy it was, after the first ghastly shock of nausea, to transmute these blasted faces into what they represented in terms of courage and daring, and how one could dance and sing to rows of distorted faces because they were not frightening, they were the masks of the spirit of man, Greek masks of Tragedy and Comedy.

It was soon after I returned to London from my *Merry Widow* jaunt that I had first met Yehudi at that lunch at my mother's house. Although

I did not know it at the time, he already shared with me that extra-ordinary brotherhood of war and the way in which the closeness of death brought an evanescent beauty of life.

In between his own professional concerts in America he had sat night after night in La Guardia, hoping for a place on a bomber, trying to get back to his beloved Europe and see if he could do something – anything: play in the park, on the pavement or even the seaside pavilion. Finally, after being turned out once for Mrs Roosevelt, he made it – not on to the pavement, but in factories and with the Navy in Scapa Flow and in other such novel concert halls. Each time he would arrive in England half-frozen after hours spent cramped into the nose of an American bomber, fall out and find how much he could cram into the two or three days before he had to fly back to the States.

He had flown under terrifying conditions to the ice-fogged Aleutian Islands, playing to the soldiers in corrugated iron sheds, dressed in a massive woollen sweater, padded pants stuffed into thick-lined rubber boots, playing anything they wanted to hear from Beethoven through Viennese waltzes to Bartók. Yes, Bartók. And they listened without stirring.

He had flown to Antwerp and given a concert while the Nazis were still in the other half of the city; leaving Antwerp on a mad impulse he had found a plane that would take him on to Paris where he rang his devoted agent Maurice Dandelot: 'C'est moi, Yehudi,' he had said in his usual graphic style. 'Bon Dieu de bon Dieu!' shouted Maurice. 'Par quel miracle es-tu là?' And Yehudi had promptly told him to open up the Opera House (closed these many months) so that he could play the next day. Years later Charles Munch, the conductor of the Boston Symphony Orchestra, told me of that historic concert; of the playing of the 'Marseillaise' for the first time since the Nazi occupation, tears streaming down everyone's cheeks; of the playing of the Mendelssohn Violin Concerto (banned because of the unacceptable Jewish origin of the composer) for the first time; of the audience who wouldn't let Yehudi go and of the US pilot who finally dragged him off the stage, hissing, 'I have no equipment on my plane to fly by night.'

But it was to be some time after that first meeting at lunch before I saw him again. One day eight months later he suddenly rang to say he was about to do the soundtrack for a film on Paganini called *The Magic Bow* starring Stewart Granger and Phyllis Calvert, and would I come to see him at Claridges and have a look at the script? I had to explain to him that after a series of doctor-shaped idiots had thumped my sister Griselda on the back and sent her away with a bottle of No. 9, by which time she could hardly stand upright anymore and was coughing all night, one of them had finally thought fit to X-ray her chest and discovered a large hole in the apex of one lung. Needing at all costs to stay in London with her, and fearful of being drafted into some Service, I had begged Michael Redgrave to let me play the part of his mistress in *Jacobowsky and the Colonel* in which he and his beautiful wife Rachel Kempson were due to star. Luckily he did and I was busy rehearsing and eventually acting in it when Yehudi called. Hardly a step upwards in my career, but a real kindness, for I was able to be with Griselda as she bore operation after fruitless operation with enormous courage and fortitude.

The Paganini script turned out to be quite abysmal – 'Oh! Nikkerlo, what gawgeous sounds you draw from that magic bow', and so on. Watching Jimmy Granger being made up at the Shepherd's Bush Studios as Signor Paganini, I asked him how he was making out as a violinist. He explained loftily that while he held the violin under his handsome chin, the leader of one of London's top orchestras stood behind him wrapping the right arm around him so as to move the bow across the strings, while with the left hand he ran deftly up and down the finger board. 'And who does the acting for you between the two borrowed arms?' I asked. Joke: sank like stone. But I don't wither that easily after so many blasting years in the Russian jungle.

Every night during that stay Yehudi used to call at the Piccadilly theatre to take me out, much to the worry of the old stage-door keeper who used to get dreadfully fussed and send me messages saying, 'Don't you remember Miss, your promised Mr Asquith tonight?' Or, 'I'm dead certain Saturday night you and Mr Stepanek [dearest 'Stoppy', who played Jacobowsky] arranged to go to the Savoy?'

But it was to the Berkeley that I mostly went with Yehudi and he slowly began to talk because I never risked asking any questions, only sensed that he was as shocked and sad as a child who has misunderstood something of great value and importance, and who cannot find the way out. His whole unique significance in life had shown itself at a very early age and burnt like a bright light. But now that light was dimming visibly, wavering in the cold and alien draught of an insecurity he had never been brought up to deal with. For, despite all his accomplishment, all his success, nothing had touched his innate modesty.

I began to realize that Yehudi was one of those rarest of creatures, driven by aspirations, never ambitions, and such are in mortal danger of falling like Icarus, doomed by the radiance of their unattainable visions. Myopic to all and everything immediately surrounding them, their power of sight begins where others' ceases. So long as they can reach outwards and upwards, they are relatively safe, but when the unseen chasm yawns, or unimagined objects fly into their path, most often they cannot even navigate with enough skill to save themselves. Dislocated and alarmed they spin, losing focus and balance and, having never grasped for themselves, they cannot perceive any object to hang on to, any lee from the changing wind that is so mysteriously blowing them off course.

The wind which was blowing Yehudi off course was the fragmentation of his marriage, and it was this private side of his life he could not deal with. He was unwilling to face its dissolution, unable to abandon a single one of those myths he had dreamed, had in fact been encouraged to believe in within the closed circuit of his family life. It was this incapacity to face facts that was slowly unbalancing him. Hence the growing bewilderment, the encroaching knowledge that a very real and deep feeling for another was no longer reciprocated, that with his typical generosity of heart it must be his own fault, hung like a cloud about him, darkening that sun he had known so long. Helpless and rudderless, he had been losing his way.

Gradually as we talked those evenings, I felt the beginnings of a release in him, the bewilderment gently diminishing.

At the time Jacob Epstein was doing a bust of Yehudi. Somehow, between playing 'Nel cor piu non mi sento' and other snatches of the invisible voice of Signor Paganini in Lime Grove, he was squeezing in an hour or two to sit for that wonderful man. Epstein seemed to be made entirely of small and big solid balloons – big for the torso, two smaller ones for each leg, two for the feet, one for the head, two for the rolling mischievous perceptive eyes and another for the nose. But the hands were no balloons. They were strong supple tools totally obedient to his brain, his heart and his mind. Yehudi was very excited after the first two sittings and asked me to come. He rang again. Disaster. In the night the cat had got lost in the studio and knocked the clay head off its stand, and what was fast becoming an extraordinary likeness had been reduced to a large pile of elephant excrement. There were only two days left to start again so I went with him and sat in a corner and watched those magical hands working away at top speed against time. And when that first sitting was over and I thanked Epstein, he said: 'Come again tomorrow, my dear, he looks quite different when you are there and I want to capture that'.

The head turned out to be as strange and striking as the Portinari portrait I was to find later in Yehudi's house, and caught the inner quality of the ruthless eagle in flight above the earth in pursuit of one single prey, one purpose.

The music for the Paganini film finished and once more Yehudi left to return to his wife, Nola, and the two small children, Zamira and Krov, taking with him all light and warmth and meaning. Meanwhile I remained in London fighting every kind of obstacle in my desperate attempt to get Griselda out of England and away from certain death.

A weary, frustrating month later Yehudi rang from California saying he was coming back and would I wait for him? Wait for what – for whom? For a man who was not free and to whom I had never allowed myself to say even that I loved and valued him more than any other man I'd known? Please don't tie yourself up with that job, he said. I did not dare think or hope, tried not to define the sudden shock of warmth and joy, suppressed the elation that kept springing up in me like a renewed source that I dammed and refused to consider.

He came that autumn in 1945, gave concerts and again we found each other, sharing like experiences of aspiration and struggle, finding so much in common, such ease and happiness. And still I said nothing, not even when he went away again to fulfil his American tour and I was left more bereft, in deeper desolation than ever, made worse by the continuing grim battle to get permission to take Griselda to Switzerland. I did at last win that battle and we reached the sanatorium in Switzerland just in time. A month later, said the doctor, and he could not have saved Griselda's life.

The enormous relief, although there was a long slow haul ahead and much danger still, helped greatly to fill the aching gap. The stifled anxiety of those fortnightly examinations which Griselda bore with her special brand of dry wit and courage, her slow climb back to health, all this came prior to any heart's dis-ease. But it was painful to have to live with the thousands of miles' stretch across which my daily letters travelled to Yehudi and the few times in those long months when his faint voice bridged the distance for a few minutes of light followed by an even deeper darkness.

Came the day when Griselda was pronounced well enough to go down to Zürich and marry Louis Kentner. Wilhelm Furtwängler, the great German conductor, and Yehudi were the two witnesses for, yes, he had at last returned. But not on his own. The long wait had ended, but I was alone, no longer even needed by Griselda.

Two and more dark years followed. Yehudi is a man who cannot believe in evil and such a man cannot fight for himself. He may fight big issues outside himself which he feels to be morally wrong and cruel, but those battles wherein he alone might suffer loss – in those he is as though paralysed. Such men are prepared to sacrifice personal happiness in the name of some strange abstract idea, part moral, part theoretical and wholly cosmic. This quality in him filled me with an apprehension sometimes so stark that once, and once only, I had allowed myself to point out to him that we might forever remain apart, because this tendency – part Parsifal, part Don Quixote – in his character would be played upon by those who wished it so. But he had only scoffed at the idea.

And my own incurable pride completed the destruction: 'Let me not to the marriage of true minds ...', I had written in an anthology of verse which I had given him on parting. But it was not the Shakespeare sonnet which applied so much as Marvell's heart-breaking poem 'My Love is of a birth as rare ...' which ends 'As lines ... Though parallel can never meet'. But the blackness and bleakness of stolen love are private pain and those two and a half years of limbo belong to the long past and were to be transmuted into a love that is the more sensitive and valuable for its near loss. On 19 October 1947 at Chelsea Registry Office the dark years finally fell away.

# ❧ 4 ❧
# *Firefly*

I suppose it was while sitting listening to Yehudi rehearsing in the Albert Hall in the aftermath of our scurried wedding that I felt the first intimations that I might have chained myself to a firefly – never still, ever darting from idea to idea, hovering barely enough to ignite, to warm, to glow and then to flit off again to the next unlikely spot in that penumbra in which all such creatures dwell. How much closer to their nature is the French word *feu-follet* with its touch of irrationality and dotty charm than the English 'firefly', for they are surely made of the stuff of magic.

Looking back I think it was the three disciplines of my youth – school, an Edwardian mother who rejected all doctors and medicines, and the Russian ballet, which didn't permit the admission of ill-health for fear of a hard-won rôle being given to another girl – all these three served me in good stead to follow my firefly, to hang on to the tail of the comet I had married, to travel through all pregnancies, ready to have the child wherever the violin was on the ninth month. They had furnished me with an enduring disposition together with a ruined constitution.

For the great advantage of the starched-upper-lip, die-with-your-boots-on, nonsense-Diana, *we* don't-have-toothache is that from a tender age one is equipped with a kind of automatic switch that turns down to a low hum the many signal-sounds of pain, above which one continues the ceaseless journey of work and obligation, responsibility and awareness. Now at last came the joyous relief of being able to be of use to Yehudi after those long, longing, heart-twisting years of waiting, of hope deferred, of mounting fear that he would be lost – not simply to me but to himself and all that he meant.

What I realized then in those early years was that somehow he must be strengthened, helped to envisage the errors – if never the evils – of which mankind is capable, while at the same time I must never spoil the essential fabric that was Yehudi. Early on he once asked me with fear in his voice, 'Do you love me because I am Yehudi Menuhin?' And I answered, 'Of course, silly, because you are one and indivisible, that is what you mean – your whole significance and what you will always be for me'. A strange look of relief and recognition passed over his face as though some knot inside him had been untied.

It was not long before I was initiated into the roving restless life of my firefly. After a couple of weeks at Alma we set out on a long American tour: planes and trains and cars; one night, two nights, some-times the luxury of three in different towns for months on end. And I was pregnant, but in my stubborn way said nothing for I could hardly see the point of telling Y that the sight of Chicago railway depot for the first time in a wave of nausea was unlikely to enhance the view of that city I have since come to love. I continued with the daily tasks of packing and unpacking, sitting at rehearsals and concerts, writing wearily in airports while the blizzards (why are US tours always in the cruel winter months?) held up the propeller planes, until Y one day noticed a change in my waistline and I had to admit that as far as I could tell, given his concert schedule, there would be a child born in Edinburgh some five months from then.

Despite my upbringing I sometimes found the relentless travel dispir-iting. Looking out on rows of chimney stacks and the tattered hoardings of the less salubrious towns, the detritus of those huge industrial cities blown about by the wind, I would suddenly feel total alienation from all that was organic, all that was logical to my whole being – a sort of hideous dislocation from the centre of oneself. And then I would have to force myself to dismiss what ironically seemed the actual, the cruel reality and swing myself up like some monkey into the branches where leaves obscured the ugliness and my mind painted a piece of scenery I could interpose. Cocooned inside one of those erstwhile splendid Amer-ican trains, spending three glorious days free of the perpetual telephone, free also of the huge packets of mail that would fall like some nasty discharge upon us at several different points along our hotel route. I could read again – not just tear through newsprint, daily, weekly, monthly in order to keep in touch with fundamental facts – but read whole books undistracted by the views of tumbleweed rolling dottily across the dry plains of Wyoming or by the sad little towns through which trains always seem to pass. All the time Y sat on Cloud Nine, the

Bodhisattva destined to carry messages between heaven and earth, either practising cross-legged in the lotus position on his bed or simply sleeping his way blissfully from Vinegar Bend to East Overshoe till we reached San Francisco or Cleveland or Los Angeles.

Madame de Staël, writing of travel, described it as 'Un des plus tristes plaisirs de la vie – cette hâte pour arriver là où personne ne vous attend'. And so indeed it is for the one who is not at the centre of the purpose. For Y there was the local agent or a group of devoted female music-lovers, the ladies who had arranged the concert and were all agog to see him. For me there was indeed a certain sense of nobody awaiting me – but it was all so new and my only agony in life having always been that *néant*, a seventeen-hour day, which was and still is our average timespan, can hardly come under that title.

Towards the close of the six-month American tour came Cuba – my first taste of Latin America – and the flat Nordic tang that is the overall flavour of the States and of England was suddenly revived by the Latin warmth that has always, together with the Slavic condiment of my ballet years, been a necessary composite of my nature. Cuba was beautiful in 1948, very Hispanic despite the American overlay. The coffee was ambrosia – never before or since have both the smell and the taste of coffee approximated so perfectly. However Y played rather oddly that night and even more oddly the next, and when I came round after the concert he looked at me as though he thought he knew me but could not put a name to this vaguely familiar female face. Terrified I got him back to the hotel and asked for a doctor. Y, patient as ever and uncomplaining, swore he was quite all right. 'You look, darling,' I said, as I got him into bed, 'like a Spanish pimento and feel like a Russian stove.' Next morning he was ablaze from blond top to toenails with large red spots. Measles, pronounced the doctor and put him on Sulfa drugs. I kept the doors of the suite locked, bribed the maids to bring me a dozen sheets and pillow cases a day, fed him with chicken broth brought by the kind wife of the conductor José Castro, and trained myself to wake every three hours to give him his medicine. They warned me my baby might be born blind and dumb, but I used my switch and turned off that gruesome idea and after five nightmare days the fever broke and Y began to focus again.

Pale and wobbly though he was I got Y back to our tiny New York flat, packed everything in a day and, loaded with eight cases and four violins, we flew to Alma, cancelling the remainder of the tour. Y, healthy in mind and body, quickly recovered and we were soon off once more, this time to Europe, despite his parents' warnings of the dire after-effects of adult measles (such as gangrene, pyorrhea, creeping paralysis of the nervous system, loss of speech replaced by incurable hiccuping and the falling out of all hair in tufts). Small wonder, I thought, that the Bible is so full of miraculous cures. Palestine must have been a fair hunting ground for those who could heal.

In Europe the Russians had blockaded Berlin just as we were about to go there. But I insisted we continue with our plans so we went, landing in Tempelhof in a Berlin still mainly a lunar landscape. There Y played three or four times a day for various causes such as the Jewish community, the Hochschule für Musik and so on. Together with Furtwängler we visited the Russian zone, greatly to the fury of the Russian Kommandantur who did not wish Yehudi as an American to disprove that his country was a land of illiterate yokels. About ten Russian officials sat in the box next to mine, looking like troglodytes out of a sick strip cartoon, sunk up to their short necks in grey-green uniforms with padded shoulders that jammed them together, giving the impression that they must come in lots of half-a-dozen and have to be prised apart. Caps on all the way through, arms folded, brows down like furry balconies, lips set tight – the very picture of official disapproval.

And Oh!, the utter fury when the East Germans rose as one man and cheered with ecstatic relief and joy at the end of the Beethoven Violin Concerto. I could feel it mount in decibels and turning towards them beamed my most idiotically ingratiating smile. I thought they would lean over the low barrier and hit me but no, they looked dreadfully discomforted, wriggled as much as their wadding allowed and one even threw me a guilty glimmer of a grin. For Russians have music in their blood, and through all the bindings of military red tape, the pride and power of conquerors bought at the price of losing twenty million countrymen, there was that Russian emotion, that feeling for poetry, the theatre, dance and music.

A little later in our journey Yehudi announced that his two children Zamira and Krov would be spending the summer with us. When I pointed out that in my present condition I wasn't exactly suited to look after them, Y suggested that we contact a Signorina Anna whom his mother had once employed for his sisters in Italy. How long ago was that?, I asked. Eighteen to twenty years, he replied. Do you expect she will still be living at the same address in Milan? I went on. Ever the optimist, Y tried and of course there she was.

In those days Y had a wonderful address book copied for him by his devoted Aba in which delicious character assessments were typed alongside the names. Thus: Morton Fitzbein, and inserted before the address, 'A ROGUE' or Henrietta Stark, 'MONSTER', care of Mr Marston P. Waveslanger, 1400 Ninety-first Street, Nickel City, Illinois'. All that was abstract and dry in the arithmetical addresses of those grid-system cities was illuminated by Aba's pithy images. Today when Y's address book would make Webster's dictionary look like one month's copy of *The Reader's Digest*, I miss sorely that first relatively modest lively tome.

As the time for the birth approached, I looked around for a base, finding one in a beautiful Lutyens house called Greywalls near Edinburgh. There we were to take a whole wing which would house the six of us, for by now Signorina Anna had arrived.

Meanwhile Yehudi had blithely gone off to Budapest with his longtime and devoted Belgian-French accompanist Marcel Gazelle and a complete silence had descended on them. I, awaiting him in London for the overnight train to Edinburgh, felt a mounting apprehension. At last Marcel came through on the telephone from Belgium breaking the news as gently as possible that two Russian soldiers had taken Y off the plane in Prague giving no reason. The plane had then left without him. I replaced the receiver paralyzed with fear.

I was now within a week of giving birth to our first child, and already had Y's children and Signorina Anna on my hands. What was to be done? The only answer, I decided, was to proceed with the plans and go on the night train to Edinburgh. Inside my compartment I sat too frozen with fear and anguish even to be able to undress, there on the edge of the bunk as the train hurtled through the night, and try though I might, and pray though I did, I could not bring myself to believe I would ever set eyes on Yehudi again. Why had they taken him off the aeroplane? I knew well enough by then that to seek reasons from Russians was a fruitless pursuit. As far as I could assess, they had nothing against him. In fact, at the end of the War in 1945 he had been the first Western musician to be invited to Russia, had been fêted night and day, and had returned to London on his way back to the States with an enormous tin of caviar for me.

I slept little that nightmare night and was still in a state of acute anxiety when we left the train at 6 a.m. and drove to Greywalls. At the hotel there was no news. All that endless day I heard nothing, sat glued to the telephone springing to answer it when it rang, only to be rebuffed cruelly by somebody from the Edinburgh Festival, or my kind Griselda seeking news.

Evening arrived still without news: I read to the children and tucked them in, tried to stop Signorina Anna from eating her way through all next week's rations carefully stored in the little pantry. Then I returned again to my vigil – to that awful hiatus I had hung in for God knows how long. It was impossible to read, to write, to concentrate, the hours dripped away minute by minute like a Chinese torture. I felt leaden as though all spirit, all life, all courage had left me and soon my reason would join the retreat – and perhaps that might mean peace.

Suddenly the telephone rang. I hardly had the will to answer it. I could not face yet another fall from hope. It went on ringing. I forced myself to get up. Lifting the receiver dully, I heard Yehudi's voice. At first I was too numbed with pain to recognize it and then I remember being totally unable to speak. He was in London and would drive up with Louis Kentner as soon as possible the next morning. Was I in bed? It was long after midnight so he'd not been able to catch the train. I managed to gasp something, hung up and fainted.

He finally arrived the following afternoon, Louis having driven his Triumph so close to an oncoming truck as to have practically shaved off the whole of one side. But nonetheless, that added hazard apart, they were there and life had begun again and Zamira and Krov were jumping round him like two puppies while Signorina Anna cried a little to an accompaniment of 'Ma, caro Yehudi', six times over. As for Y's abduction, it always remained a mystery.

That Wednesday night I felt the first pains coming on, but sure that like all dancers I would take an age to produce the poor child, I said nothing, wrote letters and went to bed alive and released. By morning the pains were more insistent but I was still reluctant to leave the children. However, on Thursday evening Y took me in his car to the nursing home in Edinburgh some twenty-five miles away. Hiding the severity of the cramps that had seized me during the drive, I persuaded him to go and get a good night's rest at the house of a friend nearby. No sooner had he gone than I crawled into bed opposite which there was a steel engraving of *The Monarch of the Glen*, intended no doubt to divert me from my increasing pains. I never had liked that conceited animal and my distaste for it grew as night drew on.

There then began what seemed like an epic battle during which I lost command of all sensation, all logical thought, all normality. I was in a limbo of red-hot pain which deprived me of everything except a terror – an increasing fear that the frightening battle in which I was involved was between myself and the baby. It was as though It and I were the antagonists and It was furious with me for denying It light and air.

Eventually on 23 July 1948, about forty-eight hours after the first pains, the poor child was finally hauled out. And the next morning when I came to they showed him to me: six pounds, battered red and blue with its struggle and its poor little eyes swollen tight shut. But it was alive and sound in all its parts and, perhaps because I had kept my promise to myself not to utter one moan or yell, the baby compensated by howling almost ceaselessly through the first weeks of its hard-won life.

Yehudi was relieved and exultant and dashed off to register the baby's name and all the other nonsenses that prove to bureaucracy that one exists. When I had first realized that I was pregnant, I had said firmly to Y that after a quick glance round the roster of names of the second and third generation of his family outside Russia, and finding that (with the exception of Zamira) most of them comprised the oddest nomenclature imaginable, I would rather propose a name myself. I did not want the wretched child to live its life out bearing the burden of Dniepopetrovsk (or Gurzoof) Menuhin.

Also I thought it high time that a nice simple Anglo-Saxon name be introduced: Smith, for example. So prenatally Smith was the baby's term of reference and, in fact, all his name-tapes were marked S.M. However, although Smithy remained his nickname, gradually to turn into 'Mita' which was his own and his Swiss nurse's approximation of it, Y did not inscribe it on his official birthday registration. He was Gerard (after my father's Irish family who were always called Gerard or Garrett) Anthony (after my most beloved friend and his godfather Anthony Asquith) Menuhin – his godmother was the kindliest of friends, Yvonne Caffin, who had helped prepare his layette with all the skill her career as Chief Wardrobe Mistress to Rank's film productions offered – and about two hundred telegrams arrived from all corners of the world to greet the battered pair.

A month later the grand tour began again. With Smithy and his Scottish nurse Craigie we left Greywalls and returned to London where we despatched Y's two older children back to their mother in New York. After some concerts in London we moved on to Paris into a lovely apartment in Passy lent by a close friend, Gilberte Dreyfus, high above and overlooking the Seine, with a cook, Emma, to match in style and standard.

How odd it was then to be in my beloved other city once more – not in my grandmother's house, nor at Kschessinskaya's classes, not dancing with Balanchine at the Champs Elysées, but married to Yehudi, and with our child hardly three months old. What did I feel? A certain accomplishment, a certain loss. I had fulfilled my role as a woman and abandoned it as an artist.

If one performing artist marry another, it is obvious that one of the two must dissolve his or her persona in the other. As there was no question as to which of us had fulfilled himself to the greater degree in his purpose, then it was for me to sink my aspirations, my visions, my hope and what talent I had had into the task of offering what help, counsel, experience were mine – much as a good gardener would deal with a precious plant. I had to learn to abandon all sense of that egotistical road known as a career, to quell the wellspring which all artists know rises unbidden to spur them onwards to the next hope of achievement. Instead this energy must be turned, redirected, whatever the pain or the loss, in another direction, the long and sometimes bitter experiences used to a profitable end, no longer for one's own benefit, but for another's.

It is tantamount to a retreat from all that one's life has signified in terms of self, a swerve, as it were, from a straight line, a curve into another direction. However there is no question of abandonment or even change in its simpler sense, merely of redeployment, of giving to someone else what once one concentrated on oneself.

I cannot pretend that on occasion I would not look over my shoulder as though beckoned by that fast-dissolving shadow of the dancer and actress. I found this especially poignant in the early years where those concerts which took place in theatres would awaken an agonizing nostalgia as I walked backstage through the dock and the wings, smelled the size and dust of old scenery, felt the boards beneath my feet; or when I glanced involuntarily at that dark beyond which had been my fourth wall and the well, dimly lit by faces absorbing what one had hoped to convey, the audience no longer mine now, but Yehudi's always and forever.

At such times a momentary melancholy would envelop me like a shroud. What shroud? I would say to myself with a shrug: a dirty old ballet tu-tu and all that went with it: the plots and intrigues, the bits of glass in my powder-box, the tintacks strategically placed in my shoes, the bestial work and the shattering disappointments. It is those I must recall – not Nijinska, not Massine, Balanchine, Lifar, Dolin, Tudor, Ashton, with whom I had danced or worked, not Pavlova nor even Diaghilev.

No, this was my destiny – concert picnic-bag, clean underwear and all and henceforward I was to spend my life on the other side of the footlights and be determined not to feel turned back to front. Mine was also the unbelievable good fortune of having been given the care of a unique human being.

# 5

# The Menuhin Caravan

How does one attempt to write about a life so clotted with work, events, duties, marriage, motherhood, step-motherhood, courier-en-chef, amanuensis and a hundred other indefinite rôles – all these undertaken at a cracking pace, all to be managed on the move, including one's entire équipage from human to inanimate, from small children to suitable clothes, from staff to schools – how can one describe this palimpsest of a life in a handful of pages? The task is a kind of 'A la recherche du temps courru', an attempt to describe part of a vivid and turbulent life through which I had constantly to canter without letting go of the reins.

Griselda had always said, from her favourite position prone on the sofa with a volume of Fielding (or Smollett or Sterne) in her hand, 'Diana, if she can find nothing else to do, spills soup down her dress and washes it off'. Unkind maybe, but extremely apt. Now it would seem in these early years of my marriage that I certainly needed neither soup nor cleaning fluid. My entire waking day was filled with tasks of so wide a span that all that torturing energy that had driven me into dancing would be absorbed without a doubt, even (dread suspicion) exhausted. I wanted to hack away the jungle that those years of war and personal unhappiness had allowed to grow across the tracks of Yehudi's life so that he should be freed to run smoothly along them once again. Little did I envisage the acceleration this would bring, the delighted speed with which he would streak down the line, with myself like some old cabooze rattling at the tail-end of his train, hanging on by uncertain couplings as he swung, gaily insouciant and with delight, bestowing an occasional smile upon the scenery, towards God knows what invisible and far-off destination. The load was heavy, indeed, but the purpose inspiring; the ceaseless movement – sorting, packing, parting from babies, travelling thousands upon thousands of miles – was taxing to a degree that scraped the very skin off one's nerves, but also colourful, exciting and (until repetition set in with its sound of a cheap alarm-clock's ticking) never boring. Trained in the theatre, I was used to thinking one leap ahead, used to expecting disasters and sudden changes. Nonetheless, I did sometimes feel like an over-aged girl guide, always prepared and married to a commercial traveller with a nice line in Beethoven and Bartók for sale.

And so the Menuhin circus swung into its stride. After Smithy no longer needed me for nourishment, it occurred to Yehudi that it might be a bright idea to have a real honeymoon – some fourteen months after those grey nuptials in SW3 in October 1947. I was to meet him in Honolulu for he had flown to the Philippines. Alone and excited, I flew that then longest of all air trips over water and arrived at the Royal Hawaii, a charming pink-iced building in those days surrounded by a forest of palms and flowering trees, not a forest of looming skyscrapers and flowering television aerials as is now the ruined scene. I rushed to the reception desk. No, Mr Menuhin had not arrived. For two dread days I sat by the telephone, only allowing myself an occasional lonely wander on the beach, eating papaya and my fingernails, sleeping fitfully in yet another of those hideous hiatuses. At last a message came. Mr Menuhin would be on flight number something arriving at the airport that morning. I sped out, my heart thumping with relief and joyous anticipation. Peering through the fence that separated the unclean visitors from the arrivals, I anxiously watched as the plane door opened and the people poured down the steps. Anguish: no sign of Yehudi. The last man had shuffled off the plane – a medium-sized Chinese trader, perhaps, in a terrible piece of gent's grey cotton suiting, a straw hat sitting like a lid from the wrong jam-jar on his head, a vast bag bulging with what resembled vegetable tops and large quantities of crumpled paper; and – wait a minute – oh dear God! could it be? Yes, that *was* a violin-case in the offside hand – please God don't let it be Manila's rival to Yehudi Menuhin going through hard times, but Yehudi himself!

I tore round to the shed of the war-time airport feeling faint. The tired passengers were filing through slowly and here at last came that lone shuffler weighted down with cases. Underneath the dreadful hat that hid his fair hair I recognized Yehudi. 'Darling,' he called 'were you *very* worried? There was no way of getting through to you – I'm so sorry.' The relief was so great that all I could say was 'Did you have to add to the agony by coming disguised as an Asian trader in his bigger brother's clothes?' Hurt look: 'Don't you like my lovely new suit? I had it specially made by a Chinese tailor – he did it in twenty-four hours!'

We drove to the hotel and I shook out the contents of that huge canvas bag – rotting tropical fruit stuck to sheets of music, socks he'd forgotten to pack, a fascinating paperback of the Agrarian techniques of the ancient Filipino farmers and, among many other odd trifles, a lovely shirt for me made of pineapple fibre and only slightly stained down the front with banana pulp. Protestations when I suggested the agrarian cultures book was now unreadable by reason of a strange black substance (from a rubber-tree perhaps?) which had glued most of the paper together. Further expostulation when I told him that though I loved him with all my heart, there were limits, and one would be his reappearing in the Mandarin overnight-made grey pinstripe number. But, oh, shame, shame, when I finally got everything straightened out and we were in bed, the total insomnia of the last two nights overcame me just as he was enthusiastically recounting the nasty techniques of the head-shrinkers (physical these, not mental) who still inhabited the wilder mountains. The memory of failing him is forever burnt into my persecution maniac's masochistic mind.

Nevertheless, we had one lovely, insouciant week in a bungalow on a deserted beach, seven days of air and warm blue water, of fresh coconut milk knocked down from the palm-trees by the Chinese house-boy every day, of time alone together, of listening to the sound of the sea, pounding the shore on its way up the beach to rustle the palm-trees in a lulling rhythm all night long, all wrapped together – all magic to a northern European – and in those days totally, or almost totally, unspoilt. The war had postponed development, package tours and all the rest of the greed of those who come solely for what they can get, giving nothing and leaving indissoluble detritus, both materially and psychologically. The traveller is a thing of the far past, the tourist has replaced him, bringing his encapsulated life, and, where he can't, demanding it to be brought to meet him.

Honolulu over, the suit and hat and soggy paperback sorrowfully and unwillingly left behind, we regained Alma and darling Mita. Walks up the hillside, my dividing the weeks between touring with Yehudi and staying with the baby. The acacias bursting out already in February all over the garden Ruth and Carl Coate, our new caretakers, and I had planted together with camellias, Chinese jasmine, gardenias beneath the nursery window, later big blue agapanthus below the living room; the excited hope that is gardening and the good fortune of Ruth's two green thumbs.

Over the next few months the nomad's life took us through a spell in an icy villa outside Rome followed by concerts in London then back to America and Carnegie Hall. Again one of those anguished farewells to Y while I flew back with the baby to Alma. By this time Craigie, his first nanny, had returned to her native Edinburgh and in her place Mita had acquired a new nurse from Switzerland, the invaluable Schwester Marie who was to stay with us for twelve years. Here at home in Alma on that lovely Californian hillside, we occasionally enjoyed quiet interludes with Zamira and Krov spending the summers splashing in and out of the pool like dolphins, I trying my utmost to compensate for my frequent absences by regular early morning readings to the children, walks in the scrubby woods full of cotoneaster and wild lilac (the latter in turn full of delightful ticks which had to be extracted from under the children's skin by applying ether to the black bump, loosening their grip and then pulling them out with tweezers); and, finally, for the two older ones the nightly serial whch I invented as I went along and which always stopped at some dramatic moment, so that on occasion Krov would burst into tears of remonstrance and have to be carried off to bed with promises that tomorrow all would be for the best in the strange lives of 'Hepatica and Jerry'. But these were no more than brief intervals in the peripatetic pattern of our lives.

And so, after settling Schwester Marie and Mita in Alma, 1949 saw us off on the first of those breathless tours in which Y cheerfully catapulted us from town to town, from country to country all through Central and the northern part of South America. On 8 May we left and by 2 July we had touched down once and sometimes twice at some twenty-three towns and ten countries just long enough to toss off a concert or two at each place, rinse out the underwear, repack, race for the airport, be slammed slap-happily into the next DC2½, and bounce and swing through intolerable waves of heat, over unsettling (if beautiful) jungle to land with a bump on mainly improvised and very primitive airports. Among the medley of concerts played to an ever-changing backdrop and a variety of unpredictable responses, I especially savoured the one in San Salvador where the cars hooted with Latin-American zest solidly through the performance so that the audience saw rather than heard Y play. Or again the time we arrived in Caracas to find that we had already missed the concert, only to be told by the local agent, not to worry, the entire audience would happily turn up at the elegant Opera House that night at 9 p.m. instead. Three cheers for the lovely looseness of Latin American time, I thought.

By now I was rapidly becoming expert in the ordained concert duties of a chief performer's wife. I was learning fast, I promise you, not to panic over a missing vest, but to search calmly, finding it perhaps stuffed between a copy of the Beethoven sonatas and 'La fille aux cheveux de lin' in Y's music-case. Next I would check on the handkerchief in the right-hand pocket and the comb before every concert, and concoct 'the picnic-bag' for sustenance during intervals, (for the Kosher rites of his ancestors had been transmuted by him into far fiercer laws of pure organic food), the necessary provisions being difficult enough to find, for plastic junk had already begun to spread its rubbery claws into all nutrition. So there was the thermos to fill with various herb teas smelling strongly to my tightening nostrils of the Augean stables before Hercules got at them, and honey to provide, honey that spreads as only it can over everything bar the violin. And besides this I had to remember a jarful of nuts and raisins of curious provenance, and several small bottles of magic tablets of hideous hue and worse taste ranging from seaweed (good for the muscles?) through bone-meal (good for the elbows, no doubt) to vitamins starting with the first letter and ending on the last of some alphabet much longer than that of the Romans. These bottles got smashed with monotonous frequency, and one of my most disagreeable tasks was to clean out a very nasty mess of broken glass, greying sultanas, tablets reduced to dandruff and the remains of assorted nuts, the lot glued together inextricably and spitefully by leaking honey. No matter, I learned to look upon that bag with its incurable periods of clotted disorder as a kind of microcosm of my life.

Of all the bizarre experiences of that colourful tour none surpassed the concert Y gave in Guayaquil, Ecuador. We had arrived at our hotel with little time to spare, climbed to our bed-and-bathroom, Y changed and practised, I put on one of the only two after-eight dresses I possessed and we were duly called for by the charming middle-aged couple who ran the local concerts. Down the precipitous flight of stairs we all went, Y with the fiddle-case, I with the picnic-bag. The slight look of apprehension on the Señora's handsome face as she flung back the wooden doors was not surprising for we were instantly forced back by an assault of what seemed to be rubber bullets. My first thought, of course, was that we had arrived during one of those coups that overtake the South American republics as regularly as measles occur in English children. Quite wrong: Señora Gomez apologetically informed me that our concert happened to have coincided with one of the seasonal plagues of flying locusts, that would we please to duck our heads, close our mouths tight (this effort agony for myself) and make a dive for the car? We followed her injunctions, shot through the swing-doors and bolted into the car like fleeing bandits. I sat down with a crunch as Sēnor Gomez swung the car round and off down the street to the concert hall. With the exception of the one I had flattened with all the definitiveness of a dancer's hard behind, the car was mercifully clear – but not so the rest of that nightmare concert.

Arrived at the hall, we were ordered to make the same mad dash through what seemed a hail of alien objects determined to exterminate us. In the blessed refuge of the dressing-room, Y and I looked at each other, panting – he, naturally fascinated with this phenomenon of ebullient nature, I slightly less charmed as I plucked one out of my carefully brushed hair. Plucked is hardly the word – knocked would be nearer, for the beasts were about four inches long, with a wing span of six inches and the speed and manoeuvrability of the newest military aeroplane. Feeling a trifle hard-done-by, I checked on Y's handkerchief, combed his unruly hair, kissed him and made for the front of the house with the Gomezes.

The concert was nothing less than hilarious. Despite efforts to keep the flying pests out, a happy few shot about the hall as though practising for an airforce display, and because of the lights on-stage, particularly favoured Y and his accompanist, an arrogant Dutchman. With his confidence fast ebbing, this man had now become a bag of nerves, twisting and turning, shivering and shuddering as the locusts dive-bombed the piano keys (black or white), chased each other through the open lid or skilfully negotiated the narrow passage between his bi-focals and the music-desk. Y was unstirred, serenely playing the Beethoven Spring Sonata as though it had been especially written for just such a seasonal celebration, although there did come a dangerous moment during the slow movement when a particularly musical-minded insect perched dreamily on the bridge of his Stradivarius and remained there while poor Y, squinting like a clown, drew his bow with dynamic force, souped up his vibrato with heedless disregard for taste yet utterly failed in this desperate attempt to dislodge the beast.

Pure Mack Sennett – and I, of course, in hysterics, stuffing my handkerchief into my mouth when I was not using it to mop my streaming mascara. The audience behaved as though it were nothing out of the common to listen to two nineteenth-century German sonatas while the concert hall took on the aspect of an open field offering a particularly delicious crop to insects. Nor did they seem to mind some very odd passages of cacophony when the distraught Dutchman, feeling a locust descend the gap between his collar and his scraggy neck, leapt four bars ('The Flying Dutchman' thought I) and left poor Y to try and catch up with him like a deep-leg tearing after a cricket ball to stop a boundary. At last, alas! the glorious comedy came to an end amid thunderous applause (whether for the very odd musical offering or for the heroic battle between man and beast, I shall never know). I rejoined Y (as serene as ever), mopped Kockingspook's huge skull with a kleenex and told him with my best British parade voice to pull himself together – he was making a terrible fuss because he'd shaken one impertinent locust down his trouser-leg. After which we were all three taken by the kind Gomezes to a local restaurant renowned for its food.

While awaiting the soup, the Señora tried to convince me of the relative mildness of this onslaught, regaling me with past stories of how she sometimes swept pailfuls of the insects out of her front hall several times a day. As she pattered on I looked with hungry melancholy at my soup in which one beast was fast drowning while the other was struggling to reach the lip of the bowl. Depressed and famished by then, I have to confess I offered it no help; I simply tried to copy the Gomezes' technique of eating with one hand and alternatively swiping with the other. Back through the barrage again and so to bed. There we took one look at the bath lined with locusts sopping up the dripping taps, shook them out of our bedding, stuffed odd articles of our clothing through the gaps in the wire netting on the windows and crawled into bed, tying the sheet tightly round our necks and sleeping fitfully face downwards through a night made hideous by the zoom and flutter of those awful monsters.

However, in Peru for once we were able to see the ruins of the city of Machu Picchu, the hallowed Inca shrine. We flew to Cuzco, the original Inca captial, situated at over 11,000 feet, soaring straight out of the damp mist of Lima into blazing blue skies. From there, together with four rumbustious South Americans, we plunged for six hours downwards on the autorail whose naked wheelrims gripping the metal tracks shook and rattled our every bone till we reached sea level, the jungle and sullen Indians who refused to supply us with mules. It was dusk and as there was nowhere for us to lay our heads, we walked straight up the mountainside for two hours, following the dried-up bed of a stream, reached the little guest house soaked and famished as the moon came up, and fell onto our iron cots.

Machu Picchu was another world – no, another planet. Nothing else can describe the weird and wonderful first sight of that group of scattered buildings spread across the long green spine that lay about two hundred feet before and below us like a beautiful oblong stage. On each side the ground fell thousands of feet to the gorges from one of which we had climbed the previous night. Dotted around were more of those jungle-covered peaks, green sentinels guarding the hallowed shrine.

Air so pure you could almost taste it. Early morning light gentle and clear and a sky clean of even a wisp of cloud. A magical hiatus suspended from the touch not only of human kind but of earthly. A dream but a dream with a meaning. A mystery, but mystery holding an unfathomable significance. The senses took it in first and later the mind. I longed to stay in that first state of bliss undefined. It could only last as long as a deep-drawn breath and then thought blurred it and it was gone. Our small group was alone and also subdued by the inexplicable strangeness as we descended the long slope to look at the remains of those extraordinary walls made of enormous blocks of stone, irregular in shape but so expertly fitted into each other that not so much as a blade of grass had managed a toehold in between them over hundreds of years.

Only occasional bird-song and the sound of our feet on the grass. No one spoke much. The spirit of the place was so strong that it imposed silence as we wandered around the long perfect walls, looked over the edge of that spur of land which seemed like the broad back of some huge animal upon which the Incas, the worshippers of the sun, had built their most sacred and secret of all expressions. Standing there, I wondered whether their worship could ever have been as cruel and crude as that of surrounding tribes, or whether that sense of the metaphysical came from a belief far higher: had they succeeded in enshrining its physical form in an ambience of height, of sight and almost of flight into the beyond?

Fortunately the mules turned up for our return journey down to the valley and back by autorail to Cuzco. There we discovered once more that peace, especially the peace of Machu Picchu, does not reign long in Y's pattern of life, whether by design or chance. Since our two-day excursion, unbelievably in that sky-high town, a deputation had assembled demanding that Y give a concert. Yes, indeed. In a population of mixed Incas and Spaniards, isolated at 11,000 feet, one could without exaggerated optimism hope that no-one would know him from a mango. But, God help us, there they were facing us – also facing us was the cottage upright in the School Hall, its yellowed teeth grinning sardonically and all its intestine hanging out of the torn canvas of its backside. Very obscene and comic – Rabelais perhaps, illustrated by Rowlandson. Unhampered by trade unions or any other such helpful bureaucratic barriers between human enthusiasm and goodwill, a band of carpenters, electricians, the garage-man and a gardener or two combined with the policeman and some of the lesser clergy to put this Humpty-Dumpty together again. Oh damn! I did so long to crawl into a corner and reflect over Machu Picchu, the Incas, this gloriously beautiful land, and here were we back in the old bent harness. Ah! Did I hear shrieking protests from van Luurpengrot, now recovered of his dread fever and back to his usual healthy grey hue? Indeed I did, but I had not yet learnt the depth and height and width and length of Y's mental deafness, and so the wretched man watched with watery eyes as they reknitted those dangling strings, glued up the straying hammers and, although it took them all day and they were still stuffing back the odd lost chord as the audience poured in, the concert took place.

This time it was vintage Laurel and Hardy. Even Y succumbed to an occasional giggle and I must admit that I enjoyed myself hugely. Beethoven, however manfully Y strove to drown the piano, sounded more like Schoenberg than I've ever heard him before or since; as for Brahms (D mi, I suspect) that well worn sonata wandered from key to key until it was finally brought to a merciful if premature end by the sudden disembowelment of the piano caused by van Nederland's furious pounding. As the strings poured out of their threadbare casing in a cascade of relief (very indecent this), the merry evening grew to a close. Y gave them a pennyworth of unaccompanied Bach and, to the sound of rousing cheers (more than earned I would say), we returned to a banquet at the little hotel.

And that, apart from a retun visit to Guayaquil where the locusts were still in fine fettle, and a quick glimpse of Quito, was the end of our South American tour.

It was about this time that I felt that things that mattered were beginning to fall into shape, the foundation seemed firmer. Y was starting to enjoy playing again and not to fight his violin, the violin he had never ceased loving but which the preceding years had twisted into a guilty object, had made him for the first time in his life feel he had no right to allow to come first in his vision, his emotions and his expression, and which perhaps did indeed absorb him to the point of unwittingly witholding from others those essential offerings that go to the making of love and friendship, of human contact and simple affection. Slowly I detected a soundness returning, a tension loosening and hoped that it was the beginning of something in which his whole being could take root and find nourishment without guilt, the soil of a plant that must grow, and grow strong and unwarped. Indeed, in those days when there were only concerts and recordings and little television, there was more time to use on the ordinary stuff of life for a comparatively young man in his early thirties with two children under ten and a baby. So he became friends again with his violin; it became his natural voice, and his hesitation disappeared, dissolved in the total application this most demanding of instruments required; the shadows withdrew. The recording with Furtwängler of the Beethoven and the Brahms concertos had already lifted him above and away from the dread and self-doubt and now I could hope for some signs of a new security, a fresh joy, some maturer version of that extraordinary and inexplicable *envolée* that had started the child of seven on his path and had set the little boy of ten firmly on the road he was destined to follow.

It was when Yehudi took part in a concert at Carnegie Hall in honour of Georges Enesco, the man whom Y had chosen as his master when, as a seven-year-old, he had heard him play in San Francisco – it was on that occasion that I sensed odd fragments of enormous importance in Y's past of which he never spoke. Collecting them together, I tried to fit them into a coherent pattern that would explain his character, his subconscious that seems to be like the iceberg, three-quarters submerged, and for whose actions and reactions he himself appears unaccountable, as though he were born to a journey rather than a life, an ever-moving trajectory with music as its heart, its generator, its guiding light. I had to accustom myself to this constant movement, always unexplained, because Y himself disliked analyzing; instead he preferred following some direction that attracted him, held a special meaning or caught his imagination because of its very imponderables.

His was the most un-prefabricated mind I'd met. Nothing affected or lured him on simply for its logical place in his life, nor does he ever pronounce upon a happening or circumstance from any standard viewpoint. This I loved, only sometimes it demanded a great deal of mental dexterity and a watchful eye to be ready for some extremely strange actions and unexplained equations. I finally conjectured that it might spring from the fact that, having played the violin since he was three, he was used to tuning and retuning his own instrument to fit the temperature, the ambience, the accompaniment, whatever adjustments were demanded of it. Therefore his whole being was like a violin, responding to the minutest changes around, not in any volatile or spasmodic manner, but steadfast only to himself and to his own vision of the world and mankind.

Erractic it is not, but eccentric certainly, and the danger lay in his avid appetite for the unorthodox, the non-conformist and the plain dotty. Nothing it would seem to me was quite off-beat and odd enough for Y not to try it out – no creature but could approach him for money, ranging from a page-turning device operated by foot, to a chin-rest for the fiddle made of foam-rubber and the hamstrings of old goats, that he wouldn't willingly and eagerly contribute towards. Only on occasion did I remonstrate: one day I caught him practising with an enormous semi-circular contraption like a lavatory seat around his head made of thick greyish felt which he told me in deeply offended tones was intended to isolate or insulate (I'm not quite sure which) the player from hearing his own sound. I retorted that if he couldn't bear what he heard he'd better give up playing and that it still was not a strong enough argument to stand there like a mentally retarded child in a Victorian bonnet. Great reproach from large blue eyes before which I retreated tactfully and the thing was relegated to one of his many secret hidey-holes where he stored all such manner of strange objects.

Every now and then I made a concerted attack upon these mouldering compost-heaps which spilled out of the warrens into every room and begged him to understand that the place had not been properly dusted for a week. With the sullenness of a small boy asked to throw away some toys broken beyond repair, he finally complied – and after an hour's gruelling excavation and the filling of six w-p-b's, Y rewarded me with a sigh of relief and a beaming smile and, of course, started refilling the nooks and crannies at once. In truth I've at last realized that Y himself is one vast compost heap. Nothing bores him. My prayer is 'Oh God! please make Y bored'. It has not been answered so far.

However, I must admit that from this compost heap has come the fertilizer he has always spread over every imaginable and unimaginable field that exists within his synoptic view. For example his Music School for the young from seven to seventeen years at Stoke D'Abernon, realized in 1963 – a boarding school that offers a complete scholarly and musical education – the only one of its kind outside Russia; his chamber orchestra; his festivals; his 'Live Music Now', an institution he formed to help the young musician leaving the music colleges to connect with a network of societies, prisons, hospitals and functions that can offer them concerts. There are countless other enterprises too numerous to mention: there are three or four pages of closely typed societies, institutions, schools of which he is either the onlie begetter or chairman or founder member.

Not long after the Enesco Memorial Concert we embarked on a journey, starting in New York and destined for London, that has gone down in family history as the 'gremlin flight'. This was still during the days of 'prop' planes, days when hazards were greater and time slower and longer.

25 January: New York. We were piled into the plane and left to cool our heels for over two hours (while no doubt the crew fiddled around with something nasty in the cockpit). Then without explanation they decanted us and sent us all by bus back to our respective dwellings. Y, delighted, exclaimed 'Now, we can go to Heifetz's concert at Carnegie Hall', and so we did and it was marvellous, fully compensating for the delay. Y rushed round to see Jascha and thank him and then we went back to our hotel, luckily found our room still free and went to bed in our underwear. At some ungodly hour, the airline rang to say we should be ready to take the bus again and go out to the airport. That we did, all got into the plane and took off at 11.30 a.m. on 26 January. Some time later there was an enormous bang, we dropped a couple of thousand

feet and through our porthole saw the impotent blades of one engine hanging like a disused windmill.

The co-pilot appeared to announce in deep sorrow that we must turn back (we were by now well over the Atlantic) and not to worry, we would easily make New York on three engines. Three and a half hours later (the time it now takes for blessed Concorde to do the whole trip) and a hundred or so 23rd Psalms muttered under my breath by me while Y slept on happily, we landed again at La Guardia. Three p.m., Saturday 26 January; since 11.30 the day before we had got precisely nowhere, while Y's Albert Hall concert was to take place at 8.00 p.m. the next day. Two hours and more later they decided to give up that old crate and wheeling out another, shovelled the by then crumpled, swollen-eyed passengers into it, taking off around 5.45 p.m. We landed at one of those wild and lonely airports in Canada with ornithological names (Goose Bay, Gander, Grebe, I no longer cared), refuelled, crawled back to our rumpled seats and took off once more over the pitch-dark Atlantic. Y, of course, slept all the way, I fitfully as we swung and bumped through January weather.

6.30 a.m., Sunday 27 January. We landed at Shannon and I shot out of the plane, found the officer-in-charge of the long row of huts that in those days comprised the airport buildings and begged him to find some fine and private place where Y could practise till we made the final lap. More bad news awaited us. Heathrow was shrouded in fog and there was nowehere else to land our stratocruiser... but 'it might still lift' said the manager optimistically as he led Y to his office. Why not, he suggested, charter a small Aer Lingus which could land in a cabbage patch, if need be. Y did so promptly, only to be told an hour later, between his arpeggios, that the plane was inexplicably held up at Dublin. Y returned to his arpeggios and I to my nail-biting. At last, our plane announced it was going to try and make London and we were levered in like a lot of battered goods at 3.20 p.m., taxied down the runway and – this is the solemn truth – stopped dead. The radio had given out. Back we went (I beginning to feel like a worn spool on a splintered shuttle). After half an hour's tinkering by some genius with the wires they pronounced the radio working so that at 4.15 we took off again. But hold: the captain was announcing over the intercom that he could not land us in London, it was by now quite shrouded. Y woke, went up to the pilot's cabin and begged him somehow to land us anywhere in England. The captain radioed. Good news, they were willing to take us at Manston, the old RAF airport near the East Coast. Y was thrilled. I hadn't a bone in my body that could any longer express a feeling except aching. We landed at Manston at 6.15 pm and were shot down the emergency chute together with our luggage (or some of it) into the icy darkness. The local officers were wonderfully helpful, gathering us and our luggage up, cursorily passing it for Customs, and courteously and quickly putting us in a car which with any luck should get us to Albert Hall in less than two hours. I counted on my frozen fingers – 8.00–8.15 – oh well, we might still keep the audience waiting only fifteen minutes. As though fate had not struck its ugly tongue out to its full extension, suddenly like the iron safety curtain in the theatre, the fog, racing across our bows, dropped and the driver slowed down as we groped and swerved through the inspissate gloom towards nowhere.

It was so cold (unheated car, of course) that I took off my fur coat and wrapped it round Y's violin case in an effort to keep his Stradivarius and his Guarnerius from losing all voice. On and on we went, our driver, a real *chevalier preux*, twisting, avoiding trees that seemed to slide over the invisibility to stand in our way, mounting some grassy verge, careering round unseeable corners until finally at 9 p.m. – lights and London and the Albert Hall! Pushing past half a hundred photographers and clattering down that familiar stone staircase, inside we heard the strains of the symphony that should have been played between Y's two concertos on that evening's programme. The backstage manager led us into the dressing room, laughing with relief. It appeared that after waiting a few minutes, for the concert was being broadcast, Sir Adrian Boult, imperturbable as ever, had gone on stage and said in his best Old Westminster voice, 'I am afraid we are without our Hamlet so I will give you the symphony first.' Cheers from the packed house. Despite all my efforts to keep the fiddles warm, Y took out his Strad and found it was a lump of ice – he only had about ten minutes to warm it and his fingers when Boult appeared, impeccable and commiserating, clapped Y on his creased shoulder and told him it was time he should go on stage. I combed Y's hair, just tore the plane label off his lapel in time and there and then in his baggy tweed suit he walked up that familiar ramp, where he had first played as a boy of thirteen, to the loudest roar of welcome I have ever heard. All tiredness, worry and strain dropped away before that wonderful sound of friendship and Y launched into the Mendelssohn as though he had not spent the last two days and more fighting his way against all conceivable odds, and was not now hungry and tired and dirty, and longing for bed. After the interval he played the Elgar, the Albert Hall audience clamouring at the end so Y managed to return their devotion with two encores and finally trotted off-stage utterly refreshed.

Back at Claridge's around midnight with the fog still swirling, and on the steps awaiting us one of those inimitable doormen. 'Now, Mr Menuhin, sir,' he admonished, 'you must never keep us in such a tizzy again! We've 'ad 'alf London ringing up to find out where you'd got to – and 'ere look at these', and he showed us various editions of the afternoon and evening papers with the stop press reading 'Menuhin reaches Shannon' followed by 'Menuhin lands at Manston' in large smudgy type. When we reached our suite, the floor-waiter, unsummoned, greet us: 'What a *dreadful* journey you and Madam have had! Now I knew that you were both partial to a nice Dover sole and I've got a pair waiting to be cooked here.' Dear Claridge's, it was run like a huge country house, with a personal touch from all the staff and a genuine interest in one's family and one's self – civility sans servility – the perfect relationship.

Over the next three months as the Menuhin caravanserai rolled on, we visited two countries in which, in very different ways, Y's extraordinary brand of obstinate courage was demonstrated. I have already remarked on his almost total inability to fight for himself. But when it came to others he seemed to possess no such inhibitions. The less likely he might be to profit from an unpopular crusade, the more likely that he would pursue it. Gradually, although I loved him all the more for it, as the years passed by and he continued to stick his neck out, always alone and determined, I began to feel like some buckle-kneed Rosinante wearily carrying her Don Quixote towards the next windmill.

South Africa. We arrived at Johannesburg with the invaluable Marcel Gazelle at 8 p.m. on 8 February 1950 after nearly forty hours travelling wedged in like tinned smelts. Usual routine, unpacking, steaming the crumpled clothes in the bathroom, three concerts in Johannesburg. Alan Paton's moving book *Cry, the Beloved Country* had just come out, making an enormous impression. Y found the telephone number of the Dietkloopf Reformatory (he never fails to connect where it concerns abstract wiring) and asked if he could do anything? Moment's pause – as Y loathes pronouncing his name and mumbles something that sounds like Youmanoohin or Yudaminin, the pause was understandable, and just as I was about to ask him to try and make it clear, the good director did some double crostic and said, 'Did you say Yehudi Menuhin?' 'Ah yes', said Y. 'I mean would it be of any use if I came and played for the boys?' Gasp of delighted wonder.

And down we went the next afternoon to find 500 crop-haired boys sitting on the ground in a big compound containing a large wooden building with a verandah. On this narrow ledge a piano (cottage upright and stool) stood and luckily suited Marcel Gazelle who was all of five foot three inches and weighed around nine stone. He sidled along and slid his knees under the yellowing keyboards. Y stood alongside and they launched into some gay snippets of Kreisler – and when that was obviously much enjoyed, ventured on Handel, a transcription of Bach and ended up with some thundering fireworks by Sarasate, Wieniawski, Paganini and suchlike, which brought the boys to their feet cheering.

The following morning to our dismay the leading paper ran a banner picture of the 500 football-like heads with Y and Marcel sawing and thumping away. Y had told no-one – never does – he is the Original Bushel, and neither, of course, had Marcel nor I. Anyway, there it was on the front page with a very nice comment underneath. The telephone rang. It was the furious voice of Y's agent accusing him of 'breaking his contract etc. etc.' and demanding that Y come and 'explain himself'. How does one 'explain' a simple human wish to give whatever one can to those less privileged than oneself? As we were anyway leaving for Cape Town the next day, Y consented to call in on the way to the airport. Naturally, I stayed in the car with Marcel. All I know is that I heard the loud slam of a door five minutes later and out came Y, flushed and beaming. 'First time I've ever slammed a door' he announced proudly. 'What happened?' I asked. 'Oh well, he said he would serve me with a writ and I told him I'd be delighted and would forward it express to the *Daily Mirror*. It was then I looked at his red face bursting with rage and decided that before it exploded I would slam the door – something I realize I'd subconsciously been wanting to do for years.' He was nearly thirty-five.

Our next stop was Cape Town, the most lovely part of the world next to the Mediterranean. There Y distinguished himself when we were taken to Parliament (House of Assembly) by a friendly ex-Mayor, William Blumberg. They were discussing the Registration Bill and when the latter translated sotto voce the speech of the Afrikaaner member, Y's eyes nearly fell out with disbelief at its medieval attitude towards the Africans. This was followed by a very just and balanced statement by an Independent, refuting the Afrikaaner. To my dismay Y rose to his feet (we were sitting by the press gallery) shouting 'Bravo!' As he has never belonged to any scholastic institution Y knows naught about what can or should or might be done or not done. 'Come on, quick', I hissed, 'before we're expelled', and seizing Y by the hand I dragged him up the gallery stairs to the long corridor to meet head-on a furious warden in uniform, demanding that we leave the holy precincts forthwith. 'I can't *wait*', said Yehudi, and walked with great dignity down the red carpeted corridor, the only drawback to his splendid exit being that he was clad in carpet slippers, the result of my having dragged him out for a walk the preceding day on his white-satin feet, which well-intentioned and mild exercise had produced enormous blisters.

Returning later to Cape Town we were invited to see General Smuts. I had long wanted to meet him and was curious to know what kind of person he would be, now that there was an Afrikaaner Government in power. The man who rose to greet us was trim and dapper, of great warmth and charm with humourous eyes, sharp nose and firm but flexible mouth half hidden in his 'imperial' beard. What animal? Too benign for a fox, too quick-witted and intelligent for a field mouse, too kindly for stoat or weasel. Could it be a red squirrel? Maybe. He thanked Y for having seized the nettle by insisting upon giving special concerts for the Africans and for playing in the townships. I noted in Smuts what I was to perceive a couple of years later in Nehru: the growing sadness of an ageing man for whom the love of his country deepened as the hope to overcome its evergrowing difficulties became more and more unlikely. A kind of self-deprecating wistfulness spread over his face as he spoke with gentle wisdom of the present and his feeling of despair if in the coming years the combination of skill and compassion, political sleight-of-hand and humane courage were not to develop in the National party. That was 1950 – the rest is history. He was the most lovable of men and as I tried to lighten the conversation by making him laugh at stories of Y's oddities and weird interests, on the day we went to see him for the last time, he seized a photograph from his desk, signing it:

'To Diana the Hydrogen Bomb, affectionately Jan Smuts'. Alas! the case in which I idiotically packed that precious memory was never found again.

The other country where Y demonstrated his courage was Israel, a far sterner challenge. It was 1951, our first visit and a dramatic one, considering that a militant group had sent Y's agent a slip of paper on which the simple typed message read: 'If the traitor MENUHIN comes to Israel, we will kill him as we killed Bernadotte last year'. Hardly conducive to a warm welcome nor to a feeling, on our part, of security. However, when Y had shown me this missive some two or three months before and had asked my opinion, I had answered that that was added reason why we should not under any threat, shirk going to a new country for which he had deep feelings and was longing to see for himself. He would thus be able to judge if his conflicting ideas of the wisdom of the country's policies deserved him the animosity of some Israelis or not.

Yehudi's sister Hephzibah was meeting us there from Australia and, as we descended the stairway from the plane, hers was the only friendly one among a sea of hostile faces turned upwards. Three hundred journalists emitting a wave of dislike is hardly a *bonne aubade* at 7 a.m. in a new country and was almost palpable in its intensity.

Yehudi flatly turned down their angry command that he should adjourn to the hangar and explain his attitude towards Israel in general and Zionism in particular, adding brusquely that they should hold a meeting to which he would be only too glad to come the next morning. With which we drove off to our hotel. It was extraordinarily moving to be in Israel in those early days, its people living on whatever food they could produce or import – ersatz tea and coffee. There was one cramped little old Palestinian hotel in Tel-Aviv, a remnant of the British 'Raj'. Outside our tiny room a hostile soldier sat all through the night, a loaded rifle at the ready across his knees. Quite a lullaby, I thought and wondered which way he really felt like pointing it.

Before we went to sleep I discussed a point or two with Y which, being myself an 'outsider', I felt might be of use. What had riled the then immigrant Jews had been Y's insistence upon going to Germany as soon as possible after the war was over. He had played with Benjamin Britten, who offered to accompany him in Belsen a short week after that medieval horror had been evacuated. And, of course, we had toured

Berlin during the airlift of 1948, Y always insisting that it was his rôle from now onwards to restore the image of the Jew in German minds from the caricature that had been Hitler's to the diligent, intelligent, gifted and cultured minority they had represented in every city where they had settled. It was not for the Jew to cry 'an eye for an eye and a tooth for a tooth', said Y. That would betray that they had emerged, those who survived, stained with the philosophy of their hideous masters. The Jews were a unique people and would show it, neither by whining nor boasting, by their work, talents and skills. I asked him to add just one point which was perhaps more obvious to myself whose family house had been bombed in the very first week of the Blitz and who'd survived several other bombings. Had they killed *my* family, I doubt I could have felt as generous or viewed the situation as clearly as he did, I said, urging him to remember those who had suffered and suggesting that he should ask them to forgive him if they believed him callous. For, although he had risked his life many times during the war, nonetheless his own family had been safely in America.

As it turned out, the meeting next day was a vital and passionate one, ending harmoniously, and although we still had to walk guarded by soldiers for a time and although my heart was in my mouth during those early concerts when anyone could have lobbed a grenade at him, the whole mood changed and gradually the military guard disappeared and a friendly crowd replaced them.

What had helped not a little was that we had found an invitation on arrival from the President, Chaïm Weizmann, to lunch at the 'White House' a day later. It was a moving experience; he was obviously already a very ill man, gentle, wise and humorous. Vera, his handsome wife, was like a home-coming to me – very Russian with a magnificent head, a splendid carriage, those Slavic eyes that looked out imperiously from beneath hoods like sunblinds, a deep voice encrusted with Russian vowels and an air as independent and aristrocratic as any of my past retired ballerina-teachers in Paris. They are an extinct breed – sadly this irreplaceable mould has been thrown away for ever. What I found strange was that Weizmann's fears were not of the surrounding alien territories, nor of the displaced Arabs – his besetting fear was that the Jew would lose his essential characteristics now that he was secure in his own Homeland at long last. 'Such as?' I asked. 'Well, my dear, his awareness, his intellect, his drive and passionate need to rise above danger and endemic persecution and prove himself, his self-containment and determination to reach the highest possible position in whatever task, in whatever profession he uses his brain.'

That was the beginning of a close friendship, for they both agreed with and accepted Y's vision of the emerging new Jew – the Israeli – and we had wonderfully instructive lunches there with Generals Dayan and Yadin, both exalted by their respective 'digs', both in uniform, both lively men of that rarest of all combinations: action *and* thought. Despite the poor food and the hard life, the subscription lists for the concerts comprised a huge part of the population of Tel-Aviv, so that in order to accommodate them all in the then small hall, the visiting artist had to play the same work with the Philharmonic seven times. I told Weizmann that the atmosphere reminded me of the London Blitz – all nonsense, fripperies and fancy furbelows discarded pared away by the sharp knife of adversity, only basics having priority, basics supported by the hope and wonder at being alive – that ever-elusive and ephemeral quality, true value, reigning. It was a wonderful moment to have seen and felt and lived with in that special period of history.

In between these two visits to South Africa and Israel there had, of course, been an endless series of comings and goings, through any number of other countries, broken thankfully by occasional meetings with Mita and Schwester Marie. Joyfully, I caught up with them in Zürich, to which they had come from Alma. No one who has not been separated again and again from a very small and first child can know the yearning and the excitement. Mita looked much bigger with a head of bright golden curls and those dark brown eyes seemed more appraising then ever. It was a full nine weeks since I had seen him, a long span in the early development of a baby. We went up to Bad Gastein for a short rest all together, and then Y whipped off to Niederdollendorf or Knocke or God knows where, and I took Schwester Marie and Mita for two weeks up to the beautiful heights of Arosa. As we got out of the train, Mita looked around at the tidy piles of snow on each side and promptly announced 'Blankets!' For a twenty-month-old child that was a pretty good symbol, and in the ensuing days I found that whenever he was at a loss for a word, he either found a synonym or simply invented a word of his own. He was great good company already, listening avidly when read to and aware of everything around him.

After that blissful respite, we met Y and Marcel again in Berne. There was a very weepy parting from Schwester Marie (who had only had one year's leave from her professor at the hospital where she had postponed taking her full nursing certificate and to which she would now return) and Schwester Hedy, cayenne-haired and sprightly, took over. Mita was, of course, beastly to her – as much out of loyalty to his beloved 'Ma' (the nearest he got to Marie) as to his already highly developed sense of personal choice and critical appraisement which traits were to make his poor mother's life extremely complicated from then on.

Later that year (1950) in August we were actually to enjoy a whole heavenly month's holiday together in Switzerland when we took the annexe of the big hotel in Bad Gastein, although for Y it still entailed practice and the studying of new works. For me it meant compensating for my frequent absences as mother as well as my summer rôle as stepmother to Krov and Zamira. But above all it meant something approaching a normal family life, picnics in the woods, long walks up the forested hills, glorious Austrian food, lots of reading in French and English, excursions to Salzburg for heavenly music and that ravishing countryside that is Austria's blessing. Unhappily the month soon grew to a close, Zamira and Krov were flown back to the States and school and, after a Paris concert, Mita and Hedy, Y and I followed them to America. Came my most dreaded moment when I would again part with Y starting his US tour and take the long flight back to California with Mita and his nurse, there to open up 'Alma', search desperately for a couple to run the house, settle the household, stay a while and then hop off to join Y for a short span.

That autumn was saddened by the sudden death of my mother, announced horribly by the hoarse voice of the telephone operator when, of course, the Black Fairy saw to it that I was alone and without Y to comfort me. Despite her childlike callousness, her egotism and her inability to worry about anyone but herself, I felt, as that disembodied voice carried the shock of her death, a pain of pure atavism, the snapping of an umbilical cord I had never known existed and I wept – there thousands of miles from away from her, knowing that I would never again see or be maddened by this curiously attractive and gifted child who had been my mother. I must also have been drawn back in certain measure to the life I had abjured since marrying Y, jerked from the three years of breathless, non-analyzing pursuit of his aspirations and my total commitment. For a moment that automatic switch so useful in facing the unfaceable had been put out of action – and the vacuum echoed with a chorus of disturbing and alien cries. What in the world was I doing out here thousands of miles from my roots and from everything that held the significance of my upbringing? Thus Lucifer, the voice of my endemic self-doubt, always whispering in one ear. For an agonizing moment, I felt totally dislocated, wobbling precariously between past heritage and present condition. What accentuated the danger of toppling was the endlessly moving current of those three years. The past had been relatively pastoral, the present nomadic, a life of a far more complicated nature on which to build a permanence for oneself and one's child, or children to come. Somehow, said the other voice in the other ear, the voice of grace, you must manage a movable structure that can withstand any amount of dismantling and reassembling and you will always be alone, for you can never betray the fact that there can never be real roots, only the superstructure adaptable to all circumstances, a Noah's Ark, sometimes afloat, sometimes aground ... always maintained so that it is seaworthy or stormproof.

Fortunately we ended 1950 with a lovely Christmas at Alma, Y peering through the unseasonable green foliage outside the huge windows dressed as Father Christmas, frightened Mita to death, until I dragged him in and he tried to placate the child by speaking in a disguised sepulchral voice hampered by a great deal of white cotton-wool. This only terrified Mita the more until I begged Father Christmas to produce some tangible evidence of the benevolent present he so singularly lacked; seizing a parcel from under the tree, he offered it with a leer – whereupon Mita retreated yelling as though threatened by a weapon. Eventually we got rid of F. C. and Y returned as his own self, greeted with cries of joy by his poor little son, and Christmas cheer was restored. Query: when a genuinely good and kind creature tries to play the rôle of an imaginary one is it a case of two plusses making a minus?

The following year was memorable for our first trip to North Africa, ancient culture, shoddy mannerisms, marvellous spicy smells everlastingly fighting indescribably filthy ones in a hopeless battle. Memorable too as a comedy of errors and surprise rather than conflict and confrontation. From Casablanca we flew to Marrakesh where Y, of course, ran riot in the souk, buying paper cornet after paper cornet filled with unfathomable purple powder, grated yellow grit, orange and rust and black spices to the huge delight of the vendors. By the time he had tasted every one, his face took on the aspect of a rainbow painted by Chagall in an off-moment.

From there on to Oran and Tangiers, dropping concerts regularly like confetti until the day we set out by car for Casablanca. That is where our adventures really began. Having negotiated the international border between Spanish and French Morocco we suddenly came upon what seemed to be a large murky lake: floods in the flat desert. Cars, the few there were in that benighted spot, up to the door-handles in water and stuck, like drowned beetles. The concert was that night and there was obviously no means of getting there – I was suggesting helpfully that we might get out and with Y's Strad across his and my heads swim breast-stroke for some miles, when all of a sudden that endemic crowd that springs out of every hole in the ground, wall or building in all Arab lands, materialized up to their waists in water and all gabbling like fowl at feeding-time.

Y had got out on to the running-board (we'd stopped just short of the deep water) and was looking around with one of his many varieties of non-expressions – all, thank goodness, benevolent but all totally un-fathomable – when a shriek went up from the damp rabble 'Mon Dieu, c'est Yehudi Menuhin!' and splashing toward us came what was, I sup-pose, the Jewish community of the small town. Y's expression changed minimally to embarrassed confusion. There was a dangerous moment when, in their excitement and enthusiasm, they all but pulled him into the water, but I hung on to the seat of his pants through the car window in British bull-dog style and he remained precariously balanced but splashed with enthusiastic mud from head to heels. When Maurice Dan-delot, who was with us, had managed to quell the yelling, by now thickened with Spanish and Arabic, he asked if there were any hope of getting through? The only reply came from hordes of children waggling soaked exercise-books demanding autographs. Maurice persisted, where-upon a splendid posse of the local village elders slowly coaxed the car towards the nearby police station where we sat crumpled and forlorn for two solid hours while a tremendous altercation went on in at least three languages.

The outcome produced a solution: they decided to drive us on to higher ground near the railway station where, standing on the platform, was a large truck. By means of planks and our splendid driver, aided by half the village pushing and shoving in the cold grey wash, they succeeded in getting our car on to that truck. A miracle of ingenuity and devotion. Unfortunately, the car's posterior hung dangerously over the edge. Immediately a perfect cat's cradle of chains and rope and string and wool was woven by willing hands into a kind of hammock that held the drooping tail more or less fixed to each side of the truck-end. To my relief, however, it was suggested that we get out of the car and squeeze along in what space was left between the car-sides and its host, while a few of the locals elected to sit on the roof of the car as look-out, dragoman and general administrators. The truck drove groggily down that sloping platform and plunged into the water its engine and part of its wheels rising into the air and away we jogged, followed by a frantically cheering mob splashing and waving after us like wet washing in a high wind. After a few miles the water receded, the ground rose, and muddy but navigable, the road reappeared.

But our troubles were by no means over. There remained the crucial problem of how to get the car off the truck again. We'd reached another of those wandering borders (Spanish-French perhaps) and that meant inhabitants and help. After more yelps of recognition for Y, drowning Dandelot's anxious announcement that the concert hour was approaching in inverse ratio to the distance between this place and Casablanca, everyone, local populace, guards, police alike, rushed around, returning with loads of bricks and stout planks, which they made into a ramshackle slope from the back of the truck – by now driven halfway up a bank and the road. While we climbed wearily over the edge of the truck, the gallant driver remained, shot into reverse and with a terrible constrained roar and a reek of his smoking handbrake, very slowly edged backwards off the truck, half-skidded down the planks emitting heart-tearing groans from the insulted engine and a very indecent black cloud from the outraged exhaust.

Shouts of triumph! Battered but in one piece, we were once more on the road – the driver heaped with howls of praise for his daring. Our tyres had miraculously remained unpunctured and we succeeded in reaching Casablanca by 8 p.m. exactly, where Y duly performed his concert kindly forbidding me to attend, so I wallowed in a tepid bath at the local hotel.

On and ever on we reached Tunis, which provided us with an experience in total contrast to the bedlam which had preceded it. I remember still an extraordinary trip to the Thermes d'Antonin at Carthage to which the American Consul General and his wife took us. There, lying on the light sands of the North African shore, were huge white marble columns and the remains of the great baths. Nothing around but dunes and a huge sky dissolving into the sapphire sea. Our perfect companions, clearly loving Tunisia and knowing it well, did not utter a word. I wandered through these fallen remains, the wind blowing like a benison across the pillars. Somehow in some inexplicable way Carthage and all its history were still there spiritually among the shattered walls and prone columns. One felt an odd presence, an immortality. For a very short spell I understood the infinity of time and knew the significance of Blake's poem:

> To see a World in a Grain of Sand,
> And a Heaven in a Wild Flower,
> Hold Infinity in the palm of your hand,
> And Eternity in an hour.

There are just a few of the many archaic ruins that still retain this strange power. The ancient gardens at Ninfa, near Rome, for instance. All are pre-Christian, yet none pagan in the cruel sense. Perhaps I caught this feel of timelessness and living significance in Machu Picchu, Ninfa and Carthage because we had the great good fortune of being all but alone and undisturbed and because all three were temples of worship to Nature?

That dream of eternity enshrined in my heart, the refreshment that followed at the French General's quite hideous Victorian house could do nothing to efface. What effect it did have was agonies of indigestion brought on by the offering of large trays of Tunisian sweetmeats set upon the plush-covered occasional tables and upon which Y fell with delighted abandon. The Oriental in him obliterated the organic food crank in one gaze of his glittering eye at the array of honeyed pastries stuck all over like porcupines with almonds, mysterious squares of nougat peppered with pistachios, greenish rolls of marzipan oozing God knows what liquid essence and pyramids of dates stuffed with what looked to my jaded eye like crystalized mammoth's teeth. That miserable wretch, Y, has the digestion of an ostrich and can swallow anything from boot buttons to alarm clocks. One or two polite nibbles at this glut of viands and I was buckled up in gastric agony for the rest of the day. The house was at Salammbô. Maybe the shade of Flaubert was getting its own back for my having found that pompous novel totally indigestible.

From there we experienced a change as complete as that of a scene on a theatre stage: lunch in the exquisite Moroccan house of the Prime Minister Bourguiba set on a hilltop overlooking the mountains. But oh! dear me, food again – and no hope of worrying it into little half-eaten piles spread diplomatically around the edges of my plate as I had learned to do as a girl at those splendid Russian meals in Paris. I was sitting helplessly at the PM's right hand and he was not only explaining every dish to me but in that generous oriental way, himself adding to my modest helpings by heaping special titbits upon which he expatiated at length. First came *briks*, a kind of edible packet containing a whole egg; then delicate baby lamb accompanied by spring vegetables (at least six varieties). Next, a heap of tiny roast artichokes; followed by a mountain of couscous on a great silver platter served with lightly spiced chicken; a vast *pièce montée* of a cake, and as an envoi, just in case we were still hungry, a more subtle version of the honeyed pastries, pistachioed mille-feuilles and almond-covered macaroons. The 'Turkish' coffee that followed did little to allay my by then agonizing spasms while the sight of Yehudi blissfully eulogizing the PM's cook, with his elastic-sided stomach bulging comfortably against the table-edge only added spiteful envy to my misery.

On our way back from North Africa – in Athens to be precise – I discovered that I was once again pregnant. Needless to say this did not curtail our travel schedule. From that day until the date of the birth, I lived for a time in Rome, acted for a spell as hostess for my stepfather, Cecil Harcourt, passed through New York and also spent eleven weeks, taking Mita with us, in Australia. On two occasions I almost lost the baby, once in London, the other time in Australia after a grim dinner in one of those less reputable Chinese resturants I call 'ptomaine taverns'. Finally we came to rest again at Alma, Yehudi having by this time persuaded Schwester Marie to leave her hospital and return to us when she came backstage after his concert in Berne and told him I was 'expecting'.

Alma – home – suitcases actually to be put away. Joy! But not unalloyed. For Alma was a beautiful vacuum. Beyond the mutual friends through whom I'd met Yehudi, the artists Frank Ingerson and George Dennison living in the valley below, the poetess Sara Bard Field Wood a few miles nearer the village and two remarkable women, Caroline Smiley and Maude Meagher (nick-named the 'Dobe Girls' as they'd built their adobe house from which they published their weekly youth magazine themselves) we had few friends of our own and I had no one to turn to in moments of stress. Every so often wild winter storms would crash through the mountains, sluicing the yellow topsoil down the slopes in thick cascades like Bird's Custard, carrying the wreckage of careful planting, cherished acacias, young poplars, a cosseted pepper-tree and the unravelled knitting of tangled masses of shrub clotted with mud. Together with it all the raging wind would drag down the telegraph poles and my only communication with Y.

And now Y was off again to Japan, the first American artist to go since the War, at the invitation of General MacArthur. After having thrown caution to three of the winds, I felt I should show respect for the fourth and elected to desert Y for the first time and not risk flying to and back from Japan in the ninth month of my pregnancy. Instead I set to my usual unpromising task of finding a 'couple' for Alma and after scouring the agencies (who, in America, wants to sit on a hillside, looking at the odd redwood and getting poison-oak swelling, between cooking frozen peas and lamb chops or sweeping the floor?) I reluctantly engaged a couple - Cedric and Fifi. They were black and presented themselves as husband and wife. At the start I had hopes, for the black Americans are full of humour and liveliness and often very kind and concerned. These unfortunately were the exception that proved the rule. Cedric was slim, good-tempered, rather sweet and totally lazy and at least forty years younger than Fifi, who was as gnarled as a sea-coast pinetree, had a face like a crumpled dirty paper-bag and never stopped whining. A veritable charcoal Electra.

I saw Y off at the airport less than two weeks after our homecoming. Aba and Mammina drove me there and were very kind and tactful, but to this day I remember the agony of loneliness and fear as I saw Y go blithely off in his Japan Airlines plane. (He put on a kimono so he told me over the blower on arrival and slept the whole way.) Oh, lucky, lucky Y to have such a temperament. There followed, for me, four Kafkaesque weeks, getting Mita back into the routine of Schwester Marie's ways. One determined character facing another, for he had got far too much of his own way, being an extremely quick-witted and articulate child, and needed to be brought to heel a bit for there was not only his strong will to deal with, but something far more elusive – his was a dreamy, explorative mind at the same time – a strange dichotomy difficult to handle. When I announced that within a month or so he would have a playmate and not feel alone, he gave me a withering look and said he would far rather have a toy.

The day for the baby's birth was drawing very close and I was over sixty miles from San Francisco. I was too preoccupied with the antics of Cedric and Fifi to be frightened, anyway I've never had time to be afraid for myself – too much taken up with the endless problems of running a running life as though it were stable – to be able to indulge in any other kind of analysis.

At last on 25 October Y rang from San Francisco. I swear I held my breath for the whole two hours it took him to be driven home. He poured out of the station-wagon, behind him a veritable mountain of crates and cases, bundles and baskets. I fell into his arms, burst into tears and begged him to sack Cecric and Fifi on the spot. He went straight down to the kitchen, returning ten minutes later without a word and made me start unpacking the cases. Out fell bolts of exquisite ancient brocade, roll after roll of silks and satins, an antique Japanese ceremonial robe of white satin inset with intricate patterns of musical instruments in red and blue and green complete with crêpe silk kimono to be worn underneath, obi, and satin slippers; vases, an ancient Chinese terracotta bull hauling a cart with enormous wheels, lacquer bowls and trays, bundles of ivory chopsticks, thick satin kerchiefs – the bedroom looked like a glorious bazaar.

Suddenly the weight had lifted. How fortunate I actually was to have Yehudi by my side – whatever the cost, whatever the burden, whatever the problems, the very sunlight of his presence was a blessing and all the more so for having to invest so much to clear the clouds and enjoy it.

So a few days later we went to San Francisco, with Schwester Marie and Mita waving goodbye, as Y drove down the mile long drive and on to the high road, and we put up on the twentieth or fortieth or whatever floor of the Mark Hopkins Hotel in a Chinese-decorated suite with a superb view of that Leonardo da Vinci of engineering – the Golden Gate Bridge – and I, impatient as ever, descended and climbed twice daily the vertiginous streets of Mason and Powell in an attempt to jolt the baby out of me. On the evening of the second day there I felt the first pains, However they decided to stop. The next day my reproduction engine started up again early in the morning and Y took me to the Stanford Hospital where Jeremy was born at 4.40 a.m. on 2 November 1951.

Oh, that special other world of after-birth, particularly when the child is born at night. Jeremy had been taken away so as to let me sleep, Y had gone back to the hotel and I lay there, gloriously alone in a kind of hiatus. The foghorns blew from the harbour, the very first faint signs of dawn came like fingers tracing a message illegibly across the dark sky and I swam, limp and delivered and in a strange state of mind unlike any ordinary feelings ranging between joy and sorrow. For a little I did not seem to be a human being, I seemed neither physical nor mental, but in a spiritual state belonging to myself before I was me. It was as though I had been where Jeremy had dwelt these long nine months and we'd both been born together. I wondered if he were feeling the same, and, longing for the clouds of glory to trail forever, slowly fell asleep as the fog bowled in white and soft and ephemeral from across the Bay.

# 6

# *India*

It was inconceivable that the violin alone could ever contain Yehudi, clear also that he envisaged music as a courier, a means of reaching out to all corners of the world, a language with no need of words, a communication rather that could be of vast and deep significance in terms of true values. So, when an old friend of Y's, Sir Alfred Egerton, passed on to him a message from Lady Nye, the British High Commissioner's wife in Delhi, that the Indian Prime Minister Jawaharlal Nehru had high hopes that the topmost musicians would include his country on their tours, even though they could not be expected to be paid the usual fees, Y suggested that Nehru should get in touch with him. He did so and I answered Nehru, saying that Y could manage a two-month visit early in 1952 and would, if the Prime Minister thought it practical, charge for the concerts, turning all the money over to the Famine Fund for Madras where one million people had died the year before. Little did we think when the idea was gratefully accepted that this would lead to a long love-affair with India, a country to which from then on, we would always feel a special affinity, finding so many people of like minds, or develop so many enduring friendships. Looking back now over nearly thirty years and even allowing for the natural thrill of arriving in a new place, I can still remember with clarity and a feeling of tingling the first sight and smell of that marvellous land.

Crawling out of the plane at New Delhi, crumpled in every limb, feeling like two old bags of biscuit crumbs, before us we saw Indira Gandhi, beautiful and serenely smiling with her delegation – looking like birds of paradise in their coloured saris coming towards this battered pair, bearing huge garlands of stephanotis and jasmine hung with tassels of sandalwood. Above was the fresh blue sky of a Delhi spring and all around pullulating crowds and the rippling cadences of Hindi, rising and falling like the chatter of massed birds in a tropical forest. Even the alien

72

ugliness and muddle of an airport could not dent the wonderful surface of the place; the plane had become a magic carpet and wafted us into a magic land.

As we drove to her father's house, Indira explained that he had delegated her to make a committee of her close friends to organize Yehudi's concerts and that these would take place in Delhi, Bombay, Madras, Bangalore and Calcutta. The Prime Minister had taken over Flagstaff House (once the GHQ of the British Army) as his Residence. Whatever other changes might have occurred in India since the British came and went, the sense of style and innate panache had survived. There on the steps of the house were several attendants in narrow trousers and white jackets sashed in red and gold, splendid turbans and bandoliers to match. Barefooted, moving with the natural grace of those who have never been crippled by shoes, they opened the car doors, swept out the luggage while Indira led us into the cool (very bank manager's Streatham) hall, up the Axminster-carpeted stairs (the British officer dies hard, I thought) and into the drawing-room.

A few minutes later Nehru walked in. My first impression was of the extraordinary aesthetic quality of this not very tall, slender man, of the combination of beauty and exquisiteness that lacked nothing of manliness or strength. I realized that I had met him before in a hundred Moghul prints, but never quite believed that such had existed other than in the imagination and vision of the artist who drew or painted them. Here was the living, breathing, moving example, (only dressed in a simple white 'Ashkan' and jodhpurs and a white Gandhi cap) – the only symbol linking him to those Persian-Hindu pictures, the red rose-bud in one of the buttonholes fastening his jacket. Something imperious but not cold in the appraising look of those immense dark eyes and a quiet humour waiting to be summoned in the mobile mouth. Lovely hands extended towards us. 'Catastrophe', he said. Krishna Hatti-Singh, his younger and mischievous sister, had opted to stay on in the room intended for us and, as Edwina Mountbatten had the ground-floor guest suite, would we mind staying at Rastrapathi Bhavan (Vice Regal Lodge) until he managed to dislodge Krishna? We should go over now and settle in and come back to dinner.

Leaving the large English villa, we drove to that most successful of all Lutyens' architectural dreams, the greatest of gestures of the British Raj standing black and plum-red on a rise outside the old city, and were there greeted by the President, an elderly man with the appearance of an oriental magician and the manner of every child's favourite grandfather. Up vast marble staircases, across tesselated floors, past gorgeous flunkeys caparisoned in red and white and gold dotted here and there like human décor to our suite of rooms, beautiful with Indian silks and brocades and sumptuously comfortable. I flung myself on the bed and looked at the decorated ceiling. I hung our garlands on chairs and picture frames, wallowed in a scented marble bath and floated like some disembodied spirit, afraid that the coloured bubble I was in must at any moment burst and I find myself in an air raid shelter brewing tea over a primus.

The speedier the much maligned aeroplane carries one from the worn world of cold wet asphalt and the rattling bustle of mankind inexorably being superseded by machines, the more shatteringly wonderful is the impact of the East. There is no slow transition, rather a juxtpositon of two extremes and I felt as I lay in my bath as though I were only a kaleidoscope shaken by an unknown hand.

And so into dinner-jacket and dress and over to 'Prime Minister's House' and up the stairs back into the long drawing-room with its Bournemouth armchairs and sofas and bridge tables, ghosts of the taste of long-gone colonels rescued by one or another exquisite Indian artefact: here an alabaster vase lighted from within so that its carving glowed unearthly and substanceless, there a box of Kashmiri lacquer, on the colourless walls Moghul prints and paintings. And then in his silent leather slippers entered the Prime Minister, filling the whole room with his especial mixture of physical slightness and intellectual awareness.

'I hear, Menuhin,' he said in his best Harrovian manner, 'that you study yoga.' Y mumbled something about having found a book on yoga in New Zealand only about nine months ago and how he had corkscrewed himself into trying to follow the instructions while holding the book with his one free foot.

'Well, what *can* you do? Can you at least stand on your head?' Y said that yes, he could.

'Well, go ahead,' said Nehru.

Poor Y divested himself of his shoes and jacket and modestly did as he was bidden.

'No, *no* that's no good, I'll show you,' was his reward, whereupon Nehru took off his Gandhi cap, clasped his hands on the floor, cupped his head in them and slowly and gracefully unfurled his legs till he stood, a perfect column inverted. Y, not to be so easily demoted, followed suit. At that moment the big double doors at the end of the long drawing-room opened and a gorgeous major-domo appeared in royal blue and gold topped with one of the most magnificent turbans I've ever seen.

'Dinner is served, sir', he announced without blinking to the two inverted figures. Behind him, aghast, in the dining-room, were about ten venerable old Congress Party members, Nehru's beautiful sister 'Nan' Vijaya-Lakshmi Pandit and Edwina Mountbatten, all thoroughly amused.

At dinner the conversation was fairly general and I, thinking it the acme of diplomacy, managed to disclose to the Prime Minister that, unlike Y (born American) I was English so as to obviate the possible occurrence of some thundering epithets against the late tyrants. I might have saved my breath. At the first opportunity Nehru engaged in a long dissertation about the near-past, ending his diatribe by saying,

'So then the British put me in prison again', deliberately turning a gimlet eye on me sitting demurely at his side.

'Now come, Mr Prime Minister,' I retorted, 'if we hadn't had the sense to do that you would never have had time to write all those books.'

A ripple of shock at such *lèse-majesté* ran through the black, tight-buttoned bosoms of the Congress chiefs and a mischievous smile from Nan.

At lunch and dinner next day the Prime Minister and I continued our parrying and thrusting greatly to the amusement of Indira and Nan.

'Now look,' he rapped in his abrupt way, 'I'm not going to let Indu and her girls work Yehudi to death – all the concerts ahead are sold out and you're not to do any more. I'm sending you down in my own plane to Agra tomorrow.' When my eyes widened with delight, he shot an arrow straight into them, saying scornfully,

'Of course, you will want to see the Taj Mahal, won't you?'

'Yes, Panditji,' I said quietly.

'Well, you're wrong. There is a far more beautiful small temple close by – Itmud-ud-Dowlah – that's what you should bother about. Don't suppose you've even heard of it.'

'No, Mr Prime Minister, we can't all be as clever as you, would you be so good as to write that name down for me?', and I handed him the menu-card. Pause. Sharp look, scribble. Name passed to me with a smile and a question in his eyes.

'Do you know,' I said, answering it,' I'm very disappointed, I thought I was going to meet my first Kashmiri Brahmin and all you've shown me so far is an irascible British lawyer.' Another pause and then laughter, and from then on a very close and endearing understanding.

Indira saw us off with typical Indian courtesy at dawn the next day, accompanied by Naryana Menon, one of India's leading veena players, an Oxford graduate and head of All-India Radio – a delightful, humorous clever man and one of our closest friends-to-be. Of course, the Taj Mahal was glorious, sailing like a white bubble against that immense Indian sky with the flat plain below. And so too indeed was Itmud-ud-Dowlah, a small gem of carved and coloured marble close behind it; naturally Nehru preferred it because it was exquisite, unheralded and unsung. Even more impressive to my mind was the vast red stone fortress of Fatehpur Sikri, built out there on the wide Deccan plain by Akhbar the Great in that wonderful sixteenth century. A great enclosure of several acres, its walls topped at the corners with capped towers, the 'Chchattri' which Lutyens had so ingeniously reproduced for Vice-Regal Lodge – its courtyards' flat surfaces broken with fountains and lovely small temples, ending in an unexplained grand staircase leading down to an emptiness of dry grey green plain stretching as far as eye could see – only broken by the poles of the occasional water-wheels sending the scarce water flowing along the narrow invisible canals. Large birds of prey wheeling above made the sky more inhabited than the land below.

Back in Delhi at lunch with Nehru, I realized he could tell by our eyes and my excitement that we were already in love with India in the way he had wanted us to be, sensing its ancientness, its especial style and its indestructible distinction beneath the poverty and the problems, the ever-growing population and the appalling difficulties of trying to drag it into the twentieth century.

One day Naryana Menon took us to meet Ravi Shankar. When someone has become part of the warp and woof of Y's musical life, it is a complex process to unravel the thread to its beginning. I remember the impact of Ravi's beauty, the gentleness of his manner, the excitement that grew up between Y and him as he explained the multiple sophistications of his exquisite sitar, the immediate contact of two masters of their own particular instruments who realized at once that their approach to music, to sound, was exactly the same. While we were there, Ravi played magically together with his tabla player (a tabla being the pair of small Indian drums that support and accompany the improvizations of the sitar) Chatur Lal, another virtuoso whose inner ear and mind seemed to anticipate every change in pitch, tempo or mood till the two of them took flight in an interlocking web of sound that was part dialogue, part song, wholly communication.

The following day Y, having now been joined by Marcel Gazelle, gave his first concert and it went beautifully. Amrit Kaur, one of Nehru's closest friends among the freedom fighters, introduced it with a moving and sensitive speech which exactly interpreted both Yehudi's significance and the nature of his gesture to India. All the strain and repetitiveness, the slow blunting of the fine edge of the meaning of music over the past strenuous years fell from my heart, I felt back in the true centre of what I had shared with Y.

After the second concert we all had a late supper together followed by the usual heaping of gifts that is so typically Indian. Panditji and Edwina and Y were on the sofa, I on the floor (my favourite seat) and Indira carrying a batch of her father's books which he signed for Y. Offered a handful of photographs of himself, I chose one where he looks straight out with sombre melancholy eyes and without his usual cap.

'Oh Diana, that's so sad!', Nan objected.

'But it's so much you caught unaware', I said to him. 'May I have it?' He looked down at me very searchingly for a moment and said 'Yes' writing, 'To Diana, Jawaharlal Nehru' in his small clear hand.

We got up a little sadly for we did not know whether our paths might or might not cross again. Wandering on to the balcony above the porch, I could smell that wonderful moment in northern India when the last of the daylight has left a faint blue hem in the dark of the sky still opaque from lack of stars or moon, when the first cool of night is freshening the air carrying a spicy smell of dying flowers and rotting dung and when the distant call of jackals rises above the stirring of heavy leaves. Panditji followed me out and we stood for a moment in silence. He put his arm round my waist and following my gaze sighed:

'I know it is an insuperable problem to which there can be no real solution my dear, but I know also that I shall and must go on trying.' There was such sadness and so much love in his voice, I longed to find some means of allaying his weariness but any words would have broken the moment and shattered its privacy. I turned away back into the lighted house. Whenever I look at that photograph I can hear that voice and the longing that was his whole belonging to India.

Our next stop was Bombay, an explosion of a place, by which I mean that it is the most onomatopoetically named town I know. Out of the elegance and grandeur of Old and New Delhi one was thrown into the hurly-burly of a modern oriental city teeming with vociferous people who only seemed to be held back from tumbling into the huge bay by the barrier of a vast muddle of houses and villas of varying Victorian seaside shapes, themselves teetering on the edge of the shore road. We had been met by a delegation amongst whom were to be our closest Indian friends: Homi Bhabha, India's great physicist, a man of about forty with a head like a splendid bull, his great friend 'Pipsie' Wadia, a tigress's head with a mane of grey hair and huge archaic black eyes, handsome 'Pan' Narielwala, one of the heads of the vast Tata industry, and a host of others including Mehli Mehta, a violinist trained at the Curtis Institute in Philadelphia and who had performed the miracle of producing an orchestra fully capable of accompanying Yehudi in the Beethoven and Mendelssohn concertos. All these were Parsees, the descendants of those Persians who had settled unmolested in India several hundred years before and formed the heart of its industrial-technological world, as well as supplying the driving force of the artistic one.

Homi and Pipsie swept us off round the immense bay to the headland, wooded and cool where the British had made a perfect enclave and built their Government House. 'Don't listen to any nonsense about being put in the "Royal Bungalow",' Panditji had snapped. 'Insist upon "Point Bungalow" right on the rocky edge looking out to sea where I always stay.' And so we did.

The Governor greeted us with the usual warmth and we were installed in Point Bungalow by at least four lithe boys in white and red and gold, grinning with delight at the prospect of looking after us. After dinner that night at Government House we returned to our quarters where I found my bed shrouded by an enormous mosquito net. Y was firmly placed in another room and fell asleep as he hit the pillow. I lay and listened to the water, lapping at the foot of the rocky cliff and to the last croak of the mynah birds as they finished their evening chat and flew to their trees. Finally, I too slept. I awoke suddenly. Something was tugging at my net, and tugging very determinedly. In the light of the moon I saw a large pair of reddish eyes gazing at me above a very sharp pair of front teeth busy gnawing a hole in my net. Frozen with horror, I let out a strangled yelp loud enough to put the rat off his job and he scuttled away. Shaking like an old flag in a high wind, I worked my way round the bed, tucking the net so firmly under the mattress that the next rat to appear slid off onto the floor and after a couple more failed attempts they must have informed their chums, for I was left unmolested and fell asleep.

The next morning the sun rose into the pale blue sky coming up out of the water like a baked orange and Y and I had a delicious breakfast of mango and papaya and guava and 'dahi' (Indian curds) and 'chow-pattis' (the flat pancake bread) in the cool fresh scented air. I told Number One Boy about my night visitor rodents. 'Ah mem-sahib,' he said, 'they have bitten through the fencing on the cliff. They come from the water. Mem-sahib shall have a cage.' Satisfied grin. Wavering smile was the best I could do, flummoxed by visions of spending the following nights behind bars.

As it happened, I was soon to discover that the cage which Number One Boy had so keenly produced as a solution to the rodent problem was not intended for me but was in fact a large lobster-pot affair of thick bamboo furnished with some very smelly bait I never dared examine into which the rats would run one after another, chattering and scratching all night. There was one slightly hump-backed one I named Akhbar, of whom I became quite fond. I also got used to their nocturnal visits and touched by the way Number One Boy, on waking me of a morning, would wordlessly collect the lobster pot, pass through the French window to the edge of the cliff, open the hatch and liberate the rats through the hole in the fence to scamper down the rocks and away. No question of killing them, nor, incidentally, of mending the hole in the wire-netting.

Mentioning my nightly chums to the Governor at dinner one night he chuckled and told me I was 'far more tolerant than Panditji who, eating his early breakfast one morning, lowered his *Times of India* to discover, my dear, one actually sitting on the butter dish licking away like mad, and so furious was he that he overturned the whole table, coffee, jam, fruit, toast – the whole jolly lot.'

All the eminences of Bombay seemed to be on the Concert Committee, including the Lord Chief Justice and Mrs Desai, one of the most prominent members of that strange religious sect, the Jains, who are so strict they will not kill a fly. Rehearsals: trumpeters wrenched from the Navy, timpani from the Army, violinists from all over. Mehli Mehta had coached them all lovingly, section after section, so that under the baton of a Goanese conductor, Mr Casanoves, Y felt quite relaxed when the concerts took place. Of course, being Y, he added a free morning recital for students with Marcel and filled up any interstices in the first day by interviewing an entire convoy of yogis until finally he settled on someone who was to be his lifelong guru, Mr Iyengar, a southern Indian whose technique in yoga was what Nijinsky's was to ballet.

Yehudi was, of course, humming like a bumble-bee over a particularly rich and beautiful flower. Everything Indian suited his soul, heart and mind, his eyes, ears and nose. We had arrived in India at the most ideal time. What routine and discipline the British had brought still kept a steady base and those Indians we met had led the culture of their country while still remaining fully conversant with that of the West, visiting Bayreuth and Salzburg, London and Paris, Rome and Florence. In no way did they find such a different variety of expressions in the arts either inferior or superior to their own, so that we shared the same language, argued over values and ideas with passion and humour, without an iota of embarrassment or alienation of fundamental taste, albeit Y and I did feel ashamed of our scanty knowledge of the Indian arts. That rather enhanced our friendship, offering them the chance to spoil us by bringing the greatest Indian dancers and violinists to perform.

The ensuing days were a feast of unforgettable experiences. One early morning we were whisked away in a small private plane with all our friends to bump about above the Gujarati plains to Aurangabad, and from there we piled into cars and drove to the extraordinary caves of Ellora dating from the sixth century AD through the Buddhist, Hindu and Jain periods to the eighth century and beyond. In a long enfilade of caves cut out of rock were temple after temple, the most striking of which was the Khailasa, which had been carved from the grassy top of the rocky escarpment downwards, digging away earth and stone till the building was complete, intricately carved and surrounded by a courtyard of smoothed rock.

The day after we drove to Ajanta, the terrace of painted caves set in a crescent in a hillside and only discovered by pure chance in the last century by a wandering soldier who, from the opposite side of the ravine, espied a dark patch in the grassy escarpment. His wonder must have been similar to ours when he discovered no fewer than twenty-nine caves all painted in glorious though now rapidly fading colours with those extraordinary Indian physiognomies: huge slanting black eyes that seem to go right round a woman's head and tie under her thick black hair somewhere at the back; fine aquiline noses, lovely classical poses; men as delicately depicted as the women only with a fierce claiming air that belied their finesse.

Most memorable of all perhaps was the morning we all embarked on boats to go across the water to Elephanta, the island where the temple of the Trimurti (the three-headed Buddha) stood. A glorious breakfast of mangoes and every possible Indian dish imaginable, served in typical style, took up all the time till we landed, sticky and gorged, and climbed the steps to the enormous opening of the building, half-cave, half-temple, that enclosed the giant heads. At first, emerging from the bright light, one saw nothing but gloom and felt a great coolness, then infinitely slowly as though materializing at that very moment, the mysterious enormous face became discernible. It reached from floor to ceiling – Buddha with great closed eyes and a trace of a smile on his lips, flanked on each side by the profiles of its other two heads. A sense of utter, total peace emanated from it that caught at one's heart and all but stopped one's breathing, so complete was the effect of stillness. Neither dead nor alive but a kind of suspension between life and death, another way of living, above mortality and yet not alien from life – immortality brought to life perhaps – an infinity that the Hindus have always recognized as contained within the process of living and which smooths the pain of parting. There was no sadness in that great head, no heavy solemnity, only a message to be perceived or missed. Mine was 'the eye made quiet by the power of harmony and the deep power of joy' of which Wordsworth spoke when he said we saw it 'in the life of things'.

On leaving Bombay for Bangalore we had an oddly moving encounter with yet another member of the Gandhi-ites who came to see us off – a very old lady called Phoebe Kaptan.

'Gandhiji would have been very sad had he known he would miss Yehudi by a few years,' she said. 'He had read in the *Times of India* how Yehudi had faced a mob of furious Displaced Persons in a camp in

Berlin in 1946, mostly Jews, who had suffered appallingly under Hitler and who had been worked up into a state of pure hatred against Yehudi by an agent provocateur because of Yehudi's insistence upon returning to Germany as a Jew to play for all deserving causes.' Gandhi had turned to her and said:

'I would like to meet him. Here is a man who knows the power of love.'

Bangalore, looking from the air with all its jacarandas in full bloom, was like a city full of gas flares. More concerts, more kindnesses, more temples. A performance of dancing where we saw the indefatigable Mrs Roosevelt, and I began to believe the story that Franklin's nightly prayer had been:

'Oh God, please make Eleanor tired.'

Yehudi, whose innocent wonder and freshness of heart protected him from all sense of boredom, fortunate creature, was determined to visit a very important Jain statue, 'The Gomeveswara', nearby. 'Nearby' proved to be an endless and increasingly hot and bumpy drive of about sixty miles during which I became more and more sullen while Y disappeared into that empyrean whereto he takes off whenever a whiff of the unpleasant reaches his nostrils. Chatter, chatter, chatter, rattle, rattle, rattle, bump, bump, bump, dust, dereliction, cracked sore earth and at last two lovely ponds with great pink lotuses floating in them, green shrubs around and before us somewhere up in the merciless boiling blue sky, a huge statue and – 630 scorching steps to climb. Aching and sticky and mutinous, I clambered silently up those stairs, slippery with the tread of a million devout Jains whose whole faith I was beginning heartily to dislike. Y, gracious as ever (till his breath gave out), performed the courtesies at which my patience had finally jibbed. Crowds of believers surrounded us concentrating on their tributes to the deity above. I kept my head low partly because it eased the strain on a back already bruised with bumping over the dusty miles, partly to cover my thoroughly unpleasant physiognomy.

Excelsior. We had arrived, panting and sweating. I raised my eyes. There before me was a statue whose vast size was only matched by its utter hideousness. At least half the height of the Empire State Building and alien from anything else I had seen in India, it looked like a nightmare from a Walt Disney cartoon. Made of God alone knows what durable material, it was painted all over in child's primer colours with a revolting dead-white face, ruby-red lips and the simper of a maudlin drunk. The whiteness, I was told with hushed fervour, was caused by the milk poured over it by the faithful for x,ooo years. I was too tired to retch and too ashamed of my lack of sympathy towards such devotion to manage more than what I hoped would be construed as a fascinated nod.

By now thirty packed days had passed since our arrival, days of such richness, of such novelty, of experience, landscape, architecture, artefacts, as to make one gasp and stretch one's eyes. But the most significant factor underlying the whole multi-faceted, multi-coloured experience was that of the Indians themselves – Hindu, Muslim or Parsee, Kashmiri-Brahmin, Harijan, or Numbers One, Two or Three Boys – they held the secret of India, bound together the disparate parts, interconnected the tremendous variety; the Indians of those thousands of years back whose thinking, skills and visions had slowly built the disciplines engraved in the sculpted temples, endemic to the votive character of their music and dance that had filled our senses, lifted up to another world; and our new friends, Homi and Pipsie and Pan, with their subtlety of mind and warmth of heart, and made us feel as though, far from being aliens, we were long-delayed relations who had postponed our journey home to them for far too long.

Yehudi was in Nirvana. Homi, who was doing a drawing of me in his big airy studio, said: 'You know he does not come from the Middle East, he comes from here. He has the perfect Indo-Hellenic head of the Gandhara period when Alexander the Great tramped through Northern India and left much Greek influence behind.'

Years later I found just such a huge Buddha with eyes closed and a top-knot on his head that is quite uncannily like Y asleep, in Kansas City Museum – alas! they had no postcard of it. Not only was the food to his liking – mainly vegetarian, full of exotic spices, not only was the plethora of fruit tantalizing, but that provider of all things bright and beautiful, Pipsie, would send round huge terracotta jars where buffalo-milk cheeses swam like white tennis balls in thick whey together with bowls full of mango ice cream. Every early morning would see him on the grass before Point Bungalow going through the strangest of contortions with his chosen guru, Iyengar, while the mynah birds rudely scoffed at him.

And so our generous friends sent us south, telling us that unless we went there too we would not get a complete enough vision of India.

Our host was to be the Maharajah of Travancore who, soon after our arrival, treated us to a two-hour concert of veena, drum and a performance by a most intriguing man, whose skill for his instrument was not commanded by the length of his fingers, nor by the strength of his arms, but by the perfect size and shape of his belly. Against this anatomical wonder he held a vast clay pot upon which he slapped, struck and thumped, varying its pitch with miraculous precision by shifting it up or down, left or right, close to or farther away from his protuberance. The result was riveting – not only to the ear but also to the eye.

Despite his unaesthetic shape and his plebeian instrument, its echoing ring and the minute changes of tone he extracted from it were weirdly magical.

Yehudi's taste for the arcane was aroused next day during a drive when he insisted upon stopping to pick every possible and impossible fruit hanging from the jungle of trees. He found one monster that not all the pleas of poor Captain Tampi, our escort, could prevent Y's eager gathering. It was an ugly and indecent great football hanging on a hairy umbilical cord from a tree, lying according to the length of that unattractive liaison mainly on the dusty roadside. 'But Mr Menuhin-Sahib,' implored poor Captain Tampi, 'it possesses a most truly horrible smell and is therefore rarely eaten except by such as are desperate in their desire for sustenance.' But he hadn't reckoned with Y's invincible obstinacy, and grimacing miserably, he ordered the driver to stop the car and slash the great hairy ovoid with his knife. 'Jack-fruit' was its name and hideous was the smell that accompanied us all the way back. The elegant and enchanting Maharajah and I sat in front. In the back the Maharajah's sister and brother-in-law jammed together with Marcel, Y and the odoriferous jack-fruit. The heat was tangible, like travelling in a perambulating armpit.

That evening over at the Palace the Maharajah gave us a delicious South Indian dinner followed by our first sight of the renowned Kathakali dancers on the wide lawn spreading like a carpet below the terrace on which we sat. By now everyone has seen a film, a show or a picture of this extraordinary idiom but in 1952 few outside India had heard of Kathakali and, if they had, imagined it to be either a Caribbean voodoo or a flea-killer. It is, of course, the most perfectly sophisticated and unbelievably subtle combination of make-up, dancing, acting and myth ever conceived, demanding of the participants not only six hours of pasting upon their faces a terrifying mask of greasepaint and rice-paper, but also a technique of such perfection that those alone who have been trained from childhood can give a convincing performance. When a dozen or so dancers erupted from behind the bushes, with spinach-faces, howling soundlessly, arms and legs bowling and swerving, pouncing, bouncing in their billowing trousers in a combination of fierce spontaneity with the most sophisticated control, one was struck forcibly by the subtle Indian gift of interpreting sensuality through the devotion to ancient religious codes and the whole gamut of human behaviour into one coordinated and coherent art form, both spiritual and physical, with none of the shameful split of demarcation that obtains in Western religion, separating the body from the soul and rendering both debtors to each other.

There, in the heat of the South Indian night under the spell of these wildly expressive creatures from a world that should have felt totally foreign to me, I thought of pre-Cromwellian England, of the sensuality of the great religious poets, of Vaughan and Herbert and Crashaw and, above all, of Donne, who even when the walls of St Paul's restricted him, transferred his passionate corporeality to the service of God, losing little in his sermons of the urge and power in that poetry he, fortunately for us, did not succeed in destroying. The natural instincts of this great sub-continent, India, had developed untrammelled by intellectual fashion or modish theories and this wonderful explosion of whirling movement under the black rooflessness of the night owed nothing to self-consciousness.

Off next day with the indefatigable Captain Tampi to the hills, the wayside crops echoing the changes of climate as we drove upwards through the rice-paddies, tapioca fields, sugar cane, coffee, rubber plantations and into the delicious cooler air where mile upon mile of tea greened the last lap. Four thousand feet and then a slide downwards through even greener tea (shades of Sheridan Lefanu, I thought) to the great lake of the Maharajah's game reserve, onto a launch and across the still waters in the last limpid light. It was clear enough to see a herd of elephants with their graceful slow-motion-camera gait coming down to drink. Bison stampeded through the long grass at the noise of our engine and an occasional group of elegant sambhars loped among the trees.

Bed: between icy sheets in the camp house on an island, and instant sleep only disturbed by the trumpet snores of Captain Tampi. Dawn:

into another launch in which we cruised up and down various waterways spreading their long fingers into the hillsides where rust cinnamon bushes glowed, flame trees burned and the reddish carob-tree described an accent amongst the thick vegetation. At last breakfast to quieten my gurgling stomach and thaw my blue limbs – breakfast on a flat rock, delicious hot Indian food eaten against a background of hosts of pink amaryllis reflected in the clear still water. Silence, pellucid light and air so pure that wine would make a poor comparison.

With the crash of 400 hobnail boots, a mighty clap of thunder erupted from nowhere. Anxiety crossed poor Tampi's face. Huge drops of rain seemed to fall from a single cloud that had shot up over a nearby mountain as though some outraged god were spitting at us. We scuttled back into the launch like so many cockroaches, packed our things, regained the boat and made our way down the lake and back to the pier. A thick mist as clammy as damp muslin covered everything. However, we found our faithful driver just as the heavens opened, loosening a downpour like a broken sewer over us turning day into instant night.

Total invisibility added to the rattle of rain in punishing blows upon the car which slithered about while the driver peered helplessly through the sluice of his windshield. Suddenly we felt a violent jolt, came to a dead halt and heard furious shouting. There before us, as we flashed our torches, were the buttocks of an enormous elephant flat up against our bonnet, and there also was his half-dislodged mahoud pouring expletives upon the head of the wretched driver.

We crawled along like penitent children for miles before the outraged mahoud finally had mercy on us and, drawing his vast vehicle to one side, allowed us to pass and continue on our slippery way, at last reaching Kattayam worn out, as damp as the underside of old flower-pots, but so filled, so glutted with the variety of this rich, dense and enigmatic country that we fell into a blissful sleep. We had also seen the oldest (Syrian) Christian church in India, passed through Cochin where Yehudi was proudly greeted by the small tight-knit and oldest Jewish community in the country, and in these two short experiences witnessed the lack of chauvinism, the open heart of this great land.

It is impossible to do justice to the rich diversity of India in so short a space so I can only skim over that extraordinary water's edge at Mahabalipuram where once the Seven Pagodas had guarded the Indian Ocean, which in scant gratitude had swallowed all but one of them; the smooth-worn top of the surviving pagoda could still be barely perceived as the waves moved inexorably over it, bent on its final engulfment. I can do no more than drag you past the wonderful rock-friezes there or the small temples stuck haphazardly all over the sand-dunes as though they were toys left by careless and highly gifted children; but I must stop for one moment to haul you with us up 600 feet of cliff at Tirakkalikaroon, up 680 steps in the steaming heat to watch the phenomenon of the two eagles who year in year out arrive at exactly 11.30 a.m. to be fed – specks on the horizon growing ever larger, alighting to pick up their lumps of raw flesh, guzzling hideously and then taking off like feathered aeroplanes to become specks on the horizon once more.

Before leaving Madras Y gave two concerts, in the second of which he had included the Bartók Sonata No. 1, because, he said confidently, 'those Hungarian dissonances approach the Indian idiom so closely they will *love* it.' For my part all I can report is holding the miserable Governor's hand while he wriggled wretchedly whispering, 'Oi, oi, what terrible noises.'

Our next stop was Calcutta, where to our delight we caught up with Nehru again, using every opportunity between his work commitments to talk, argue, explain, toss queries and grab answers about our mutual absorption in his country. Such intimacy reflected the sudden growth of that especial kind of fond friendship, rare in any circumstances, but rarest of all in our nomadic, hard-working lives. It was one of the saddest moments in my life when a few days later, back in Delhi we said goodbye for the last time.

As a parting present for Yehudi's concerts, Nehru had arranged for us to visit Kashmir. On the morning of our departure that incorrigible devourer of all that is strange and novel, Y was up at the ungodly hour of 5.30 and off to a nearby glade to see a demonstration given by the guru of all yogis and a team of his followers. He returned full of joy just in time to join me, the luggage and the ever affectionate Indira and Narayana Menon (who was to be dragoman) to drive to the airport. I asked Y how he had enjoyed his dawn diversion and was horrified to hear him say that it was so enthralling he had found it irresistible not to comply with their demands and had divested himself of his outer clothing and joined in. I gave him a withering look which, of course, never so much as touches that hardy perennial and asked apprehensively, 'And what did you finally appear in?' Silence (Y's great and stainless steel armour). Sometime later they sent me smudgy photographs of a large circle of venerable old dhoti-clad gentlemen in the centre of which, standing on his head, his loose underpants drooping dangerously around his buttocks was the recognizable and otherwise naked figure of Yehudi Menuhin, the violinist.

Kashmir was Nehru's greatest love affair, it dominated his whole life, his being and his heart. He chose a Kashmiri girl as his wife, a slender and delicate woman who was to die of tuberculosis when Indira was only twelve years old. Therefore his fight to keep this lovely land within Indian rule may have appeared illogical from the purely political point of view, but once one divined his passion for that dreamlike country, one relinquished dry reason and understood the heart and depth of his emotion. And once one had seen Kashmir, one did not need the excuse of being – as he was – a Kashmiri Brahmin, to fall prey to its power of seduction.

We flew to the border town of Jammu, hot and dusty as a bowl of dry cereal, and from there the little plane struggled upwards against the forbidding wall of the giant Himalayas like an amateur climber with borrowed grappling irons. I bit my lips as we fought and tossed our way ever nearer to this terrifying barrier, for all the world like some insect clumsily attacking a garden wall, falling off backwards and sturdily trying again until (so I prayed) it would finally make it, and lumber over the top trimphantly to safety. By the time I opened my tight-shut eyes at the sound of a lessening in the grind of the two small engines, I found we were indeed just over the crest of the mountain wall and there below us lay the plains and water-meadows, the great golden carpets of saffron, the silver ribbons of narrow streams, an early spring greening the trees with its benediction. As we skimmed down the runway and clambered from the plane, smelled the freshness, saw the extraordinary light, it was as though we were on the roof of the world – aloof and aloft, lifted on to another and stranger plane.

Srinegar – what a solitary and echoing name. Small wonder Panditji, escaping here whenever he could afford the time, was so deeply and incurably in love with Kashmir – even the brief glance as we floated down had caught at my heart with that immediacy that is like a state of grace.

The guest-house put a sharp stop to all that kind of poetical fancifying like the slap of a British governess wielding a wicked ruler. It was pure and unadulterated lower provincial suburbia. The shock of the dreadful bedroom with its shabby flowered carpet, its twin Tottenham Court Road beds with their shiny sateen bed-covers, the awful matching dressing-table with its determined doyleys and the rest of that terrible furniture family: wardrobe equipped with tin hangers, chairs with Baptist chapel backs, bloated purple armchair looking like a fat alcoholic in the last stages of DTs; the shaggy fringed plush curtains, guardians of the wild and doubtless dangerous beauty beyond, the blistered wall-mirror, the whole loveless unlovely symbol of sad, grim, sex-frightened England.

'Yehudi,' I cried 'I can't – darling you don't know the significance of this, you're not English. I must escape.'

After a dinner of cubed mulligatawny soup, fish fried in an overcoat of browned gravel and 'cold shape', I tossed under my multi-floral eiderdown thinking savagely of all the awful 'digs' I'd had to live in in my ballet days from the renowned horrors of Ackers Street, Manchester, to the prissy drearinesses of the ground-floor-backs of Edgbaston. It revolted me that I should be here in Nehru's beloved Kashmir, barricaded from all that was beautiful by the durability of the British boarding house.

Next morning (after leather toast and manure coffee) Narayana turned up with Shamblu, who was to be our guide and who soon found us a houseboat. It turned out to be very damp and smelled of mould, but it was moored to the green and sloping edge of a wide and beautiful river and on the bank were those huge and benevolent grandfather trees, the deodars. Across the waters were saffron fields beginning to spread like delicious scrambled eggs lightly powdered with curry, and the light and air joined in a pellucid companionship that held all the fairy tales of one's childhood – cleanliness, innocence and purity. But it was freezing and I huddled in the tiny cabin moaning in middle register. Y promptly leapt to his feet, cracking his head smartly on the ceiling, and dashed out to find Shamblu who returned a quarter of an hour later carrying two small iron braziers about the size of an incense-burner full of glowing coals. 'There,' he said proudly, 'this is what all the peasants carry underneath their outer clothing. It is called a kangri.'

Wondering vaguely about flaming bed-clothes and charred cloaks, I got back into my bed, hugging my kangri, had my breakfast, dressed and then drove with Y, Narayana and Shamblu into the town.

A world apart from India, a total entity: people with Asiatic faces, either Central or Southern Asian with olive skin and great black Semitic eyes under their very dirty woollen hoods; stone houses, greyish with wooden balconies, open bazaars selling hot, flat, circular loaves like the Arab ones to be found in Morocco; donkeys, noise, cool air and matching sky. Shamblu - eponymously named, so we were soon to discover with shambling ways and shifty eye - led us from one exotic shop to another. In one, carpets stacked on the floor, hung from the ceiling, smothering the walls, added to the deepening feeling of Asia. All that was southern Russian in Y caught fire and he gloated as he wandered through - he has a passion for carpets and rugs and had already quite a beautiful collection - to another shop full of exquisite lacquered boxes and trays, bowls and jugs, Byzantine in colour and fantasy. Yet another where whole families worked on the intricate embroidery with which the Kashmir wool is adorned - worked with such minute care that some of the best pieces were completely reversible - cloaks, covered with flowers, gowns, capes, shawls, big and small. Narayana kept on pressing me to buy but I held back, choosing only a few things for myself together with a marvellous mediaeval-looking long coat in musk-brown, embroidered all down the front and across the hem with very pale beige silks which I felt Y must have. Again and again Narayana returned to the attack pressing me to buy more. Afraid that he might think we did not appreciate the exceptional beauty of all these handicrafts, I whispered: 'Narayana, Y has given all his fees for the Famine Fund, I'm *not* going to make him spend money on my fancies - please.'

Afterwards Shamblu took us in a rickety car to a spot by a stream on the wide plain where I enjoyed one of the most momentous meals of my life: fresh trout (expertly caught and cooked by Shamblu) and big pads of hot bread, fruit and wine, all in solitary peace, the ring of snow-capped mountains guarding us, together with the plain and some fallen Greek pillars to remind one in this timelessness of past time. The only sound was the running brook and the occasional bird floating and wheeling and crying in that high pure air, the soft spring sun catching its coloured wings and flicking the water with flecks and flashes of gold. And that light - softer than the beautiful Greek light which is like wide-opened eyes - Kashmiri light is more elusive, more peaceful, the half-open lids of innocence and shyness perhaps? It was only on the aeroplane next morning that Narayana told me why he had so doggedly urged me to buy more on our shopping expedition.

'Nehru ordered me to encourage you to buy everything and anything you wanted, Diana – but he did not want me to tell you for fear you would hold off!' Damn, and Damn anew. Virtue is indeed its own – and sole – reward.

Back in Delhi we found most of our Bombay friends bearing gifts. They themselves were gifts, they had warmed and expanded our lives, were to dwell forever in our hearts, had coloured what is for the main part a very demanding, exhausting and sometimes monotonous life with their bright minds, their affection, generosity and the peculiar imagination that is particularly Indian and which suited Yehudi's own very original and searching mind and brain. Panditji rang from Simla to bid us goodbye and to thank Y again, telling him that the concerts had raised $38,000 for the Famine Fund. 'Please come back soon', he said.

Two years passed before we could repay our debts to India. It turned out to be a true home-coming, Indira with garlands at the airport, Panditji running down the staircase to hug us at his house. Concerts, happy meetings and at the close another $38,000 to offer.

For a year I had become 'Aunty' to a young boy, Pema Tulku Tenzing, one of the many Tibetan refugees camped outside Delhi who were being looked after by Indira's friend Freda Bedi, helped by a group of the most inefficient, fussy, devoted old female muddlers I had ever met. One of them was awaiting me in the drawing room of Nehru's residence, a very odd effigy from outer South Kensington dressed in long robes and at least three coats of many colours and different lengths. Sidling up to me and raising her head as though she were a crab and I a bump in the sand, she drew from behind her a frightened small boy. 'Heah', she piped, 'is your *lama incarnata*'. At a loss, I shook him by the hand. He grinned, showing a set of dazzling white teeth. A lot of dithering followed accompanied by fluttering gasps, fluting sounds and crescendoes of gushing. I must, insisted the lady from South Kensington, I must come to the Tibetan camp which was only ten minutes away. We should have to leave Pema here as there would be no room in the jeep for him. I asked one of the beautiful silent valets to keep an eye on him and bring him some sweets, and very reluctantly followed the lady still a-twittering down the stairs.

Outside was a venerable jeep with a very friendly, quite mad woman from Fulham at the wheel. Her name was Joan and apparently she actually *lived* in the jeep. After a hair-raising drive we stopped by the side of one of those large banks of dusty earth that stretch over the plains round Delhi decorated with the tumbling tombs of past maharajahs, abandoned and desolate. There stood an old bungalow and dotted all over the bank, squatting and crouching, the most fatally lost lot of human beings I had ever seen. It was not so much an air of despondency that they projected as one of total meaninglessness. Dear good Freda, dressed in saffron robes, emerged from the bungalow with a glazed look in her bright blue eye and asked me to meet 'one of the highest and most exalted of the Great Lamas'. I had not the faintest idea of how to salute him and stood stock-still, hoping at least that I emitted waves of respect and humility. After fifteen minutes of mime during which he hawked and grinned a great deal and Freda looked increasingly *exaltée*, I begged her to come down from Nirvana and get me back to the Prime Minister's house where the wretched Pema was sitting alone. I pushed some money into her hand and said I would make a covenant for him as there was no other way to get money into India. I also asked her whether I might pile some of those mothers with the rash-covered babies into the back of the jeep and drop them at the hospital. After much dithering I got my way, delivered my sad load, returned to the house and racing up the stairs, found Pema beaming before a huge empty sweetmeat plate. Oh, do-gooders, why are you always so disjointed?

Pema grew into a charming lad and decided at the age of thirteen that he was not a *lama incarnata*. With the help of the Maharajah of Kashmir, I managed to get him into an ashram at Pondicherry and now he is a married man with a four-year-old child and we still correspond a little.

On my return I reduced Panditji to tears of laughter over my Tibetan morning. Despite his evident amusement, however, I noticed that he looked frailer and more worn. He was truly a man apart, a being of unusual qualities whose English conditioning had both been an advantage and a disadvantage to so deeply romantic a nature, Gandhi was the practical man, Nehru the dreamer. With the battle against the British won, and Gandhi assassinated, he was left very much alone in his struggle to drag India into the twentieth century; very often perplexed before the huge complexities which faced him every day and which challenged his pride and independence. He would appear sometimes arrogant and self-righteous in his pronouncements and there was no-one other than his wise and gentle sister, Nan, who could give him counsel. Slowly he was to kill himself with overwork. The most difficult moment in all countries' histories is the aftermath of battle, and the supremest of all complexities lies with those who have won – not those who have lost.

# ❧7❧

# *Family Taking Shape*

Aeroplanes and trains, hotels and concert halls, strange places, strange people – these were our staple diet during those years. But we did manage in the occasional pockets of time that such a crowded and ever-moving life allows to fit in and gradually build a family life, enjoying albeit all too rarely such communal adventures and misadventures as other people take for granted. Alma always meant a breathing-space, however short a time I stayed, either alone or with Y. Its beauty, calm and detachment from the circus that comprised most of our life together offered a hammock of sorts in which to try and swing into a rhythm, soothing to the nerves and above all, a chance to take stock – that imperative effort without which no joined lives can run smoothly.

The male is the romantic, the woman the practical, She cannot afford to dream, to take her eye off the way ahead, even to linger for fear of missing the priorities upon which the entire family is based. She must constantly be orchestrating the whole score that is the slowly expanding family, the multiple changes, the endless additions that accrue, all must be harmonized, either by recognizing their value within the lives of those she loves or by detecting the dissonance that may prove destructive.

How was one to try and give Y the life, the family life he in his undefining way desired so deeply, how to be by his side physically and mentally, supporting, encouraging, sharing; how not to deprive the small boys and Zamira (who was not yet permanently with us) of some kind of nucleus that would give them that sense of a nest, when the parent birds, singly or together, were constantly flying away from it? Over four months had elapsed, for example, when we returned, with various diversions, to Alma to see Mita and the now eleven-month-old Jeremy. That Mita looked like Long John Silver with a patch over his eye from having cut it to the bone, did little to reduce our joy and excitement. Jeremy seemed enormous, rather plump, with large slate-coloured eyes and a thatch of dead-white, dead-straight hair on his round head. Mita's was a lovely wavy corn-coloured mop and they (apart from the cut eye) were flourishing thanks to Schwester Marie.

Unpacking with Mita's help, listening to his tales and adventures – at just short of four years old, he had a large vocabulary and read quite well and was as ever a responsive and delightfully sharp-minded companion. Presents from India distributed all round – Mita excited over a dark red lacquer bedside lamp and box (for secret treasures) to match – bedtime story and at last bed. Our very own bed in a room without a suitcase in it and before us the summer holidays; Zamira and Krov would arrive by mid-June and stay on till the end of August – the evening serial continuing during their supper, the strangeness created by the long absence dropping away like a 'winter weed outworn' and plenty of walks, swims in the pool, visits to 'Nonnetto and Nonnina' (Mammina determinedly kept to her Italianization of family appellations), picnics, reading, music on the radiogram, Schwester Marie very strict and quite rightly so; either the children sat still and listened or they went off to play – no 'music as background colouring'.

Family reunions did not, of course, always take place at Alma. Later that year we rented a chalet at Mürren, in Switzerland, and early autumn found us in London where I took the children down to see their step-grandfather, Cecil Harcourt, at Chatham. 'Mar charld,' said Cecil (his version of 'my child'), 'would you like Jeremy to be christened at Rochester Cathedral? The Bishop would love to be one of the godfathers. Chavasse, you know, a very splendid fellow who lost a leg in the First World War; I would be another if you agree and you can choose godmothers if you will. It can be very quickly arranged.' Looking apprehensively at the rather large lump, all of eleven months, which was my younger son, I thanked Cecil and told him to go ahead. My apprehension was in the event to be justified, but all my passion for Dickens was aroused at the idea of Jeremy's being christened in that part of the world and I loved the great old church sitting by the Thames.

So one day Cecil, Schwester Marie, Mita and I drove to Rochester, which still bore the traces of an elegant small town, and up to the delightful eighteenth-century vicarage. There we were greeted by Jeremy's handsome future godfather and his charmingly pretty wife. We chatted for about half an hour in a pleasant room overlooking the widening estuary. The Bishop then rose and, limping across the parquet floor to the far corner, bent over and lifted up a large square of it, revealing steps leading downwards to the ancient Saxon crypt upon which the original cathedral had been built. With mounting excitement in inverse ratio to our descending steps we all clambered down the stone stair, finding ourselves in a small stone chamber with a few rows of pews, an altar and a pair of candlesticks. Mita, solemn and a little wondering, sat by my side; Jeremy, a solid beaming infant in an Italian knitted suit, was quite another kettle of fish. He was handed over to the good Rochester who proceeded in his beautiful voice to pronounce such words as were required to make of him a good soul. Suddenly the Awful Child snatched the Bishop's gold spectacles with a chortle. There followed a rather vague mumble while the denuded prelate, peering at the blurred print, made wild dabs at Jeremy's plump hand waving the spectacles delightedly just out of reach.

At last the patient Bishop gave up all attempt at finding his place in the prayer book, closed it, recaptured his spectacles, put them firmly on his nose, reopened the book and continued his service. But he hadn't counted on Jeremy's capacity not to recognize the right and proper form of any occasion (inherited from his father). Showing total lack of respect, the Horrid Child seized the Bishop's elegant nose firmly between his finger and thumb with the result that the final passages from the Bible were delivered in a weird nasal whine over which the poor man's beautiful oratory lost all power. He ended swiftly, handed the joyful monster back to me (Mita and I were laughing so much we could hardly get up) and we all went up to one of those glorious English country teas I had not seen in decades.

One day Zamira, now twelve years old, announced that she 'wanted to be a child before it was too late', and could she come and live with us? I was very moved, told her she must work it out with her own mother, and if she succeeded I would welcome her with wide-open arms. After a few tussles all was happily settled and we sent her to stay with English friends in New York where she subsequently for a time attended the excellent Dalton School.

Despite the eccentricity of his life, or perhaps because of it, Yehudi undeniably occupied the centre of the stage with his energy, unpredictable gestures and irresistible attraction for the outlandish which never ceased to surprise us. There was that memorable time when he dropped in at Alma unexpectedly early one morning in the middle of one of his tours. The door burst open and in he rushed, beaming like the barely risen sun and bearing a huge paper parcel which he plumped on my bed. I was too happy and excited and comforted to notice anything except him, but at last he prodded me into opening it. It was an exquisite small Boudin of a sailing boat! He knew how much I loved the Channel painters. Hugs and masses of brown paper and ribbon, and the little boys running up shouting 'Daddy, Daddy!'. Schwester Marie asked about breakfast and suddenly that look I had got to know so well compounded of shame, wistfulness, guilt, embarrassment and pleading spread over his face. He had only twenty minutes left to drive back in the waiting car to the airport to catch the plane to the town from which he had diverted his route in order to give me this lovely Boudin. I tried to hide my tears of shock. I'd known it could only be a day or so at the most but one and a quarter hours seemed a cruel taunt, although totally unintentional. I turned my head and ran downstairs, begging five minutes more to choose the whereabouts to hang my treasure. Y, happy as a puppy who has brought one his best bone, gathered up the pyjama-ed children, and together we found the exact place in the hall, then, standing hand-in-hand shivering in the doorway, we waved Y off as his car swung down the long drive to the bottom of the valley and off up that beastly highway to the airport.

Y's fascination with all manner of fads and fancies we found especially baffling. There was the day on which some genius turned up with a sinister contraption which when unpacked from its wrappings looked nothing more nor less than a cross between a crucifix and a deckchair. When finally disjointed and rejointed, it proved to be a music page-turner, complete with pedal upon which the standing player pressed at the requisite moment, thus releasing a ghostly hand which appeared, grabbed the page and with great if jerky deliberation, turned it over and patted it into place, flipping itself back into 'position no. 1'. No amount of sarcasm from me as to whether this sci-fi invention might not detract from the total dedication necessary to the rendering of an inspired mus-ical performance wrought the slightest effect. I was left to enjoy the sight of Yehudi looking like a one-man-band, sawing away at some sonata movement with strained eyes, muttering lips and plunging foot, sweating with the effort to coordinate what might be so easily achieved by the quick flick of his own agile hand. And in any case, Y only uses music when playing with other chamber-music players.

That miracle eventually died a natural death when the hand developed a nasty habit of either turning three pages at a time or occasionally knocking the whole stand over. Y himself had always been a compulsive inventor, once coming up with a plan for hydraulic brakes only a short time after the archetype had been patented. He was highly commended by the astonished aeronautical engineer to whom he diffidently took it. Shoulder-rests, chin-rests, mutes, some in conjunction with others, some alone – all these were at some time or other the product of his fertile mind. The last solo effort I recall was the self-stirring saucepan over which we used to have eternal arguments. But admittedly his is an all-inventive and scientific mind as he once proved when he deftly picked the lock of my hotel bedroom door by means of a strong hairpin.

Then there was Y's growing obsession with yoga which on more than one occasion caused various members of the family acute embarrassment and confusion; one such occasion occurred in New York where we had gone to visit Zamira. While there Y agreed to demonstrate his yoga exercises in a long photographic session for *Life* magazine. I kept a beady eye on every 'asana' (pose) and then when all seemed well and proceeding safely, dashed out to buy Y two more rehearsal shirts. During that unguarded thirty minutes he had, of course, fallen into the trap he never sees. Two or more weeks later he adorned the front page of *Life* with bulging eyes and his tongue stretched full out, revealing his tonsils and uvula. The rest was silence. Poor Zamira didn't go back to school for two days. Y, of course, thought it all quite natural and splendid.

That summer the whole family joined together for a holiday in Italy where we had rented a summer villa in Lerici. I had taken my boring pains to a Swiss clinic for eight weeks, ending with an appendectomy, and Y as usual was touring, so Schwester Marie and the children were the first to move into the villa. Y fetched me and together we travelled to join them. I awoke the next morning still physically and mentally shaky from my operation, but the Italian sun poured its importunate way into our pleasant room, the small boys and Zamira were in the villa below and at long long last I was in circulation again. All round me in the villa I could smell that aphrodisiac odour of Italian coffee, hot rolls, fresh butter and jam. At last a little relaxation, a little luxury, an end to medicines and diets. However, I could not know that Y was in one of his culinary rabbinical moods. He bounces into the room and sets my breakfast tray on my lap. 'There, darling,' says he with that fanatical gleam with which I was becoming more and more familiar. '*There* is a breakfast that will really strengthen you and do you good!' I glared at the jug of hot water and lemon, at the plate of rusks looking like nasty small bath-mats, at the honey (I've always disliked honey). 'Butter won't do you any good, so I left that out,' added Y triumphantly. Suddenly I saw red and with a yell, picked the whole tray up and threw it through the open window. Y looked deeply hurt, like a priest with egg on his face, thrown by a recalcitrant proselyte.

'Darling,' I said, 'there are certain limits to self-control, added to which there are differences in approach to food. Goodness knows, I have followed your precepts from bone-meal, through seaweed patties to horse serum, I have just emerged from nearly two months of cabbages and ether. Would it be too great a stretch of the imagination to think that I might like to begin this lovely Italian day with something sensual and appetizing and not Spartan and improving?' Wistful and disillusioned, dear Yehudi ordered me coffee, rolls and jam and went down to pick up the shattered crockery and health food where it lay like a martyred saint amongst the lobelias below.

Christmas that year we spent at Alma, Y now really getting into the rôle of Santa Claus without sending Jeremy into hysterics and with a lovely Christmas tree decorated by Schwester Marie. Except for the wrongness of the climate, for once I experienced a real feeling of family and home and a little firm centre growing despite the jangling arrivals and departures. But almost simultaneously I was beginning to wonder whether Alma could forever remain our base. We had by now taken Zamira from New York and installed her in an excellent school in Switzerland. For a long time I had realized that I could not bring up the boys here in Alma, where in all the luxury and lavishness they would develop no anti-bodies against physical, mental or psychological germs; that, hard though it would be for them and for myself to leave this sunny paradise, I must give them their early education in Europe where they would learn languages by osmosis, see in towns and streets more of the ugliness and reality of life than could ever happen in this exquisite vacuum.

1954. Mita's sixth birthday took place on board a ship in the Atlantic and we invited all the children he'd made friends with to a birthday party. I'd left it to Y who had little enough chance to be a parent to arrange the tea. Everything was going very well until the 'cake' was brought in. I had not reckoned with Y's health laws. Mita's eyes filled with tears of disappointment and embarrassment when he saw a kind of flat platter of fresh and stewed fruit held together by what looked like a great deal of wet rope, but which turned out to be the poor chef's attempt at making a decent pie crust out of wholewheat flour. Since that débâcle, Y has not been nearly so rabbinical about special occasions and bendable rules.

For the summer we rented a chalet in Gstaad, one of those horrid chocolate-brown villas with a real dining-room and suburban-Swiss suite plus lace tablecloth and an inspiring view of the back of the Palace Hotel (architecture: Snow-White and the Dwarfs) around which, like mushrooms beside a forest-tree, stood the machine-made toadstools of Mercedes-Benz, Rollses, Porsches, old uncle BMWs and all. I shut my eyes and thought of the excellent schools for the boys I would soon dig out. As in all such chalets the money had been expended on the encaustic-tiled fireplace and Dubarry damask five-piece suite, leaving the bedroom to the attics with a six-foot head clearance and beds like coffins upon which had been frivolously placed a couple of huge cotton meringues. Sighing, I went to bed in this eyrie among the bird-droppings and listened to the all-purpose Swiss rain. Y, of course, disappeared under the hideous duvet and was out of this vale of tears for the following ten hours.

Next morning I awoke, sat up, caught my head a sharp crack on the ceiling, swore, sighed and nudged the neighbouring meringue with an irritable foot. Slowly, like the beginning of an avalanche, it moved, one blue unfocussed eye appeared followed by an arm and finally Y's whole head. I waited for the crash of his final awakening, which was announced by a cracking of all his joints, first knuckles, then shoulders, hips, knees and finally ankles and toes. Y was awake. Beaming of course.

'Darling,' he said with his delicious smile, gazing at the cracked lime-green paint, 'isn't it lovely?'

'Well...' I said, trying not to be disagreeable so early in the day.

'What's the time?'

'Seven-thirty'.

'Ah, I must hurry' and with that he threw off the enveloping shroud and was gone.

Half an hour later Mita, Jeremy, Schwester Marie and Y and I were all breakfasting in that dainty dining-room when suddenly I looked through the window at the long pretentious drive. The improbable spectacle I beheld was not calculated to raise my spirits. Up the drive, his soaking dhoti clinging to his muscular legs, strode Mr B.Y.S. Iyengar, Guru-in-Chief to Yehudi Menuhin. With a muffled sound, Y scuttled from the table and shot into the hall to open the front door and give Mr Iyengar a welcoming hug. I stood while the puddle round poor Iyengar gradually reached his ankles and waited.

'Darling, didn't I tell you?' asked Y innocently. 'Mr Iyengar is spending the summer with us'.

Nor had he told us that yoga sessions that summer were to be a communal activity. We were all, including 'Miras', as the small boys called Zamira affectionately, required to rise at 7 a.m. for the day's exercises. At the end of these sessions one lay on the floor with closed eyes and was supposed to empty one's mind while the good Iyengar laid his hands on one's eyelids. I went through agonies trying to empty a mind black with ill-will and red with suppressed rage and kept wondering whether he could read my hostile thoughts. I shall never know.

The Chalet Flora was found as a school for Mita – we'd arrived there on foot on one of those days when Switzerland seems to be one great sponge, looking like tramps, bedraggled and soaked, with the intended victim in tow. 'Tante Flora' listened to my précis of our endlessly moving lives, of having to abandon our children so often and of how much a child needed to feel supported by her and the school during these absences. She responded sympathetically, agreed to take him 'on trial' for both sides and see if he were happy and could settle. Relieved, we got up and Y passing an upright piano in the hall, ran his fingers up and down it and pronounced it out of tune. Suddenly Tante Flora looked at this figure with plastered hair, muffled in an old raincoat, mountain socks and boots and exclaimed, 'Bon Dieu, vous êtes Menuhin!' Y admitted it. I liked Tante Flora all the more for being willing to bend her school rules to help an unknown and distraught pair of parents to settle their child.

Griselda and Louis came to stay, and in between musical sessions we all had mountain walks and picnics and almost a normal family life. Gaspar Cassado, of whom Casals had said 'this is my Crown Prince', joined us and there were enchanting evenings of chamber music. Gaspar was the warmest, funniest man I had ever met and interrupted the playing with 'I have tremenjos story to tell' which enlivened every occasion. That summer was a good one even though I loathed the rented chalet and its proximity to the richissismes of the neighbourhood.

The following year I discovered that I was pregnant again. For some obscure reason of my own I never announced a pregnancy – not until the third or fourth month when the first obvious signs were visible. I had always wanted three children – also I hoped that Mita would feel the part loss of me less if there were three in all, and, instead of a sense of competition, would gain as the eldest child. For the first time, however, I felt an inexplicable sense of *Angst*, a horrid foreboding which, try though I might, I could not expel, although I never voiced it all through the ensuing months.

As the baby was due in August, and after touring the statutory eight-and-a-half months, we returned to Alma for the approaching event. What I found most difficult of all was to match the optimistic joy and eager excitement of Yehudi and Schwester Marie and to conceal my silly unfounded anxiety. A week later Y thought it best to take me into San Francisco for a final examination and to stay in the hotel. My gynaecologist, who had handled Jeremy's birth so beautifully, greeted me with warmth and pronounced himself totally satisfied. I hesitated on the threshold as I was leaving and turned, longing to pour out to someone the unreasoning fear that had never left me all nine months, but I found it impossible. Two days later, after waking at 6 a.m., I went into Stanford University Hospital. At 4.35 in the afternoon a perfect boy weighing 7 lbs 3 ozs was born. He died twenty minutes later. They never fathomed the reason why.

When I finally recovered from the sadness of this event, our long-laid plans to move to Europe began to crystallize. Zamira had already transferred from Switzerland to a finishing school in Paris, and by now I had regretfully decided that the two boys should eventually go to boarding school. Slowly and even surreptitiously I prepared for the Hegira – the flight from Alma with its hollow beauty and its false sense of security. Knowing the devotion Y felt for his parents and his fear of hurting them, I felt nonetheless that one could not forever dwell in a kind of ancestral worship and filial duty. The children's future was just as important a factor – for were they not, as I said to Yehudi, tweaking his worried nose, to be one day themselves ancestors and did they not deserve to be the best of their kind? He gave his whole-hearted approval. And Mammina, I was convinced, with her sixth sense knew and also approved. And so I packed and stored and one spring day, after saying a loving but vague goodbye to Aba and Mammina, we took the train eastwards – Schwester Marie, Mita, Jeremy and I. The two Siamese kittens, Hansel and Gretel, I had committed to the care of TWA. The parting with the parents-in-law had been clouded by the fact that Yehudi had put in their hands return tickets to Europe as a kind of earnest of our ties – our unbreakable ties – with them. Aba with his volatile nature had been very excited at the prospect. Mammina at her most Russian had coolly refused, giving Aba's frail health as an excuse.

In Chicago we had a one-day stop-over where we went to the zoo. There I was bewitched by what from then on has become my favourite animal – the symbol of all I can never be – viz., the sloth. There he lay in a tangle of dirty orangeish hair, looking like a discarded hearthrug, his feet and hands emerging from the hirsute muddle, tipped with long revolting nails curled into an infinite uselessness. I never did quite find his eyes, nor delineate his face, but I was convinced it held a secret contentment, a glorious lack of focus, a bemused happiness quite lost to us in this world of fuss and fidgets.

In New York we joined Y and caught the boat for Europe where we split up, Schwester Marie and Jeremy returning to a much nicer and genuine chalet at Gstaad while Y, Mita and I took the train to London. I looked out at the streaming rain in Dover, the glaucous grey tiles of the acres of small houses, and my heart filled with fear as I recalled the sunny paradise from which I had uprooted the children. Mita and I were playing Questions and Answers. I wrote on my slip of paper 'Do you like England? If so, why? If not, why?' and folding it up, passed it to him. The answer I unfolded was 'Yes, because it is so cosy.' Totally bewildered I wrote 'How?' and the answer came, 'Because of the rain, they know how to make Inside better.'

## ❧8❧
# Log-book (part 1)

As organically as the flow of a river, the current of our lives over those early years had carried us ineluctably towards Europe as our true centre of gravity. The articificiality of a home-base on the West Coast, Yehudi's world-wide concerts, the growing necessity of Mita's education, had all combined towards a decision to move the young family nearer the core of everyone's needs.

I have leap-frogged ahead over the perennial schedule of Y's working life as it would be wearisome to chronicle every detail of our movements, thinking it better perhaps to provide a diary of the main events of those years, memorable either for their intrinsic importance or for their incidental qualities, the range and variety of which evinced either a sense of exhilaration or sadness, of exasperation or disbelief and, on occasion, of outrageous comedy. Let me then start with South America where Y and I found ourselves once again a few months after our return from India in 1952.

MEXICO CITY, 23 FEBRUARY 1953
Almost immediately on arrival Y had a long television session. Next day we decided to lunch at a club whenever Y finished his practising. The telephone rang. A European voice speaking fluent English reminded me that he had been involved in last night's show. Could we have lunch? he asked. No matter how many excuses I made he persisted until I finally told him that we would not lunch till very late at a garden restaurant and hung up. At about 3 p.m. Y and I walked to the restaurant, having locked Y's violins in their double-cases in the wardrobe and given our key to the concierge. There to our dismay we found the pest at the entrance, greeting us like long-lost friends from Outer Siberia. During lunch Nudnik (Russian for pest), as I mentally called him, left the table to make a telephone call, saying a friend was due to join us. Friend

unable to come – fulsome apologies, etc. At last I reminded Y of that night's concert and resisting Nudnik's attempt to accompany us, we returned alone to the hotel. 'Señor Menuhin,' inquired the head concierge, 'did you not ask us to send your violins to the concert hall?' I grabbed the desk feeling faint. It appeared that a voice 'just like Señor Menuhin's' had called soon after we had left the hotel making such a request. After some hesitation, the concierge had entrusted the violins to his two biggest and toughest boys telling them they knew what Señor Menuhin looked like, and that the violins were to be handed over to no-one but him. On the outer steps of the concert hall the boys had been accosted by a man who tried to grab the case but, eyeing the gathering crowd, had fled. Returning to the hotel, the boys gave the precious instruments back into the safe-keeping of the concierge. Since that near disaster we go to bigger, grander and more anonymous hotels where the bigger, grander and more anonymous guests are carefully catered for by callous, disillusioned and thoroughly untrusting professional guards. Sad tale.

PARIS, 23 APRIL 1953
In Paris we found our beloved Enesco, by now bent almost double with his progressive spinal disease, reduced to living in the 'appartement de la basse cour' of the block of flats on the third floor of which had been his lovely flat. There, uncomplaining as ever, he sat in a miserable little dark room just large enough to contain his cot, his grand piano, a chair and a piano stool. 'Eh bien, chers enfants', he said with a heart-rending mixture of defensive pride and hidden shame. 'Me voilà!' Y talked to him of music and at one point Enesco turned to the piano and ran his sadly twisted hands over it as though it were an extension of his own being, part of his circulatory system without which he could not survive. There was nothing he could not hold in his encyclopaedic head: whole operas, concertos for any instrument. His entire mind was music and simply to spend an hour with him was magic. I noticed the frayed tie, the shabby jacket, the waxen face with its clean, beautiful bones and serene eyes and detected in it a kind of diffusiveness. Was it that this vast synoptical knowledge and comprehension had hindered his ever bringing himself to one single great accomplishment? Or was it that fatal slip in time that misplaced a genius two centuries too late into this commercial era?

At that moment 'Marouka', la Princesse Cantacuzène, whom he had finally married, having been her faithful, handsome and brilliant lover for so long, made one of her sudden royal appearances in the doorway. If you can imagine a No. 2 Company Zobeïde from some *fin-de-siècle* theatre who had once seen better days and who still refused to accept the ravages of time – merely adding layer upon layer of make-up to commemorate as it were the passing of each unkind year on top of those already ingrained from that famous first unforgettable night when she had taken fourteen curtain calls before the fluttering gas footlights; if you can take in the multi-coloured satin caftan wrapped round the massive trunk and above all the extraordinary head held with great dignity, scarlet-rouged, purple pouting-lipped, be-kohled eyes sombrely smouldering like two charcoal fires, the whole adorned with 'bigoudis', those large, crescent-shaped hair clips, beloved of the Marcel-wave era, set in symmetrical rows in her iron-grey hair and which she contrived to transform into a kind of 'kakozhnik' (the traditional Russian tiara); if you can take all this in without either flinching or fainting, then you will have absorbed this extraordinary Balkan effigy that was 'la Princesse Cantacuzène, Madame Georges Enesco' – imperious, totally self-absorbed and not a little mad. Just exactly what that chivalrous, wonderfully gifted and highly principled man, Georges Enesco, did *not* need to ease his way out of the life he had served so unselfishly and in such an aristocratic and generous manner. Leaving Enesco and Y to talk about a concert in which they were to appear together, I led the Princess down the dingy passage to her own room. There I found the typical vast divan covered with carpets, silk scarves and shawls of bizarre bazaar colours. On to this Marouka heaved her vast bulk, I squatting at the other end and in between us a huge Turkish tray containing a dozen dusty hard-boiled eggs, rather stale brioches and several of those tiny Turkish handleless cups of coffee. For two hours I sat there listening to the Princess till my head spun.

At long last Yehudi appeared in the doorway, very pale and with that expression of his that can only be described as 'silent'. I took his hand and went in to embrace Enesco. He seemed tired and white, lying back with a peaceful incandescent look on his face. I kissed his eyelids and we went through that dreadful dank courtyard and down the Rue de Clichy, and back, hardly speaking, to our hotel.

PARIS, 24 APRIL 1953

A small switch to the side to describe a meeting and an atmosphere so utterly different and yet in character the same – that of the total disruption and uprooting of human beings who had once lived in the greatest luxury and at the summit of the society of their erstwhile countries. Yehudi not needing me that afternoon, I raced out in a taxi to one of those little private enclaves in Auteuil, a double row of modest two-storey villas set in a small tree-lined avenue with gardens as their forecourts. A charming fake eighteenth-century house fronted by a small conservatory rather in the style of a little lodge at the gates of a large property. There, sitting on her tiled verandah amongst her favourite hydrangeas, surrounded by multiple cats whose smell wove a kind of exotic spell, sat Mathilde Felixowna Kschessinskaya, the last great Ballerina Assoluta of the Maryinsky Theatre, at seventeen the Tsar's first and most adored mistress and so powerful a courtesan that the Bolsheviks had never destroyed her house in St Petersburg. On the contrary, it was from her drawing-room balcony that Lenin had chosen to announce the Revolution of 1917. Delicate, tiny, sparkling with her own very Russian brand of mischievous coquetry, she sprang from her straw chair. 'Dianchik!', she cried and caught me and my huge hydrangea in a double embrace. Through the stained white doorway ambled one of the most beautiful men I was ever to know – her husband, the Grand-Duke André, first cousin of the ill-fated Nicholas II, whose escape had been made possible through the love of his peasants, 'Diyanna, deeerest!' he said with that lovely Russian nasal drawl and we sat there while his devoted old batman 'Monsieur Georges' brought out the tea and we talked of her ballet classes, of her pupils, of me and my babies, of the love we had had and kept for each other since Arnold Haskell, the foremost English ballet critic, had picked me up under his arm away from the abrasive screams of Rambert and deposited me in Kschessinskaya's classroom in Paris in 1932. There was no allusion to past grandeur, no sighs for lost treasure, just two completely devoted, distinguished and attached creatures who had found it possible to re-create their own diminished home as naturally as will a pair of very rare transplanted horticultural specimens adjust to another climate. How I loved them, and all they stood for in their proud poverty and threadbare elegance, their liveliness, simple acceptance and grace.

A guilt-heavy journey back to my life with Yehudi where all was so different – young, flourishing, bursting with work, plans, projects, a life prismatic in its brilliance and its achievements, past, present and hopefully the future, a life that was so crammed that there was no crack through which a cold draught could reach him. A sunlit boy, I suddenly thought, as I looked at his eager, sweet-natured face, and one whose total modesty, whose longing to give, to help, to encourage earned him the right to be so blessed. For by now he had cast off the scales of neglect and unhappiness and bewilderment and was leaping forward.

### PARIS, 27 APRIL 1953
Lunch with Marie Laurencin, sitting like a Watteau *Marquise* among her paintings, and talking to my delight of the ballet she designed for Diaghilev, *Les Biches*. Looking at me suddenly she asked if I mightn't be a dancer.

'Il-y-a six ans, chère Mademoiselle', I said, 'et il-y-a seize ans j'ai dansé le rôle de l'Hôtesse dans votre *Biches*.' Whereupon she picked up a large book just published on her work and drew me the most graceful pastel sketch of a dancer with 'à Diana Gould, Marie Laurencin'.

### PARIS, 28 APRIL 1953
Leaping is the operative word. To keep up with Y you need six legs, four minds, two brains and a ventilator to keep the lot cooled. I returned from my little Auteuil visit with its touch of *grisaille* to be hurtled straight into a conference convened by some of the wealthier Rumanians over the problem of rescuing Enesco, the proudest man on earth, from his present plight. We drove to the Belgian Embassy villa on the outskirts of Paris where one of Y's most loved and respected friends, Queen Elizabeth, the Queen-Mother of Belgium (an old pupil of Enesco herself), fortunately happened to be. Between us we cooked up a plan for Durand, his publishers, to reprint all his works, we paying him a monthly stipend. Whether Durand ever did publish or not I do not know, but in that way we were able to support him. On one last visit to Enesco I came bearing a pretty Sulka tie. He turned from the piano 'Mais comment, chère Diane, vous me trouvez tellement mal affublé?'

I went scarlet and stuttered something about its being 'mon plaisir, ma joie, si vous voudriez bien l'accepter'. He nipped my nose, took the frayed one off and tied mine on. It would be the last time we'd see him sitting at his beloved piano. The relief at not having to run the gauntlet of being waylaid by the egregious Marouka was not to be. As we emerged from the dismal archway into the Rue de Clichy, there, resplendent in purple satin, her head blatantly adorned with six rows of her crescent wave-clips, sweeping majestically through the traffic from the café opposite, the remains of the breakfast adorning her bosom betraying a menu of croissants, jam and coffee which in no way detracted from the grandeur of her carriage, sailed Marouka waltzing through the taxis to our side. Hooting in her barn-owl voice, 'Yah-hoodi! Diyanni!', she clasped us firmly to the detritus of her morning meal.

ALMA, 1-5 JANUARY 1954
Horrendous news that a plane carrying William Kapell (the great white hope of young American pianists) had crashed that night some twenty miles away in those very mountains where we lived, with the loss of all lives. I felt sick, wondering how much longer I could bear the strain of waiting for those telephone calls from Y telling me of his safe arrival. The telephone rang. It was Y. He had learned of the ghastly accident. 'Darling,' he said, 'I've decided to stop flying until such time as they've equipped all commercial planes with radar. I have too many people dependent upon me to risk it. Both Ginette Neveu and Jacques Thibaud have died recently in exactly the same way, crashing into invisible mountains.'

I could have cried with relief for I had never felt justified in begging Y not to fly while it held no fear for him. I myself had hidden my own growing terror of it for nearly three years. Unfortunately, Y had given an interview to a reporter in Vancouver which, like all things negative, winged its way top-speed to London where a week later a very unpleasant and sarcastic 'boxed' article on 'Yehudi Menuhin's Decision Not To Fly Any More' appeared, accusing him of stupidity, cowardice, lack of commonsense and other such delightful characteristics. It was, of course, written by the Air Correspondent who, one supposes, could only see it as bad propaganda for the airlines. Followed the most fascinating and admirable correspondence in *The Times*, attacking the reporter from all angles, pointing out that Yehudi had been the only artist to fly from America alone in the frozen nose of military bombers all through the War to play three times a day in factories and army encampments, in the Albert Hall to raise funds for the Free French and the Chinese, etc. etc.; that to choose such a man as an example of physical cowardice was disgraceful effrontery and insulting innuendo – and more of the same. The controversy raged on for days and was great fun. It made Y love England more than ever, not for the nice things they were saying about him, not even for the marvellous protective shelter they had erected around him, so much as the civilized way of a land whose leading newspaper had provided a voice in which such diverse opinions could be read, heard and bandied about with good or bad humour, and above all in a tone of voice that was always supremely human. We also got letters by the cartload sent to us. My favourite came from a double-barrelled-name colonel with a Wiltshire address. 'Damme, Menuhin, travel by camel if you wish to.' Short and to the point.

LONDON, 14 MAY 1954

Y was to give a concert in St Paul's, three Bach solo sonatas which H.M. the Queen Mother was to attend in aid of the restoration fund for the bomb damage. We went to St Paul's to try out the acoustics. As we walked up the nave we met Robert Masters, the then leader of the Mozart Chamber Orchestra, who was being 'stand-in' for Y. Robert stood in the transept and fiddled away dutifully. Total muddle – the engineer counted an overtone of eight seconds which meant that a fugue would sound like jabberwocky translated into Chinese. The setting was so magnificent, it seemed a sacriflege that the music should ruin the occasion, and, were Y to play very slowly in an effort to unravel the knitted sound, it would be pure parody. Someone came up with the brilliant idea of erecting a kind of shelter at the corner of the choir-stalls that would at least help to contain the echo and cut down the overtones.

The splendour of that great drawing-room of a church, the packed pews, the Queen Mother sitting on a throne-like chair at the front of the nave, all made one harmonious whole, but I have to admit that the sentry-box into which Yehudi stepped did somewhat blight the grandeur, and I was afraid that there might be a dreadful undertone (to replace the overtones) of 'They're changing Guard at Buckingham Palace'. I need not have feared. As soon as the first notes of the heavenly Praeludium from the Bach E major Partita welled out under that great dome, travelled down the nave and reached round the great pillars into every corner of that most beautiful of baroque churches, I knew it would be all right. Y looked very small in his black suit, half-enclosed in his sentry-box. He seemed to dissolve until there was nothing but sound, pure and clear, belling out in a kind of benediction.

SANTA BARBARA, 24 JUNE 1954
I got my first dose of poison oak and carried my swollen face and itching arms to Santa Barbara where I was much cheered by an Awful Concert. I have a weakness for theatrical disasters (a very nasty trait) and this was a real beauty. There was disposed, grouped one side of the huge and beautiful swimming pool at the Casino by the seashore, in all their model dresses, rattling with diamonds and borne down with emeralds, the richest community in the United States. On the far side sat the humble musicians of the orchestra, all in white tuxedos, and on came the equally humble Antal Dorati and Yehudi (*not* in a white tuxedo because I think he looks like an abortionist in one). Up goes 'Toni' Dorati's commanding baton, up goes Y's bow and up goes the wind in perfect collusion, lifting the players' music off their stands as would some playful zephyrs, tossing it around to let it drop like the contents of a filing-cabinet into the pool. Chaos. Cries of alarm and horror rustling among the rich (who'd paid $200 for their seats and were obviously not going to get their money's worth), I in transports of delight. Pure Marx Brothers. Y waiting patiently. Dorati looking efficient in a vague sort of way and some of the musicians rolling up their sleeves in an attempt to retrieve the floating Mozart from the pool. Eventually new parts were found, wet ones shaken dry, and the orchestra moved back as far as possible from the danger of further dousing. Toni and Y launched with redoubled vigour into the concerto. No sooner had they played a few bars than another kind of drowning happened. With a jolly roar speed-boats shot off right and left into the moonlit night. I sat in a state of bliss watching Y and Co. playing a Mozart concerto and guessing whereabouts they'd reached in those few moments when no speedboat roared happily up and down the bay. Around me were outraged millionaires seething with, I must admit, righteous fury. When I ran round to see Toni and Yehudi afterwards, Y was, of course, perfectly happy simply to have played the work with Toni, and said he was afraid he didn't really mind if he was the only one who heard himself. Toni said 'I just got on with the work and suddenly as I listened to Yehudi, I had the crazy idea – what if one had a whole violin section with that sound, what a miracle it would be.'

ANSBACH, 1 AUGUST 1954

Drove to Ansbach where a magnificent Bach Festival was held every year and where Benjamin Britten and Peter Pears loved performing. The splendid point of playing in a festival is that you can enjoy other concerts as well and Ansbach was a real musical treat – except for the rain which poured down in a thick steady drizzle from a bulging sky that seemed to hold eternal supplies. Day followed grey day and I took to my bed – that is to say, sitting up under the coverlet writing endless letters while Y stood at the foot facing my dressing-table mirror, steadily practising that dreary drone that is apparently the only means by which a violinist can keep himself in trim. Suddenly there was a tremendous crack followed almost simultaneously by a crash and a huge part of the swollen plaster ceiling fell from a point exactly above where Y was standing. With the agility of an acrobat he leaped backwards as it came thudding down, the mirror cracked from side to side and the poor old Lady of Shalott's feet were buried in a hundredweight of huge lumps of plaster mixed with glass. The slow deadly soaking of the past weeks had penetrated centuries of replastering in the old inn and, we were lucky to be alive. Y was spattered with nodules – his violin miraculously untouched by his swift backward leap. My feet and ankles were bruised, the coverlet torn, but the glass had not cut through. There was a stampede of feet up the stairs and a banging at the door and in rushed the manager and his staff, fully expecting us to be either badly hurt or at least quite dead. Above my sore feet gaped the rafters while the whole room was a quarry full of differing sizes of plaster chunks. We moved to another room, I limping gracefully, and Y, with a small cut on one finger, and resumed our tasks.

PARIS, 25 OCTOBER 1954

To Y's concert at the Châtelet, where I made one of my better gaffes. At that time the artist's room was a kind of small gardener's hut containing a wooden table, two naked protruding light bulbs and a single bentwood chair. Knowing that Y, the least fussy of all creatures, nonetheless had a horror of being pushed backwards into a dressing-room by a panting horde at the end of the concert, I flew round the corridor to the pass-door, smiled glowingly at the fierce official and begged him to hold back the encroaching wave until I could safely extricate Y from the *oubliette*. He was most co-operative to me but hardly courteous to the

Diana aged fourteen, when selected by Diaghilev.

Diana and Griselda.

Diane Gould as a wood-nymph in
*The Miracle.*

*Right:* Diana with her first baby, Gerard –
Mita' – at home in California in 1948.

*Above:* Gerard and Jeremy, 1952.

*Below, left:* Yehudi allowing Mita to break the rules. Austria, 1950.

*Below, right:* Zamira and Krov in Switzerland, 1947.

iana and B.B. on an outing in the woods
ound I Tatti, 1958.

Jeremy's and Yehudi's first sonata together.
I Tatti, 1958.

Zamira, Gerard and Jeremy in fancy dress for Yehudi's
birthday at the Villino, 1959.

*Above:* Nehru and Diana.

Yehudi and Mr Iyengar at dawn in
the grounds of Government House,
Bombay, 1952.

Yehudi with Hephzibah (*left*) and Yaltah, Bath, 1963.

Yehudi playing at the Wailing Wall, Jerusalem, in celebration of the Camp David agreement.

In the garden at Gstaad.

Gerard, Zamira, Krov, Anne, Jeremy, Diana, Yehudi, and Zamira's son Lin Siao at the chalet in Gstaad.

crowd: 'Ecoutez, vous,' he yelled to the mass of eager fans, 'restez-là, un peu de patience, voyons!' I turned to smile at the mob hoping thus to palliate the official's stentorian orders. At my elbow stood a furious elderly woman dressed in a schoolmistress's tweed suit, her grey hair topped by a large black cowpat, edged with white veiling, the whole completed by a formidable pair of pince-nez. She stabbed me with one glance from two hatpin eyes:

'Madame', she announced in the kind of deep voice that seems to have a beard somewhere entangled in its vocal chords, 'Madame! JE SUIS MADEMOISELLE BOULANGER!' with which she pushed me aside with her umbrella and marched on to the stage. Oh dear! I crept quietly after her like one of the many cockroaches that infested the ancient stage and did manage gently to extract Y from his cell to meet her and, valour being the better part of discretion, stayed guarding the violins amongst the dust and heat of those naked bulbs.

LONDON, 14 NOVEMBER 1954

To one of Y's concerts at the Albert Hall. There is a magic in that great elephant of a hall that is communicable to artists and public alike. All 7,500 of them always seemed as one in their attention and delight. I swear it emanates from the ghosts of all the great artists who performed there, Melba, Caruso, Galli-Curci, Ysaÿe, Rachmaninov and how many others, who left behind some of their spirit and their art, infusing the vast hall with an atmosphere that keeps it always warm and curiously close. Modern halls reject any such magic revenants, antiseptic and aloof they cleanse themselves expertly from all lingering wraiths.

It was after one of those concerts that someone detached themselves from the usual crowd and came up to me announcing that she had never missed a Menuhin concert since she was a girl, that she knew I had an extremely complex life and if there were any way in which she could help me - either shopping for the children or doing other chores - she would love to do so. Her name was Angela Marris. Delighted at the first offer of help I had ever had, I asked her if she could possibly find some grey socks for the boys. Since then she has knitted Y all the elegant cardigans he has been seen in at rehearsals all over the world, and has become a close member of our family.

LONDON, 8 DECEMBER 1954

Richard Buckle held his marvellous Diaghilev exhibition, now one of the high points in ballet history at Forbes House. A series of lectures were given by all the surviving dancers from that inimitable era: Sokolova, Idzikowski, Dolin, Markova, many others and of course the still beautiful Tamara Karsavina, my beloved 'Madame Tata', with whom the Rambert Dancers had made their début season at the Lyric Hammersmith during the great days when Nigel Playfair ran it. To my delight and confusion she told Dicky Buckle the story of how I had been the last dancer Diaghilev had chosen when I was fourteen and that on that score she would like me to be included in the roster of lecturers. Out of sheer fright and rustiness, at first I turned it down, then (thanks to the insistence of Domini Crosfield at whose house we were staying) I found two days in which to scribble it and just time to pull a presentable dress over my head, go to Forbes House, drop my coat in the wings and say my piece. I was twice happy when the BBC chose that one out of all the lectures to record for them.

LONDON, MAY 1955

Dined with Khatchaturian, the Russian composer, and David Oistrakh, the leading Russian violinist and one of our favourite musical colleagues (Y and he had played the Bach Double Concerto together in Prague in 1945 and many times since). David looked like the nicest of all teddy bears with the fur shaven off; as for Khachaturian the Georgian, his bulging brown orbs (peppermint bull's-eyes a quarter sucked) and greying hair as crimped as the corrugated iron roof on a Baptist Chapel, he looked more like a respectable Armenian carpet-seller.

David told Y that all Russia was clamouring for him to return and Y, very touched, said he would indeed very much like to find time to go.

'Why', said Y, 'don't *you* come to America, David?,' whereupon David threw his hands up and said something to the effect that all Russians were anathema to the Americans and there was nothing less likely than that he'd be invited nor would his government hear of its citizens being fingerprinted. This incidentally was during the height of the McCarthy Reds-under-the-bed period.

'Nonsense,' said Y. 'Shall we make a bet, David? I will get you your invitation, visa, concert tour, and all quicker than you will get the same for me in Russia?' Y that very afternoon, sent cables to the State Department and his agency, Columbia Artists Management and within two days had the promise of an immediate visa (sans fingerprints) and a tour of the most important towns in the States at Y's fee – (the highest there was) for November and December 1955.

Delighted, Y rang David to come to Claridge's as he had some news for him. David duly arrived and Y spread out the cables for him to see and take back to Russia to his boss and prison wardress, Madame Furtseva. David was thrilled with the speedy reaction of the Americans, but mortified that Y had given him such a heaven-sent opportunity and he had nothing to show in return. Giving one of those resigned shrugs that was the graphic speechless gesture of all his countrymen, he said, 'You know, Yehudi dear, with my country it has to pass through five or more Government departments before your next visit can be arranged.' Yehudi hugged him, saying that he had only made the bet as a joke and a way of proving to him that MaCarthyism was but a passing phase exaggerated by Russian propagandists to vilify America.

### ATHENS, 10 DECEMBER 1955

On board the Orient Express on our way to Athens Y discovered to his fury that there was no communicating door between our two cabins. Undeterred he smashed through the thin panel above the washbasins so that at least we could poke our heads through and maintain some kind of contact – the splintered remnants of the Orient Express's best and most ancient marquetry he hid under the bed. Arriving three days later in Athens we found Hamish McKenzie, the First Secretary at the British Embassy, a marvellously humorous future friend, waiting to meet us. 'We must collect our baggage,' I said brightly. 'Luggage?,' incredulously from Hamish, 'but the Orient Express *never ever* carries a luggage-van!' Dreadful moment, Y was due to give a concert that same night. However, it appeared there would be a train later coming from France and it should be on that. Off we went to the British Embassy where we were staying with Ambassador Charles Peake and his wife Catherine and waited anxiously for news of our belongings. Y didn't, of course. So long as he had his violins and his wife, no other possessions worried him. In came the baggagiste. Very sorry, no luggage – maybe tomorrow. I looked appraisingly at the Ambassador – not less than six foot four inches tall. '*Your* tails won't be any good,' I said, 'we'll have to have a sweep around all the embassies and fit the fiddler up for tonight. We've only got about seven hours left.' So while Y went off to snooze, unperturbed, we mounted a search. (I had been kindly lent a velvet dress by Catherine Peake.)

The trousers of the first secretary fitted round Y's waist but were too long, the tails of one of the French Embassy's staff fitted his extremely broad shoulders allowing him the extra looseness needed for playing (to the despair of his tailor) and some other member of another foreign mission lent him a boiled shirt, while yet another a pair of black boots. I left Y standing like a statue while a ravishing Greek housemaid pinned up the wastage of trouser-leg floating around his feet and went down to dine, making slightly distraught conversation, having left my mind behind in the upstairs bedroom. As soon as the pudding was served, I begged to be excused and ran up the broad parquet staircase clattering like the Charge of the Light Brigade. I stopped short at the sight of Y standing in the doorway of the bedroom. The maid knelt at his feet while she proudly patted the hems of his trousers into shape (having pressed them sideways). They were now at half-mast exposing the black lace-up boots (Y has very small narrow feet and obviously these relics must have belonged to some diplomat's distant boyhood). The top half consisted of an enormous boiled shirt which lent Y the bosom of Dame Nellie Melba adorned with a made-up white bow-tie like a helicopter; from over the butterfly-wing collar Y's head emerged, blond and fluffy, exactly like that of a duckling breaking the shell of its egg. The tail-coat dangled within a few inches of the bottom of those angular trousers; the starched cuffs drowned his small paws.

'Do I look all right?,' he asked so disarmingly that it would have been sheer cruelty not to stifle my yell of laughter and not to say: 'Of course, you look splendid – what luck, you're a veritable League of Nations, darling,' and bolt before I collapsed.

Y went to the theatre ahead of us while the great German pianist Wilhelm Kempff, Zamira and I came with Charles and Catherine to their box. Never have I been more grateful for and less irritated by being handed a bouquet of flowers, for as soon as Y and Kempff walked on I exploded behind it using it as a screen. I was not alone in my mirth – a subdued giggle floated from several points of the semi-darkened hall and the only box from which there was no sign of laughter was that of the Russian Embassy for their own sartorial inadequacies brought the level to about par. Most agonizingly funny of all were those cuffs stiff as boards which kept sliding down over Y's hands, so that when I should have been in raptures over a particularly beautiful phrase, all ecstasy was dissolved as Y, barely managing to reach the end of a lovely down-bow passage, had hastily to haul up his sleeves before the starch hit the strings earlier than his fingers.

I went round in the interval as usual and was feeding Y an orange when King Paul and Queen Frederica came round. Being German, she loved music and was enjoying herself; I felt I had to explain the reason for Y's Chaplin-appearance, whereupon both admitted they had thought his clothes a trifle odd. The comedy concert over, we all returned to the Embassy where the Peakes gave a reception. Out of the crowd a small dark man emerged: 'C'est bien Madame Menuhin?,' he asked me, whereupon my not having denied his conjecture, he proceeded to introduce himself as the Italian Ambassador, adding that neither his friend (introduction) nor he could bring themselves to believe that Menuhin had such a poor tailor? Irked, I replied loftily that our luggage had not arrived and that many kind diplomats (amongst whom I trusted there was *not* one from his mission) had kindly done their best to help fit him out. Acidly, I added that I hoped their concentration on his clothes had not interfered with their enjoyment of the music and walked off to look at my favourite portrait of George Gordon, Lord Byron, that hangs above the drawing-room sofa. Our cases arrived the following day, minus a beautiful négligée someone had pinched from one of my bags.

MUNICH, 6–9 JANUARY 1956

On the way back from Eastern Europe by train, kind friends, knowing the paucity, even non-existence of food on such journeys furnished us with a sumptuous picnic. A welcome gesture considering Y had no money. After nearly nine years of marriage I should have realized his loathing of cash and his invincible faith in credit, and learned as I did soon after, always to carry some form of acceptable currency in my bag. Luckily he had confided in the American Ambassador in Athens (both the Athens concert and the following one in Belgrade he had given free) so that when we reached Brussels we were met by two charming American officials bearing $100.00. In those days that went quite a long way, enabling us to move over to a second-class carriage and just catch the boat by its tail as it left Ostend.

## LONDON, CLARIDGE'S, 16–17 JANUARY 1956

Mysterious telephone calls from strange people, and knowing the skill of Claridge's switchboard and listening to the cadence of the voices, I poked my head out of the window to have a good look at the flags, and saw the Indian one. 'Yehudi, do you know what I think,' I said. 'It's Krishna Menon's calls we keep getting.' I rang down to the concierge and he duly confirmed that Krishna Menon was in the hotel and confined to his bed with suspected appendicitis. When we called Krishna, he said that he in his turn had been getting mystic Menuhin calls and invited us to come down and cheer him up.

There he was looking like a Far-Eastern John the Baptist who'd exchanged his goatskin for a pair of bright green pyjamas – managing somehow to appear more like a fanatical prophet than ever in them. He was just returning from his spell as Indian High Commissioner to the United Nations, where he'd been busily unravelling all the good relations with the United States that Nan Pandit during her term there had so meticulously built up. Without further ado he plunged into excoriations against America; his marvellous head with its sharp profile, prow-like nose and mane of grey hair furnished him with the perfect adjuncts of any demagogue. Y gently demurred at some of his wilder condemnations. I became more and more irritated. The wild and wonderful head swung from side to side thoroughly enjoying its imprecations. Suddenly I rose, seized the knobs of his brass bedstead and said: 'Oh Krishna, for God's sake, who do you think we are: Senator John Lodge? You're in the wrong play,' and giving the bed a good shake, I walked out. Y followed me with that bemused look he wears on those occasions when I blow up. Next morning I was woken at 7.30 – Krishna from the airport: 'Darling Diana, don't be angry, I know I was so rude!' How sad it is when passion overtakes intelligence and burns away all its usefulness.

## LONDON, 20 JANUARY 1956

Yehudi's guardian angel rarely blinks, but sometimes such is the pressure put upon this Gabriel that he has to fold his wings and snore. One such occasion was when Dr Paul Czinner, one of the foremost theatre and film directors in Germany, approached Y and asked him to take part in filming some of the more important operas so that cities owning no opera houses could at least see them in the cinemas. Y, always ready to leap at a new idea, asked Czinner in what way he could be of use. 'As narrator of the synopsis to *Don Giovanni* and to lend your name to an unusual form of showing music which may be difficult to attract sponsors' was the answer. Of course Y was fascinated and we spent a whole day in a rather cold small studio in Ebury Street while he ploughed his way through the tangled synopsis. So much for that day's work ... the envoi comes later (accompanied by a passacaglia of the Archangel Gabriel's snores).

LONDON, 23 JANUARY 1956

Another lapse by Yehudi's guardian angel! He was to take part in Patrick Saul's innovatory idea 'The Institute of Recorded Sound'. This society would not only serve as a library of recordings, but would make recordings of as many lectures on music as possible. Y was, as usual, the first person approached. He offered to give the first lecture at a hall in a Bloomsbury square, the tape of which would be the initial one baptizing the new library. He talked at length, without notes, on Georges Enesco, with a short interval to enable the engineer to change the tape on the recording machine. He was in great form, the hall full, and at the conclusion there was quite an ovation. Delighted at having helped launch a splendid idea, Y and I were somewhat surprised to see Saul emerge from the wings with a doleful, hang-dog look on his face. It appeared that the rather amateurish team he'd engaged to record the lecture had turned the tape over in such a way during that interval that it had erased the first half entirely while making jabberwocky of the second.

NEW YORK, 26 FEBRUARY 1956

It is chronologically here that I owe you the envoi to the event to which I referred when Y's archangel nodded, viz. the recorded script for *Don Giovanni* he had so innocently done for Dr Paul Czinner in London. The results were now to be shown together with the film of *Don Giovanni* at a Gala Evening at Carnegie Hall - followed by a grand reception at one of the few remaining great houses on Fifth Avenue. The lights dimmed and out of the darkness came Y's canned voice announcing the opera followed by a light résumé of the first act. I had already been worried at the vagueness of the synopsis and soon my worst fears were confirmed. As the singing began, slap in the middle of Donna Anna's most agonized trilling, Y's voice was heard explaining that she was fending off rape from Don Giovanni, whose impassioned if crude courtship was likewise half-drowned by the drone of Y's inexorable explanations. And so it continued, the wretched Y's voice flooding on like some unquenchable river, or as though the leader of a conducted tour in a bus persisted in pointing out the scenic wonders to his captive prisoners who could perfectly well distinguish a mountain from a waterfall. Y and I agonized – and the audience (amongst whom were many cognoscenti of opera) began to hiss and say 'shut up'. But relentlessly Y's recorded voice thumped on, ruining the top notes, drowning the delicate pianissimi, turning the whole evening into a black farce. I looked on in misery while Y, knowing as the audience did not, that he was helplessly stuck to the sound track and could only be removed when Don Giovanni is finally engulfed in the flames of hell, simply relaxed and took himself off figuratively on to that happy Cloud Nine he had, in perpetuity, rented as a refuge from all unpleasantness.

LONDON, 13 MAY 1956
Lunch with Nan Pandit, India's High Commissioner, who at Y's suggestion has invited the Soviet Ambassador. Five of us altogether: Nan at the head of the table, the Soviet Ambassador on her right, Y on her left, I next the Ambassador with Nan's very intelligent and quick-minded first secretary opposite me. All through the luncheon the Soviet Ambassador, a large imposing man with the face of a satisfied wolf, shot poisoned darts at the West and its policies across the table. Nan was her usual courteous unruffled self, Y made a few mild rejoinders. Finally the pudding was served and we helped ourselves in a rather tense silence. Nan's secretary made some remark anent the multiple difficulties facing India, whereupon Soviet Ambassador snarled:

'What you expect? If India so stupid to try and be democracy, she deserves troubles.'

My blood boiled. I seized his untouched plate of meringues and cream, saying: 'Just for that remark, Your Excellency, you deserve to go without your pudding' and plonked it down out of reach. He turned an empurpled face to me and, as I met his eyes, for a split second I thought he might hit me (I would have been delighted). But he dropped his hand, swallowed hard and then grabbed my pudding: 'So, I take yours!'

'You're welcome, Your Excellency', I said, 'but I consider I've won that battle, for my helping is much smaller than yours ...'.

Poor Nan and poor Y. They both sought comfort in exchanging soothing glances. The Indian secretary was delighted. I merely felt I had not spent some twenty-five years of Russian training in the ballet for naught.

## PARIS, 7 JUNE 1956

The unveiling of a bust in honour of Georges Enesco at the Ecole Normale. Anyone who is cognisant with this kind of French ceremony will know the grim torture of listening to half an hour of delighted – but not delightful – delivery of the spokesman's pet ideas delivered in alexandrines whose determined rhythm drives one into a kind of very special purgatory. For once, because his deep human love for his master and mentor roused him from his usual good-natured uncritical acceptance, Y was furious and followed this costive self-absorbed nonsense with a veritable burst of anger, giving the audience a vivid, colourful and splendid portrait of all that Enesco signified and all he represented. I enjoyed hugely the battered amazement on the bureaucratic faces that comprised most of the audience and longed for a latter-day Daumier to be there to depict it in all its dismay and intellectual demolition.

## BUDAPEST, 12–13 JUNE 1956

Following a whole series of concerts (to a variety of Hungarian audiences), the US ambassador invited the leading spirits of the intellectual world to come to the Embassy Residence. To his delight, for the first time since the war and its occupation by the Soviets quite a few had the courage to come. As he saw us off by the dirty old train the next day, the Ambassador told Y he had cabled the State Department saying Y was the 'best US Ambassador we have yet had'. Comforting for all the physical hardships and incessant work.

## LAGO MAGGIORE, SEPTEMBER 1956

Seized a spare day (now becoming increasingly rare) for a dash down to see Toscanini, an angry old Maestro in his villa on Lago Maggiore, inveighing furiously against America in general and the company whose orchestra he had worked for with such magical results in particular, and who, he roared, had so arbitrarily dismissed him. A memorable day, shining summer sun, reflecting off indigo waters in front of which Toscanini's white and handsome head vibrated with fury, finding a perfect audience in Yehudi, and above all having at his command one of the languages most ideally adapted to excoriation and abuse while still retaining all its music – Italian. Histrionics at their topmost continued right through luncheon, Y (to whose gentle interpolations he barely listened), providing him with a sublime catharsis. As the sun went down he rumbled to a rousing finale, hugged Y and alluded to that first wonderful meeting when he had conducted the sixteen-year-old boy in the Beethoven concerto in New York. It was the last time we were to see that splendid head – on 17 January 1957 Toscanini died.

LONDON, 3 OCTOBER 1956
To the première of the Bolshoi Ballet. Fascinating to see the Russian school before it was filtered through the sophisticated French taste of Diaghilev, and horrifyingly dated to the audience at Covent Garden of whom the older generation had actually seen the Diaghilev Company and the younger had been brought up in the tradition. Very obviously the Bolshoi was built on the bureaucratic principle of hierarchy, which offered one a Romeo on the shady side of fifty who had evidently inherited the rôle because of the long-awaited demise of his predecessor. He spent more of his time flailing his arms about in vivid mime than he did using his legs. There was a vast amount of scenery of enormous weightiness and a splendid piece of functional plumbing in the shape of a real fountain spouting real water and taking up the greater part of the stage. Juliet was the one-time Prime Ballerina Assoluta who, much against her will, had been dragged out of retirement because of her position in the hierarchy. She still retained a lovely fluidity of line and a passion rarely seen in those days amongst the cooler English dancers.

I slept little that night thinking of that world upon which I had deliberately shut the door, sadder than ever now that I had actually seen the clumsy, artificial lumpishness that Diaghilev had transmuted into that unbelievably inspiring and exquisite expression of the Russian genius for dancing.

CAPE TOWN, OCTOBER–NOVEMBER 1956
During a tour of South Africa Y underwent an operation for a slipped disc which turned out to be a complete success. However, I was warned

before visiting him in hospital the morning after that he would be muzzy with painkiller. Imagine my disbelief when I found him propped up in bed, shovelling breakfast into a face that bore the first colour it had worn for two weeks!

'Good morning darling,' he said, waving a spoon at me, 'did you sleep well?' Delighted but as thrown off balance as an actress who had dried up, I searched for my missing lines and managed a shaky 'Bravo!' So astounding was his lack of pain that a whole posse of surgeons, neurologists and orthopaedics came to visit him on the third day. I found them standing mystified at the foot of his bed, agreeing that it could only arise from his continuous practice of yoga, which gave him the power to relax - pain being, of course, at least fifty per cent tension. The huge relief I felt was tinged with guilty loathing of enforced yoga for obedient wives. I soon found that my role of hospital visitor was being totally usurped by a gigantic Xhosa woman with polished black face, ivory teeth and huge eyes, whose duty it was to tidy up Y's room from time to time. Y had established complete rapport with her when he discovered that her diet consisted of various seeds, pulses, fibres, grains and organic dust. In ecstasy he begged her to bring them one and all, cook such as were inedible when raw and leave those alone that should be eaten as nature intended. And there he was joyously gulping down an enormous soup plate full of a revolting chocolate-brown substance that looked to me as though it had already been eaten once. Joy abounded; with sparkling eyes he raised a glass of some greyish fluid like liquidized worsted socks and drank it off as though it were ambrosia. Knowing my place, I shrank back against the door-jamb; there was no left-over space for me with this ebony Brunhilde. Modestly I wished my husband well.

GSTAAD, FEBRUARY 1957
Reflecting on our last meeting with Toscanini, I realized that slowly, inevitably, the great figures that had adorned Yehudi's life since early childhood were disappearing. Because of his precocity he had belonged to an era almost a generation older than himself. He was like a young plant growing in the rich soil of a great forest, shaded from the harsh sun by benign and beautiful trees, nourished by the leaves that fell and fed the ground in which his roots were becoming stronger and deeper embedded. Lucky child indeed to share with and learn from such great

figures as Bruno Walter, Weingartner, Furtwängler and Toscanini, to be guided by such batons; even though in the case of Weingartner it usually meant standing for an hour listening to a long verbal dissertation on the chosen concerto (when he might have been rehearsing) before finally being offered a chair by one of the equally long-suffering players, so that he rarely got past the first movement. And there were Kreisler and Hubermann, Thibaud and Heifetz as colleagues, to say nothing of Adolph Busch to whom Enesco sent him at the age of twelve to study Bach, and who replied when some musician asked him what he thought of this small American boy: 'Ach, he already plays much better than I!'

To my mind it was this paradise of great musicians about whose musical interpretations there was neither commonness nor meanness, that bred in Y his innate and immutable modesty. No matter what fame, what praise, what adulation became his, it never touched that longing to be worthy of them, to speak the musical language they had inculcated in him from the very first. Alive, they fed his aspirations, and as he grew older and they faded from his scene, the obligation never to lose the visions they had opened up in his young mind, the assurances they had made him feel were indeed attainable – these never deserted him. Rather they kept his mind's eye ever fixed upwards towards their standards and their quality. Fortunate, indeed, but at the same time burdened with a sense of the vast and ceaseless application, the invincible courage needed to preserve that vision from falling into something cheaper and easier – an ever-present danger in an increasingly commercialized era. My task was both clear and complex. It was to help him conserve a world which, with the gradual loss of his mentors, was dissolving around him; also to protect him from hardening into the persona of the mature man who had, in actual practical terms, attained their eminence without in the least becoming conscious of it. Mercifully, his own sweetness of heart, his generosity of spirit and his ebullient optimism helped.

NEW YORK, 10 FEBRUARY 1957
During a shopping expedition to Bloomingdales to buy some of their delicious bread I lose Y amongst the corridors of preserved foods. After a while he emerges triumphantly carrying clutched to his overcoat three cans of tinned bees, one of Mexican worms, a fourth containing Japanese quails' eggs and, to complete the fantasy, a bottle of lily bulbs preserved

in syrup – for which, of course, he cannot pay because he only has a handful of South African cash. I dig up the dollars and ask for one of those winsome American shopping bags into which Y carefully slips his precious provender and with my modest loaf under my arm *à la française*, tow Y home (to hotel).


NEW YORK, 15 FEBRUARY 1957

Lunch at the Pavilion with Billie and Stanley Marcus (Top Boy of Neiman-Marcus and possessed of a beautiful dry wit) during which we caught sight of Artur Rubinstein dolefully eating alone in a corner, looking like the condemned man failing to enjoy his last hearty breakfast. We called him over to join us. It appeared that he had been in such a state of nervous despair over a series of Chopin recitals he had agreed to give, of which the first would be tonight, that his family had turfed him out to cry alone over the marvellous menu of that restaurant. And 'restaurant' it proved to be, for his irrepressible Polish humour burst through the mood of gloomy regret while he regaled us with comic anecdotes and wicked comments for the next two hours. My favourite one was of a concert where he had played a concerto with an American Orchestra, after which he was begged to attend a party given by a very generous sponsor better known for his bank account than for his culture.

'Well, Mr Rubinstein,' shouted this Maecenas, 'I did not attend your concert [typical] but I hear it was a huge success.' Here Rubinstein gave a marvellous imitation of himself being suitably modest and simpering.

'Where are you going next?' bellowed the Important Man.

'To the next big city, where I will be giving a *recital*,' murmured Rubinstein.

'Is that so? Who'll be your accompanist?'

Only for one split second was Artur flummoxed, then he looked up brightly saying: 'Yehudi Menuhin!'

'Jeeze, that's just fine, I know he's just about the tops.'

Mute nod from Rubinstein subtly imitating himself as a 'diplomat manqué'. . . .


WASHINGTON, 20 FEBRUARY 1957

Dinner in Washington with Robert Murphy, now Assistant Secretary of State, talking over long past days in bombed Berlin, after which Bob took Y over to the State Department to discuss various countries behind the Iron Curtain with Ambassador Lacey. As the manipulators of that nasty farce were constantly lifting it in order to invite Y to step under, he wanted to establish with Lacey an understanding that if it were not acceptable for him to go to certain of those countries for political reasons, Lacey, who dealt with 'East-West', would let him know. For the moment both he and Bob Murphy were only too delighted that he should accept.

LONDON, 9 MARCH 1957
Y *does* get a cable from the State Department (East-West). Would he please not go after all to Budapest as the American Ambassador has been recalled? Damn that Slav colonial regime; damn their hard eyes; damn their closed faces that look as though they had locked them against all danger of becoming human.

NEW YORK, 6 DECEMBER 1957
Sandwiched in between like anchovy paste were the usual ghastly television programmes in which, for vast sums of money, Y would be incarcerated all day in some derelict theatre in order to play five minutes of the shadier classical snippets for easy money; also, one must admit, somehow intriguingly different from the concert hall routine. These TV bonanzas were purely artificial in approach, bereft of all artistry, offering an audience that queued up outside and then poured into the theatre looking for all the world as though someone had lifted the manhole covers in the sidewalks, added to which was a desperately serious compère who 'organized' the applause with signals from the stage. My favourite one of such oddities (Y and Hephzibah squeezed between five minutes of Merle Oberon and five minutes of some famous singer whose name eludes me) was when the No. 2 camera, rolling his trolley towards brother and sister for a close-up of the divine pair, had neglected to remove a large can of film from his platform with the result that during an exquisite lyrically soft passage, said can slipped off, propelling itself with a metallic clang all the way across stage, klankety-klank, klank, klank, to end up with the knell of a sunken bell at Hep's pedalling feet. As it happened to have arrived at the irredeemable 'live' shot, several million listeners must have wondered at the strange percussion intro-

duced so arbitrarily into a performance of Debussy's 'Maid with the Flaxen Hair'. I had a lovely time stuffing Kleenex in my shaking mouth and clocking up yet another Reviving Disaster. Hep and Y were quite undisturbed and rippled on regardless.

# 🌸9🌸
# *Polish Interlude*

If I have omitted one particular journey from the diary of these years it is because in my mind and heart it holds an especial place, not simply as an archetypal adventure behind the Iron Curtain, but more as a variant in the character of such experiences, a mutation as it were whose colour and form, taste and smell differed basically from any other in Eastern Europe as will the spore of a plant type. This was Poland in 1957 where Yehudi had offered to give two concerts in Warsaw – incidentally his first visit to that unconquerable country that has known so many conquests.

I suppose for me the adventure really began in a dismal grey villa in the suburbs of Vienna where I spent two hours telling the Polish officials what our respective grandfathers had died of, how many children I had decided to bear and (apologetically) why none of our relations as far as I could trace, had ever been inspired to belong to the Communist Party. At last I emerged triumphant though haggard clutching the two visas, collected Yehudi, and we crossed the city to the Ostbahnhof where, with our usual eight pieces of luggage, we boarded the ancient carriages which most countries whose trains venture across the Iron Curtain prefer to choose in the event of their possible disappearance into the Carpathians, the Urals or the Siberian tundra. In this case it proved rather an advantage for we had two large shabby Franz-Josef-ish compartments with wide-open doors between worn mahogany panelling, plenty of ornately decorated, slightly fly-blown mirrors, lots of shabby plush, dusty velvet and darned yellow lace. Very Schnitzler and very chilly. I took off my dress and put on a big bed-shawl, kicked off my shoes, sent for two more pillows and, as the train drew out, settled on to the wide and comfortable bed to read. Y did the same only without the bed-shawl and with some score or other.

A slowing-down not long after leaving made me look out of the wide window. All sense of smugness was instantaneously shattered by the sight of a great barrier of barbed wire edged on either side by deep ditches and commanded by a frightening wooden tower about twenty feet high with a covered platform upon which stood stone-faced soldiers armed with swivelling machine guns. We had reached the precarious rim of civilization and were about to cross into Totalitaria. Across this modern dried-up Styx Charon was armed with more than a simple oar and there was no Cerberus to whom to throw a loaf of bread. Spine- and heart-chilling. Nothing else in my life has ever struck me with such an instant icy blow. Is this what we idiots had fought for for six years; this, the sole memorial, cynical and brutal, in honour of the millions of dead and destroyed?

For a long time I could not bring myself to read again, to rejoice in my crumbling comfort. I felt I had at last and quite literally seen No Man's Land and what it must be to be a non-person. Would the spirit of man rise yet again to dismantle this apparently inhuman non-world or was it forever buried by the irreversibility of our utter stupidity before Communist cunning?

The train rolled on into a countryside already greening with spring and I was eventually able to return to my book. Suddenly we stopped at one of the Czech-sum-Slovak stations with names composed entirely of consonants: Grmdz or something approaching it. My book was en- thralling and it wasn't until I had picked it off the Turkey carpet for the fourth time that I registered that the train, or anyway our part of it, had been performing a strange kind of folksy contredanse, fifty yards or so in one direction and fifty back with singularly little grace and a great deal of jerking, this manœuvre affording one a monotonous view of several kinds of warehouse and one-half of a dilapidated station.

A knock at the door and the servile face of our 'Schaffner' (attendant) appeared.

'Gnädigste,' he began, wringing his hands, and proceeded to give us the dire news that our through-carriage to Warsaw had for some inex- plicable reason been rejected by the Authorities (here his voice trembled somewhat) and would we please descend as we were to be shifted to another train?'

'Nonsense,' I said crisply, 'kindly go away' and returned to my book. The poor fellow reappeared some ten minutes later begging me to take him seriously. Furious, I looked at Y deep in his double-stops. 'Oh well,' said he philosophically, 'I suppose we have to get out.' 'Aber, warum denn?' I snapped at the shaking Schaffner. He shrugged his shoulders and rolled his eyes in true Viennese mime, so, sighing I got up, repacked my cosy shawl, pulled on my dress, shuffled into my shoes and summoned the Schaffner again.

'Also,' I said, 'get someone to carry the cases and we'll get out.' I might as well have asked him for a couple of sure-footed dromedaries. His jaw dropped. I folded my arms, and waited. Convinced that neither I nor Y had any intention of lugging eight cases, and seeing his tip fast disappearing, he shuffled off on to the platform, now full of wretched people in the same situation as our own, and eventually returned with two strong, square, rosy-cheeked farm-hands who hauled down our suitcases from the racks as though they were crates of potatoes. I pointed out the handles to them and we exchanged grins. They waddled off down the corridor followed by Y. I took one last longing look at my enticing shabby nest, picked up the two biggest pillows and shouted to Y through the open window to run quickly and secure the best seats he could, and I would catch him up.

The Schaffner, mollified by Y's usual generous tip, gasped as I passed him by with an 'Adieu'. 'Aber, gnädige Frau – Sie dürfen nicht den Kissen wegnehmen!' 'And why can I not take the pillows at least, considering we have paid for a comfortable journey and are now being deprived of it?,' I replied angrily, jumping down and running fast along the platform with one under each arm, pursued by the baffled Schaffner expostulating in incomprehensible Viennese dialect. Y was waving at me from a carriage. It was as awful as I had expected, with bright green plastic seats offering one's buttocks about fifteen inches of convex space to sit on. Whether the Sovietized Czechs were provided with rubber suction cups which they applied to their bottoms to enable them to grip the narrow bevelled surface, or whether their nether portions are equipped by nature with the necessary shape to adhere to these impossible constructions, I do not attempt to analyse. But never was I so glad that I had in my anger purloined the pillows. In fact, I cursed myself for not having pinched the blankets as well.

Eventually, after a dumb show in which we had offered the gaping farm-hands four oranges and a lump of chocolate and they had left laughing with joy and wonder, the train moved off. 'Eventually' in Iron Curtain language meaning two hours later. It appeared our Vienna carriage was declared UNSAFE, a ploy used every so often in order to discourage the adventurous Western European from peeping through that hideous barrier.

Anyway, 'eventually' we did go rattling and bumping and skidding off those slimy green seats, till finally dark descended and with it the whole weight of the classical chain of totalitarian officials like some black-joke Gilbert and Sullivan chorus. First the passports. (None of the erstwhile German-speaking Czechs is ever employed so that there is no hope of communication whatsoever.) Grim-faced and Gradgrind, the chosen officials, looked accusingly at every bit of small print, transferring that jolly expression onto our faces, as variation. Y retreated to Cloud Nine. As for me, I automatically become unrecognizably Archduchess the minute I transfer from West to East Europe. I, the slave, willingly washing, darning, ironing, mending and lugging loads suddenly cannot lift a box of matches, a very effective metamorphosis and a psychologically fascinating one. After the passport-scrutinizing act and the grudging withdrawal as though they had been cheated of finding some miniscule defect that had obviously become the stale spice of their dreary lives, there followed a very unappealing lady clad in greasy grey uniform with the biggest beam I have ever seen this side of the Hottentots. More dumb language which was eventually translated into her desire to know what monies we carried. Poor woman, little did she know what she had undertaken. Y first produced a quite considerable sum of Austrian schillings, which she raked through down to the last insignificant pfennig (I waiting to see if she would bite one or two with her aluminium teeth to verify their right, as viable currency). Disappointed at being unable to find fault, she pointed at our cases, my handbag and even glanced towards my large feet. The devil caught me: I emptied my handbag, took off my shoes and shook them under her nose (which looked like a big toe), made Y turn out his every pocket and push his hands with solemn enthusiasm into each corner of the inside flaps of his suitcases. All along I maintained this comedy with a hopefully translatable series of gestures in the form of deep frowns of serious concentration followed by excited cries of inspiration, topped off with flourishes indicating yet another quarter where Y might possibly find some incriminating currency with which to feed her greed. More and more bewildered both at this show of willingness and at the, for her, totally weird and wide collection of coins and notes, the poor thing was by now sweating visibly: pengös, Swiss francs, Deutschmarks, French francs, pennies and sixpences, pesos from a half-dozen South American republics, Filipino odds and ends, South African rands, all manner of North African colonial coins, Moroccan, Tunisian, Algerian, Turkish, Greek drachmas, all the coinage known to Scandinavia, the odd crumpled American and Canadian dollar bill – all in miniscule quantities. It became a veritable archaeological dig. There they all lay, rolling off those dreadful benches the while she scrabbled after them underneath, her huge seating area showing at its grossest best, her reddened baffled face staring helplessly at us as she straightened up, puffing and at her wit's end.

Finally with commendable mercy Y shovelled the lot together and pressed them affectionately on her. Uttering a muffled shriek she pushed his hands away as though they were poisonous and fled the carriage, sideways, managing her vast hips in two swift well-practised swings and was gone. Y and I collected the rubbish and shovelled it back, locked the door and lay down on our hummocks, very grateful for the stolen pillows.

All through that endless night the train stopped, people clambered on, banged at our door. Y got up wearily, spoke a few words of Russian which stopped them in frozen alarm from forcing their way in and we would return to the torture of the green plastic rack. Came the dawn. Ice had formed on the inside of the window panes. Pulling up the blind cautiously we saw the corridor jam-packed with standing bodies and not the slightest possibility of reaching the loo, not that there would have been any likelihood of finding water to wash one's grimy hands. So we settled back and did our best with eau-de-cologne, grateful for having both been trained like camels insofar as our inner organs were concerned. At 6.50 a.m. we drew into Warsaw with an angry hiss accompanied by huge clouds of very dirty smoke, as though the train were tired to death with towing human-shaped objects and had done its dreary duty as unwillingly as it could. Clambering stiffly down from the green plastic I remembered the two purloined pillows and picked them up. The three officials from the Ministry must have thought us an odd pair, gritty, crumpled and I armed with bits of bedding.

We and our luggage were shovelled into one of those funereal motors only to be found behind the Iron Curtain with nasty stained upholstery and heavily veiled windows. Pulling back the dirty net I saw piles of rubble on each side, half-demolished buildings sticking out of the mess like broken teeth, doorways leading to nowhere, windows like empty eye-sockets. Thirteen years had passed since the war, when the Russian armies had sat on the opposite bank of the river waiting for Hitler's soldiers to do their best worst before crossing to take over the remains of this once great and beautiful city. I thought of the Canaletto drawings I had seen and my gorge rose.

As we reached the centre there were typical signs of clearing up visible in slabs of housing designed either for human or office files and constructed of that sinister and depressing rough grey material, a composite of gravel, dirt and dandruff combined with some wetting substance and rolled and hardened into large lifeless blocks. Streets of them stretching on without physiognomy or character as though resigned into battered obedience and hopelessness, to match the people who lived and worked in them.

We reached our hotel. It was one of those large pre-First-World-War buildings patched like an old warrior and netted with scaffolding supporting groggy balconies and gap-tooth excrescences, the remains of an exuberant *fin-de-siècle* decoration. A dirty vestibule led to a very uncertain lift which groaned its way upwards with rheumatic reluctance to the first floor where sat, like some more sinister and feminine St Matthew at the seat of custom, the inevitable 'Dujournaya'. This one, being Polish perhaps, was not one of your Russian wardresses. Painted to the edge of her thick black hair which fell to her uniformed shoulders, she looked more like a retired prostitute waiting in line for a post as the Madam of a local brothel. With a pleasant smile showing the regulation amount of tin teeth, she handed us the key to our kingdom, the porter brought in our luggage, the Ministry officials bade us a polite goodbye and we were free to examine it. As usual, we had been given the erstwhile 'Grande Suite' which in totalitarian terms inevitably meant that it would be the only one whose decayed grandeur was regarded as an untouchable glory, while lesser and more humble rooms benefited from relative modernization.

We looked cautiously around. A large sitting room faced us like a wind-swept prairie, furnished with an enormous cracked marble table, two dubious armchairs with peeling gilt trim and three windows through which blew an icy gale. The rest was composed of the customary Central European alcove with a vast and lumpy double bed. Worn out and longing for hot water, I searched out the bathroom. It was not a long search. My nose led me to a door on the far side of the bed. Bravely, I opened it; and staggered back, retching. As far as I could detect the suite had been occupied by a dozen or more horses over the past couple of months, incontinent horses who had made frequent use of a lavatory of the ancient type with the cistern high up on the wall from which the broken arm projected impotently, shorn of its most important feature, viz. the chain. The resultant overflowing of their digestive tracts had therefore collected till an immodest amount had amassed within and around the pedestal at the base. Shutting the door with a bang and a whimper, I ran across the half-mile of threadbare carpet to Yehudi wailing, 'I don't think I can take much more – oh, please help!'

Y was splendid; unfolding his metal travelling music-stand to about half its length, he removed his shoes and socks, rolled up the hems of his trousers, advanced upon the stables, flung open the door, surveyed the hideous scene unmoved, climbed on to the rim of the seat, inserted the hooked end of his music-stand into the gaping hole of the cistern crook and with a determined yank of his bow arm forced it downwards. A mighty rush ensued and to my immense relief the lavatory swallowed the contents, calming my besetting fear that, having reached the point of no return, it might do exactly *that*: vide: choked by its generous contents it would indeed throw the lot, as it were, back into our laps. Y got down, flushed and exultant. I hugged him and willingly mopped up the scattered remains while he pattered down the corridor to bring the Dujournaya and a piece of strong string.

That afternoon we were driven to a quarter that has remained for ever after in my mind as an example of the spirit of man for whose resuscitation I'd felt utterly despondent as we crossed that hideous No Man's Land the day before. There in front of us lay the proof of at least one country, one people who would be hard to kill in soul or spirit – street after street of seventeenth- and eighteenth-century Warsaw exquisitely restored in all its fantasy and beauty. An entire district of houses, small, medium, large and almost palatial ones rebuilt with such panache that the whole looked like scenes designed for a play by Goldoni. While the inhabitants of Warsaw lived at plumb level in their dreary, chipped housing, here was a corner illustrating an invincible pride, Polish style and significance, indestructible by any oppressive outsider's heavy hand. Back in the hotel, bemused by the beauty of what I had seen, it was harder than ever not to shudder as we passed through the penumbra of that vestibule where stiff-faced men in peaked caps wandered about aimlessly in long grey overcoats like reject dressing-gowns while others sat slumped in hideous armchairs that contrived at one and the same time to be rectangular and yet bulgingly overstuffed. A revulsion at this shabby puritanism passed over me mixed with a cold fury I found difficult to control. I would willingly have shaken all the frowsty palms and loosened a shower of dust on those dismal caps. Up in the 'Grande Suite', having reclaimed our key to the dubious kingdom from tarty Dujournaya, I felt even more futilely angry.

We proceeded to go through what in twenty-four hours had become the ground-bass of our day, viz, pull the chain of that egregious loo irrespective of whether we had taken advantage of its services or not. Gradually the rank Augean savour was diminishing, helped by liberal sprinklings of eau-de-cologne dispensed like holy water, which ecclesiastical duties Y and I divided between each other: acolytes of the water-closet. We bribed Anastasia the Dujournaya to deflect the inevitable stream of importunate mamas with prodigious children, or papas with genuine Strads made in Germany in 1897, but we did enjoy meeting Mr Abel of the *New York Times*, a brilliant and very handsome young journalist who knew all the ropes as well as the facts, political, international and human, about Poland. And the diplomats too, all, from Mr Roy the Indian Ambassador, and friend of Nan Pandit's to the American Ambassador who sent a car to get us to the iciest rehearsal I've ever shuddered through, the admirable Y blowing imperturbably on his fingers during the *tuttis* (Beethoven). We were in fact grateful to the whole Corps Diplomatique for giving us lunches and generally rescuing us from the sad prison pallor of our haunted suite.

Next morning Y played a solo sonata concert of Bach and Bartók. I from my viewpoint in the stage-box, flanked by Abel, gazed down on the rows of Politburocrats and their smug wives *endimanchées* like pre-war parlour-maids on their day out. Incensed, I saw rows of shabby students, girls and boys, standing lining the sides pressed against the walls. As soon as Y had finished the first half I said: 'Abel, I'm getting those young on to that stage,' and I ran to Y's room where his nasty agent, who had a face like an uncooked muffin, hovered about. Y agreeing with me, I told the agent in my lofty Iron Curtain manner to order all the standing students on to the big empty stage.

'Impossible!' he cried, the rolls of dough shaking.

'Nonsense', I said. 'Do as you're told.' (Shades of nanny and bed-time.)

Accompanied by a laughing Abel I ran down the stairs, he translating for me and together we guided the students like a pair of collie dogs on to the terraced stage where they squatted to the fury of the privileged guests and to the delight of Y, now surrounded and embraced by several hundred devoted music students.

'Attagirl,' whispered Abel as we clambered back into our box.

It was a marvellous and moving concert and hours before they would let Y go – but at last it had been worthwhile coming all that uncomfortable way.

Less moving but more aggravating was the advent of Doughface in the vestibule the following morning explaining why, after all, he could not pay Y the contracted money, neither the small dollar amount (which anyway Y was donating to various musical causes) nor the remainder in zlotys. As he mumbled along, his little Sunmaid-raisin eyes shifting as though they were trying to dislodge themselves from the damp flour, another remarkable character appeared, so British as to belong to a past backed by an Empire that ruled the waves.

'Cavendish's my name, howdy-do' he said – about thirty-five, dark-blue blazer and grey flannels, old Borstal tie just frayed enough, delightful pink moon face. 'London *Times*. Now what's this you're saying?' looking at Doughface as though he'd first had to put a pair of gloves on his eyes to remain uncontaminated. Glancing at his wrist-watch, he went on:

'My copy goes out in about an hour and if you're not back here pretty damn quick with *all* the money, it will be my immense pleasure to let my paper know that on Yehudi Menuhin's first visit to Warsaw you absconded with his fee.'

Doughface scuttled off through the potted palms like the cockroach he was and we turned to enjoy this sudden and enchanting apparition from the Raj. 'Skunk', he said, following him with a cold eye, 'know the type. Black market, rotten fellah. He'll be back. Let's have a drink while we're waiting.'

He was as interesting in his disclosures of 1957 Poland in his laconic way as had been Abel, and sure enough Muffin returned panting, half-cooked, with a fat packet in his hand. Cavendish accepted it coldly, counted it deliberately, handed the incomprehensible official paper for Y to sign, flicked it over to Muffin who shuffled off never to be seen again. Y arranged with Cavendish in what manner he wanted the money distributed and then I said:

'What do we do with the remaining zlotys?'

'Well, old girl,' (we were by now firm friends) 'what about coming along with me to the pawn shop where all the wretched ci-devant aristos have dumped their stuff and see what you'd like to buy?' Y returned to Suite w.c., and Cavendish and I drove to the pawn shop.

It turned out to be rather a painful experience. Small heaps of family silver, porcelain, paintings, prints and fine laces were presided over by a weary cold-faced distinguished woman who once had lived amongst just such beautiful objets d'art. I felt acutely embarrassed. Luckily she spoke French – but although I tried to show some of my shamed feeling, she remained cold, proud and totally indifferent. I chose all that was left – about 40 pieces of a *circa* 1830-50 Meissen onion pattern porcelain dining set – mercifully untrammelled with gold – and paid. Impasse. It appeared to be impossible to pack it. Cavendish with his useful vocabulary of two hundred of the ruder and more forceful Polish idioms, marched into the warehouse at the back and found the usual useless louts especially bred by Totalitaria. Within no time he'd got them to their feet, the straw and packing cases appeared and the job was done. I tried to say goodbye to the Countess Potowska and tell her how much the china would be loved and cared for. But she was too bruised in spirit and heart to respond and merely gave me a cold nod. Cavendish restored my humour.

'Cheer up, me dear, you had a pretty tough war yourself.'

'Oh, Cavendish, but I wasn't drained of all meaning and left with the rest of my life to kill slowly.'

Next day we said our final farewells to Suite w.c., feeling we had done our bit for the next occupants (until the string would inevitably fray and break again) kissed Anastasia, our Dujournaya, goodbye as we gratefully and dutifully returned the keys, and looking back found her crying a little, tears coursing down her splendid rouged cheeks, for she had fallen slightly in love with Yehudi.

The scene at the station was very Slav. Crowds of people going nowhere, poor devils, shrieks of steam and smoke; the dear young daughters of the British Air Attaché with fudge they'd made for Y; a most delicious cold collation prepared by them for our supper; a host of diplomats - and an adamant Schaffner utterly refusing my vast crate of Meissen. But I had not counted on Cavendish, that outpost of Empire who had already persuaded the recalcitrant porters to load it on their trolley, using what was undeniably basement Polish. Loosening some more of his stock of crude Polish words, he pulverized the Schaffner, ordered the porters to heave the vast crate on to the corridor where it stuck fast at exactly the junction of two coaches, thus cutting off one half of the train from the other.

'Quite all right,' said Cavendish, 'save the Schaffner from having to walk up and down all night.'

We climbed into our carriage - thank God one of the *Alt Wien* ones (the famous pillows by the way had been returned, graciously handed over by me to the wagon-lits the day after our arrival in Warsaw: I might have been releasing the Crown Jewels). Leaning out of the windows, we felt again that heart-racking jab when it is forceably brought to mind how callously one accepts the liberty which is one's birthright and how deep the guilt, as we gazed at those upturned yearning, trapped faces, so grateful for the miniscule gesture of the music Y had brought, cheering as the train drew out - dear Cavendish glowing like a lighthouse amid a grey and rocky sea.

Arrived in Vienna next morning, the Austrian porters roared when Y told them the crate contained Khrushchev's corpse. I was carrying the carefully wrapped remains of the whole cold turkey supplied by the English Air Attaché for our supper (anyone who has ever tasted Polish turkey would understand why one wouldn't leave so much as the wishbone behind) and clutching the bottle of St Emilion. So our entry to our hotel was somewhat strange. The imperturbable concierge at Sacher's greeted us as though we did not look like the tail end of a travelling circus and we settled into our suite (I putting the turkey out on the balcony) and flung open the bathroom door and gazed with a mixture of respect and admiration more aptly due to the high altar at the Stefansdom. Wallowing in a boiling hot bath, my relief to be back was only diminished by the vision of having had to repass that dreadful No Man's Land with its great wooden outposts, stone-faced soldiers and swivelling guns but a few hours ago, rising like a Doré drawing in the steam.

That was 1957. Twenty-five years and more have passed and the Poles have shown the world that my fears for the extinction of the soul and spirit of man were ill-founded insofar as a country of such indomitable courage is concerned. What exercises the mind is the unanswerable question, the odds and evens between the sacrificial heroism of a handful of brave patriots and the grim costive bureaucracy that holds all the power in its hoary fist. How many blows to the head can a people sustain before they suffer irreparable brain damage?

# $10$

# Log-book (part 2)

VIENNA, 21 JUNE 1957

A typical Menuhin marathon: Y playing the great Bartók Concerto with the Philharmonia Ungarica in order to raise money for this refugee orchestra one evening; the next night a recital with Hephzibah containing the new Bartók Solo Sonata; the third day a concert in which he both conducted and played the Bach A minor, Mozart E major and Bach E major concertos at the Konzerthaus. The occasion also provided a friend from the past. The young Zubin Mehta, who had come from India and who was then studying to be a conductor under the great teacher Swarowsky, turned the pages for Hephzibah during the recital of the second concert. We had not set eyes on him since he was a boy in his teens when the whole of his family had come and seen us off on the boat from India three or four years earlier.

ANSBACH, 25–26 JULY 1957

Happy company again. This time at least we were not buried in plaster. Among those attached to us, there was an enormous Teuton lady, upon whose form the fat was so evenly and firmly distributed that she seemed as upholstered as an up-ended sofa. She was also extremely imperious and very clever about artists' taxes, therefore to be seen wherever her clients were, which meant just about where all the star performers performed. She too performed, rolling into concerts and meals on oiled castors and surveying all and sundry with a sharp financial eye. I nicknamed her Frau Doktor Hammerklavier and we all became so accustomed to referring to her thus that one unforgettable day a charming musician introduced her to an assembly of friends as 'Frau Doktor Hammerklavier' in dreadful innocence. She corrected him with an outraged iciness that blenched the poor man. And I stood there helpless and guilty, surprised that a German musician of great knowledge could imagine anyone actually bore the name of a set of Beethoven variations for the early hammer-piano. Beware facetious jokes.

SALEM, 1 AUGUST 1957
A visit with Benjamin Britten and Peter Pears at the suggestion of our good friends Peg and Lu (Prince and Princess Ludwig of Hessen) to Salem, the huge thirteenth-century Cistercian monastery belonging to the Markgraf and Markgräfin of Baden. I wanted to see the famous school founded there by Kurt Hahn (who subsequently created its sister-school, Gordonstoun, in Scotland). I must not dwell on that marvellous building where the boys could bicycle down the vast corridors, nor digress about the then Headmaster Prince Georg-Wilhelm of Hanover and his entrancing wife Sophie, who were to become close friends; enough to mention that the whole atmosphere was such that I at once asked if I might enrol Mita for one of their 'prep schools', Hermannsberg. It was the cosmopolitan atmosphere, the unwritten discipline, the stern lack of luxury amid surroundings of great architectural beauty that drew me (and also Yehudi on a later visit) to Salem. An added attraction was that one-third of the pupils were chosen gratis from those families who could not afford the fees. Among them at this time were a great many Hungarian refugees who had escaped their country after the 1956 Revolution.

LAUSANNE, 8 AUGUST 1957
An expedition with Yehudi and Zamira from Gstaad to lunch with Alfred Cortot and his wife who lived near Lausanne. I had not met him, although I'd heard him many times as a child and a girl in London. Y said Enesco had brought him often to the Paris suburb of Ville d'Avray when the Menuhin family were living there as children. He must already have been an old man when we met that day but I still recognized from my childhood that odd Red-Indian-shaped face with its bleached skin and plastered black hair – a face I found unfathomable, skin stretched like a drum, a strangely pedantic man proud of his magnificent library. His wife, Renée, was very sweet and warm and took Miras and me up to see a cabinet containing 500 lovely rings she'd collected over the years, pressing upon us one each with an eager delight I found rather disturbing.

## LONDON, SEPTEMBER 1957

Returning from Vienna to the usual spate of recordings, Y received news from the Bartók Trust in New York that since the recent death of the Hungarian violinist and one-time fiancée of Bartók, Stefi Geier, his first violin concerto, which he had dedicated to her and which she had kept unplayed since she had broken off the engagement all those decades ago, was at last free. Victor Bator, chairman of the Trust, knowing in what esteem the composer had held Yehudi, offered it to him personally for a whole year before it would enter into public domain. Considering Y's passion for and support of Bartók in the last years of his life in America, this inevitably excited him enormously and he could hardly wait for the moment to come when he would be able to get hold of the music and perform it.

## NEW YORK, 12–15 DECEMBER 1957

The year ended with a right royal bang. Y, knowing that the composer Ernest Bloch was dying, determined to play his violin concerto which had not had a major hearing for years. Mugging it up in his usual manner between concerts on tour, he played it in Carnegie Hall with an Italian conductor, Previtali. It is a shortish work, a very lyrical one and received an ecstatic ovation. Returning three times to acknowledge the applause, Y was touched at the reception and happy for Bloch. Usually he has to be forced to give encores, and on the rare occasions when he does, his custom is to ask the conductor's permission. Previtali agreed at once and Y launched into the Praeludium from the Bach E major Partita. For those who may not know it, it is a beautiful fanfare full of confident joy, and not surprisingly it was rapturously received. As always, I went round backstage afterwards where to my astonishment I found a colossal row in full spate. Bruno Zirato, the manager of the New York Philharmonic who, incidentally, had been a friend ever since Y at ten years old had made his début with them, was yelling in Italian at Y as though he were the bad boy of the Lower Third. How dare he have the colossal impertinence to play an encore? Didn't he know perfectly well that such vulgarities were never permitted by the management in these sanctified walls? And more of the same, accompanied by a great deal of waving arms and hot rolling of black eyes and saliva à l'italienne. Y, very pale and quiet and half Zirato's height, waited like a surf-rider to get a word in when the wave of wrath might recede sufficiently to give him a chance.

'Ma, Bruno,' he said firmly, 'I knew of no such set rule. I rarely play encores but I don't know of one other major orchestra where I am not free to do so if I feel the audience really wants it. Their reception of the Bloch was so unexpectedly warm and enthusiastic that after I had returned to the stage for the fourth time I asked Previtali if he objected. As he did not, I played as a gesture to the dying Bloch, some of whose family were out front, the Bach Praeludium. Incidentally, this must be the first time anyone has, to my knowledge, called Bach "vulgar".'

More pyrotechnics ensued and I, feeling sick, turned to the leader, or concert-master, as he is called in the States, the much loved John Corigliano. 'Don't worry, Diana dear,' he said, 'we enjoyed it and the Bloch was a superb performance.' Silently Y put his violin away. Previtali, new to the scene, looked stunned (coming from the land of the birth of the encores, he was completely flummoxed that his compatriot Zirato should show such incredible rigidity). We went back to the hotel. There were three more performances to come. Oh God, oh Montreal. . . .

The following day in the *New York Times* Howard Taubman tore Y to pieces for his lèse-majesté. Y read it, said nothing. I got his things ready for that day's matinée and off we went to the hall. The orchestra greeted him warmly, laughing. That lifted my flattened spirits a little. I attended to Y automatically, kissed him good luck and went to my seat, apprehensive at the sight of his quietly set jaw. Same ovation from a packed house. Same return four times to bow. Up under his determined chin went the violin and he swung with added vigour into the clarion call of the Praeludium once again. I was torn between admiration and fear. Of course the audience cheered. He could have played four encores, but he just bowed smiling and walked off. I sped back through the delighted chattering crowds pouring into the corridor, my heart beating. The orchestra was highly amused, Zirato's door was shut and Y was wearing his wicked schoolboy face. We finally got through the backstage fans – 'Attaboy Yehudi' – was their attitude and walked back to the hotel. I could only think of the third concert the following night. I had noticed one particular music critic from a weekly magazine slipping into Zirato's room, talking to the orchestra, and deliberately avoiding Yehudi. I knew what to expect from him.

Next day the *New York Times* had 'Menuhin fiddles while orchestra board burns' or something like it, followed by an amusing paragraph subtly favourable to Y. So that evening down we went for the third time, I, reinforced by our dear friend Norris Houghton, founder and director of the Phoenix Theatre. Backstage was like an ice-box. My erstwhile great pal, the man on the pass-door, icily refused to return my greeting and the orchestra for the first time looked apprehensive. There was no other soul about. I went through my usual ritual and said to Y 'Don't exaggerate darling, it would be unsporting,' and joined Norris in the stalls, cold and shaky and glad to have him by my side. The house was crammed, they were even standing at the back of the boxes (another law broken). When Y came on a great cheer arose. Oh! dear God, I prayed, please, please don't let him overstep the mark.

The concerto went beautifully. Same ecstatic applause – not really all that gratifying as one was sure they were egging him on to repeat his defiant gesture. He returned to the stage his usual three times and on the fourth held up his hand for silence. I clutched poor Norrie and shook. Y's clear light voice rang out: 'I am not *allowed* to play. Soon *you* will not be allowed to applaud. If Bach could have known the irreparable damage to the tradition and budget of the New York Philharmonic that only two minutes of music could cause, I am sure he would be deeply grieved. In spite of the fact that these concerts, unlike those of other great orchestras, seem to be directed by non-musical and extra-musical forces I would like to assure you on behalf of my colleagues on the stage and for myself how much we love and are grateful for your enthusiasm and support. You may applaud as long and whenever you like.' Roars of delighted approval.

When I went round to see Y, the man on the pass-door tried to bar me. On the door was written something to the effect that no-one was allowed to go backstage. I sharply snapped at him: 'You will please let me through at once.' Reluctantly he opened the door a few inches and slammed it after me. Upstairs was slight pandemonium. Y in a quiet rage (for, of course, the audience had cheered and applauded after his short speech and he had *not* returned), his own loyal manager Kurt Weinhold very upset as he well knew how dangerous it was to strike at any power centre in those days and the orchestra, poor dears, very 'piano' and afraid – for they had long loved Yehudi and he them, but they had their jobs to think of and he had, let it be admitted, put them in a quandary. I went to John Corigliano and told him I fully realized the situation and only hoped that this idiotic storm in a tea-cup would soon blow over and we would be forgiven by the Holy of Holies. John was affectionate and rueful. The newspapers were splendid. The *New York Times* contented itself with a verbatim report of Y's statement and left it at that.

The final concert: I, trying to hide my cold jitters so as not to affect Y's performance. Normally one of my tasks is to stand watch-dog until the last moment so that he will not be importuned by the unthinking, the self-seeking or the plain loony. This time I need not have troubled. I begged him to be well behaved and went out front. Y, however, is stimulated by battles. No-one would believe it looking at his quiet face and gentle manners but when he has a cause at heart, beware! Suddenly he sprouts a wispy beard, dons his barber's-dish helmet and his armour and off he goes to tilt at his newest windmill. Dear Don Quixote! But I sometimes wish I did not have to be Rosinante, Sancho Panza *and* the donkey. Ah! well. This time Y played with even more fire and emotion. The whole audience stood and cheered for a full five minutes (I looked at my watch). He returned several times bowing politely and smiling until the audience gave up.

Next day came a perfect deluge of congratulatory telegrams not only from all over America but from Europe as well. The doorbell rang. It was Norman Cousins, editor of the *Saturday Review* and a good friend of Y's, who had come to tell us that the next issue of his magazine would contain a virulent attack on Yehudi by their music critic, but since he had never interfered with his staff, all he could do was to offer Y as much space as he wanted in which to reply. As a matter of fact that particular little article was entirely swamped by a spate of leading articles from all over the States, editorials as they are called there, all in praise of Y's stand, some calling the veto 'the act of a lot of stuffed-shirts which we Americans deplore'. It was a comfort not only for its support, but for the fact that it showed so clearly the American love for an individual spirit, 'a loner', and one who risked taking a stand against the Establishment.

AGATE BEACH, 14 JANUARY 1958
Settled on the West Coast with time to spare for once, Y restless as ever, decides to drive north to Agate Beach to pay what might possibly and sadly be a last visit to Ernest Bloch. We were to be accompanied by one of his daughters. The prospect of a fascinating journey up that glorious coast was, however, soon transformed into an adventure com-

pared with which Wagner's Ride of the Valkyrie would have seemed a children's gymkhana. No sooner had we gone a half-hour up the road than a howling gale descended, rattling hail on the roof of the small car and buffeting it from side to side like so much tumbleweed. Valiantly, Miss Bloch drove onwards ever more blindly, the windscreen wipers swiping at the torrential rain with all the effect of a pair of feather dusters. Y cheerfully mopped and dabbed the streaming water – by now entering the side-windows and leaving ice-cold puddles on the floor. Whenever the view ahead cleared enough we glimpsed pine and fir trees swooping and bending like drunken dancers, while every now and then we thudded with a gigantic splash into a forty-foot stretch of pure pond which doused gallons of water over the roof of the car in indignation at our defiance. At last after several hours we came upon a small building crouched on the edge of the cliff with a sign on it indicating food (EATS). Gratefully we parked the car, slopped our way out of it and pushed open the solid, sodden door.

There before us was what appeared to be the cast-off set of a Grade B film depicting Hawaii. Dusty paper palms bent over bright red oil-cloth tables adorned with pots of paper hibiscus; tubs of jungle-ware, *viz*. plastic cacti, very dirty sand in which large lumpish pebbles lay separated by tufts of dispirited grass and cigarette stubs amongst which cardboard snakes slept, while clamped to the listing fake saguerras tropical birds moulted mournfully. Perversely I chose a table right up by the 'picture window' against which the raging Pacific tossed great balls of fluffy yellow spume from the rocks below. The whole scene was a marvellous comment on the sturdy refusal to accept an unkind and vicious Nature. Outside the howling wind, the raging ocean, the beautiful ephemeral spume knocking on the glass – reality at its most savage; inside, the shoddy décor determined to create a factitious world of beatitude and bliss. We had a filthy hurried lunch as plastic as the cacti, then resumed our journey splashing along the road until at last we reached the sturdy cliff house above Agate Beach where the Blochs lived. A great fire was burning before which Y and Ernest sat down talking happily, discussing the solo sonatas Y had commissioned, mulling over the days of old while we slowly dried off and were given glorious coffee by his wife. Before we left Bloch filled my pockets with rough agates gathered from the beach far below.

HOUSTON, TEXAS, 4 FEBRUARY 1958

Y indulges in another of his bright enthusiasms, this time a contraption called a Sturmdranger Home Exercise Machine which he had read about in a magazine. When I expressed scepticism that it might be impossible to ship it to Gstaad all the way from Houston, Texas, my doubts were waved away with the observation that such genial inventions were by their very nature and function collapsible and portable. Another of the lessons I had learned – not without trial nor tribulation – was never to shoot down Y's fancies but to wait patiently and watch them fall of their own accord. The Sturmdranger Home Exercise Machine duly arrived carried by a panting Demonstrator sweating profusely. When unpacked it proved to be all of seven feet long and its weight imponderable. By moving furniture to all four corners of the hotel room and opening one window, he managed to extend this mobile device sufficiently to show off its indispensable use to everyone concerned enough to maintain themselves in the pink of condition. Metal joints creaked, odd springs squealed, hidden extensions appeared at the touch of a button all of which, vaunted the Demonstrator, would cause such a complete circulation of the bloodstream through every tired muscle that years would drop away and a new supple man be born. Feeling that Y was quite young and fit enough for me, I prayed silently that Y might feel the same. However, I had to endure another half-hour by which time the monster had expanded as far as the bathroom door before the beginnings of a cloud appeared on Y's beaming face. And it was only when the Demonstrator, in a last vigorous effort to show the effect produced by the machine upon the coccyx, got himself inextricably caught in a wandering coil of steel, that the cloud took total possession of Y's face. As he helped disentangle the poor fellow, Y asked blandly:

'Aren't you from the Relaxacisor?'

The look of disgusted fury that greeted this question would have pulverized anyone other than Yehudi. 'Why,' said the angry man, 'that is a pocket-sized steel and elastic contraption for stretching the lumbar region alone – and of no use whatsoever.'

I escaped into the bedroom only to re-emerge half-an-hour later when the clatter of steel had subsided and the demon machine been spirited away. Y was sitting rather self-consciously on an upturned sofa, a magazine in his hand.

'Well,' he said with a shade of defiance in his voice, 'I must somehow have muddled the two machines, I suppose. I've found the right number now and I'll ring up Relaxacisor.'

'Oh no! you won't,' I said with as much firmness as I could muster. 'Come and help me put the room to rights before the conductor arrives for your *Sitz-Probe*, please darling.'

I enjoyed quite a long span of peace after that splendid morning – nor did I ask whether he had to pay a vast sum for the visitation – nor, thank God did he summon the Relaxacisor.

NEW YORK, 18 FEBRUARY 1958
Y's inexhaustible supply of ingenious, if eccentric solutions to life's daily challenges finds new expression. Since we no longer travelled by air, the winter tours across America were usually negotiated by rail. At many stations, however, we were unable to find a porter, forcing Y to carry his violin case rather than perch it on top of a trolley of luggage. This growing discomfort finally persuaded him of an alternative method: he would henceforward carry it on his head. I objected, rising to the defence of his lovely Lock's tweed hats (of which he had already mislaid countless numbers in various colder parts of the world). It appeared he had no intention of sacrificing the only remaining one. He had decided to buy a deerstalker and would I please take him to Bloomingdales or Saks or Maxwells (no, I said, the latter is in London and makes your shoes) – well Hawes & Curtis (no, I said, they are in London too and make your shirts and suits). Well, he said, refusing to be put off, you go to lots of shops here, please get me one. I did everything to dissuade him. Smiling blandly (danger signal) he insisted we go in search of a deerstalker, and damn it all, at Bloomingdales we found one. It was of bright green and red tweed and with the flaps down made him look like a cross between a shorn sheep and a Gandhara Buddha. I do not by now have to tell you how delighted he was. A few journeys later, the rumour I suppose having got around, a large picture of him appeared in the papers smiling serenely walking down one of those endless American platforms, deerstalker strapped under his chin, large violin case sitting atop held in place by a fur-gloved hand while the other grabbed me to prevent my dodging the photographer. My head was both bloody in expression and bowed and I suspect that awful photograph went all around the world.

It was far too long before he lost the deerstalker and I suffered deeply. I could not bring myself to drop it swiftly into a street letter box, nor could one toss it from any train window for they are all hermetically sealed. Besides, dear thing, he was so very *fond* of the horror. All I could do was to pray he did not order himself a Norfolk jacket and knicker-bockers to match. Darling Y, stubborn as a mule yet tender as an angel, sensing my anguish as I shuddered away from the sight of him firmly tying the Baker Street horror on his head, crossed the street and bought me a lovely pair of drop-pearl and diamond earrings from Van Cleef & Arpels which (until the day some cold-hearted pig smashed open my case and stole all my family jewellery a year or so ago) meant always Sherlock Menuholmes to me.

## GSTAAD, 11 MARCH 1958

Y's communications seem to be purely by cable (telegram or telephone). Desperately I ask myself whether he is entirely governed by string: four on his fiddle for one kind of expression and any other carried on complicated wiring systems above and below the earth. Whatever it might be, he seems completely satisfied, divested of all other mode of connection.

## GSTAAD, 12 MARCH 1958

In his efforts to play Happy Families Y engaged a skiing instructor for himself despite my begs and pleas. Poor dear Madame Caillat, what agony she went through, what sleepless nights we both spent until Y had managed a slope or two without breaking anything important and only emerged with a few fruity bruises. Proud as a peacock he had himself photographed on the Eggli mountain in full ski-rig flanked by Jeremy aged six and Mita, nine, both proficient skiers. After which, wobbling fearsomely he took the slope at an uncertain angle and reached the first stop all of a piece. Poor Madame Caillat was released from a month's anguish and we all went off to celebrate Y's triumph. No other achievement of his has ever evoked such a glow, nor had I ever before or since seen Yehudi bereft of his modesty. It was an enchanting moment. All my three men with glowing cheeks sitting in the Stübli drinking Glühwein.

## LONDON, APRIL 1958

Assailed by a multitude of trivial preoccupations: deposits of luggage, of children; loading and unloading of same; lists of same for fear of forgetting where Y's winter overcoat might be, or when a child needed to be transferred or to what part of the world; who might be having a birthday and how near the date one could celebrate it without the celebrant feeling hurt or neglected; whether I could squeeze in a hop over to see one or other of our scattered progeny in what school, how much time it would take from one or other Top Important Concert during Y's endless tours? I was becoming like a thumbed-over dog-eared Bradshaw.

## LONDON, 1 MAY 1958

Suddenly I felt that the prediction of Pagliacci's 'Laugh clown laugh' was overtaking me and unless I detached myself for a week or so my face would stiffen into just such a rictus and the rest of me no longer be able to hide exhaustion, worry and lack of sleep. Asked Y for a week or two to clean my mind while he did a non-exacting short tour of Scandinavia. He agreed so I asked Clare Strafford, a close friend, whether I could stay in her house on the Chelsea Embankment. She was away, it was May and the spring had at last deigned to appear. I went for long lone walks along the riverside just as I had as a child and a girl, the seagulls wheeling and wailing in the clear sky, Battersea Park's trees fringing the opposite bank with early green, the Apothecary's Garden on the other side and, further along, the graceful building of the Chelsea Hospital amid its gardens. Sunny by day, Whistlerian grey by twilight, swans shaking themselves clumsily at low tide among the riverboats and the glaucous mud. Tugs and barges and pleasure-steamers ruffling the water and, across from the house, the church where Turner had sat on his wooden chair painting his visionary sunsets. My whole growing-up waiting for me to revisit and greet it. Even the 31 bus terminal where I would jump off and race the three or four streets home to Mulberry House, sore of feet and torn in heart from Madame Marie Rambert's caustic ballet classes. It was a home-coming in the best possible sense, for it 'rinsed the eye' as the French have it, cleared my mind, helped me regain my own rhythm and heal the bruises and scars that the past ten years had inevitably inflicted, obliterating the slightest sense of nostalgia, of wistfulness or the silly whimsy of the might-have-been. As I leaned on the window sill watching the last grey light fade beyond the hideous towers of the Lott's Road Power Station (christened by us children the 'Ogre's Palace') I knew there had been no break in my life, no change, that I must guard a suppleness of mind and a strength of heart whatever further strictures upon my own will or weights upon my shoulders lay ahead. Yehudi was a challenge and one so valuable and worthwhile that it would be criminal to lose heart, and wicked ever to falter.

LONDON, 8 MAY 1958

I allowed myself one outing before I left London, going to the Festival Hall to hear Oistrakh, Oborin and Khuschevitsky play the Beethoven Triple Concerto. To my mind even such great performers cannot redeem that clumsy work, but what they did manage was to enhance, as it were, its monstrous weightiness by their shape and sartorial appearance. All three were stuffed into those extraordinary Moscow dress suits whose tails sweep the ground and were wearing ballooning starched shirts with wing collars and vast made-up bow ties like signposts pointing east and west. To complete the picture each had enormous padded shoulders squared up to the ears as though fulfilling some strange tailor's conception of balance. The resulting spectacle was so gloriously Victorian that it seemed an error not to have had Oborin playing on an ornamental cottage upright or to have decked the stage with one aspidistra and two potted palms. I have never heard the concerto better played nor more adroitly put in its rightful place. Nor, when on occasion I have to sit through it again, does the image of those three dear Slav penguins heading northwards off the stage to roars of applause ever leave my mind.

SANTANDER, 17 AUGUST 1958

From Biarritz by train to Santander where Yehudi, Louis Kentner and Gaspar Cassado were to appear at the Festival. On arrival Gaspar announces he has, like Bo-Peep's sheep, left his tails behind him. However he is much consoled when he finds another lot in the dressing-room of the theatre grateful that 'someone has been so "tremenjos" kind'. The three then adjourn to the hotel room to practise for the evening concert while I, in the first stages of bronchial pneumonia, am confined to bed in the adjoining room. The telephone rings. Hoarsely I whisper 'Hallo!', and am greeted with an avalanche of fury in a mid-West accent:

'See here, can I speak with one of those three? I happen to be the conductor of the American Ballet Theatre and we've held the curtain up for half-an-hour trying to find my tail-coat. Did one of your lot take it from the dressing-room?'

I croaked, 'Wait a moment,' wobbled out of bed, opened the adjoining door and, unable to shout, made frantic signals. Deep in their Brahms or Mozart or Schubert the damned trio played on, Lou shooting me an outraged look at such unexpected *lèse-majesté*. Desperate, I threw some soft object in their direction. Gaspar and Y looked at me with a mixture of worry and horror. Obviously I was in an advanced state of delirium.

'Gaspar' I muttered 'conductor of ballet on telephone – please talk.'

Distantly that gentleman could be heard still keeping up his flow of invective. Finally Y picked up the telephone:

'Yes, can I help you?' The roar reached even Gaspar who followed Y into the room.

'Oh I *see*,' said Y, 'how very upsetting. Mr Cassado indeed has your tails. He imagined some kind musician had left them there as his own are somewhere between Florence and here. I will see they are sent round at once.'

Furious, only half-mollified snarl as Y hangs up hastily.

'What is?' from Gaspar who had in fact been rehearsing in the very tails 'to see if comfortable'.


SANTANDER–PARIS, 23–24 AUGUST 1958

Having stuffed me to the eyeballs with penicillin, my good doctor let me leave nine days later on another of those horrific Menuhin caravan journeys to the border, three-hour wait, on to Biarritz to catch the late night train, an hour's standing stranded by the barrier. Why? Because the lights had fused. At last pushing fractious, exhausted children into their bunks and fitful sleep. Early morning found us in Paris, Jeremy and Schwester Marie dispatched plus a third of the baggage to Gstaad; Zamira, Mita, Y and I across to the Nord, only to discover with horror that two bags were missing. Zamira was splendid, leapt into a taxi and returned triumphantly with both just before the train ferry for England puffed and shrieked out of the smoke-darkened station leaving an echo of puffing and shrieking humans behind, the whole scene taking on that look of Daumier peculiar to all French platforms, a drama of uplifted faces straining to scream the last goodbyes, angry injunctions, admonitory yells wetted by a few rationed tears. A thriftily emotional race.

PARIS, OCTOBER 1958

We called on Casals and his lovely bright-eyed Martita on their way to New York to play at the United Nations. We teased him: had he not vowed never to play in public again in any country that recognized Franco? Slyly his cunning Catalan eyes slid behind metal-rimmed spectacles and looking at the carpet he declared the UN 'neutral ground'. Poor old lamb, he was still playing so extraordinarily well that he was bursting to appear again. Tolerance. It would be too cruel to tie him hand and foot to his great gesture of moral uprightness even though the latter had also brought him vast respect and grudging admiration. Yehudi hugged him, wished him a good journey and a successful concert, and a laughing Martita showed us out.

# ❧11❧

# *B.B.*

Out of the welter of going to and fro in the earth, and from walking up and down in it (see Job 1:7) came one of those rare gifts that were to alter the tenor of our lives profoundly. The Marchesa Origo – Iris Origo, the author, who was a beloved friend – had asked Yehudi to play for her Italian Red Cross in Florence in 1954. After the concert she wanted to know if there were anyone I would like to meet in the remaining evening that was ours before we would be going to India next day. I promptly said, 'Bernard Berenson, of course.'

It appeared he was free and delighted – and so, for the first time in a friendship that was to last only, alas, for the remaining few years of his life, we met the King of Florence. Nicky Mariano, the charming elderly woman who had cared for him and supervised the library for years, greeted us and we were taken very ceremoniously into the long cool drawing-room, half-shuttered against the lowering sun, past a superb triptych by Sassetta to where 'B.B.' sat, a tiny figure in the corner of an engulfing leather sofa. It was his exquiteness that first struck one, that fineness of detail in the bones of hand and face which dismisses size as unimportant and replaces grandeur by perfection of proportion and a kind of finish to the whole, thereby creating a work of art at its own evaluation. Smooth bald head, lidded black eyes, white beard and moustache and beautiful long carved fingers. He was enchanted to meet Yehudi, twice-over delighted to find how simple, how easy and how restful he was. I left them to talk about this and that and chatted with Iris and Nicky Mariano. Then B.B. called across to me to join in – I don't remember what the subject was, but my answer made him laugh and we continued like happy budgerigars to chatter and laugh until, to our horror, we realized we'd been there over two hours and poor little Miras (who was travelling with us) had all the time been waiting alone in the hotel. I jumped up saying, 'Our treat, Mr Berenson, is at an end,

154

I must take the Fiddler back to his daughter because tomorrow we are going off early to India.'

'Good God, my dear, is that all?' cried B.B. and I nodded, looking round me at the cool peace of that room a little wistfully. 'Come again just as soon as you can and make me laugh some more,' said B.B. and we raced back to poor Zamira who was indeed becoming nervous.

It had been the following year, 1955, when I was marooned in a Swiss clinic in an effort to give my third pregnancy a little repose for six weeks (and of which I have already written the sad dénouement), that I had read in my *Times* that Berenson had celebrated his ninetieth birday. On an impulse I wrote, congratulating him and apologizing for the intrusion but telling him the memory of that delightful visit to I Tatti was as a distant light in my present depressing circumstances. From I Tatti came a warm and enchanting reply within a few days and a request to write to him regularly because my letter had regaled him so much. And so started a correspondence with B.B. which lasted almost until his death, written by me from all over the world to B.B. who would reply punctually, as I imagined him, sitting with a rug over his thin knees surrounded by beautiful things in that immaculate villa.

Over the years we had made further visits to I Tatti, invariably forty-hour sorties by train since we were still not prepared to fly. Florence is, in so far as the international railway services are concerned, well below the salt: one is decanted at the most unwitching hour of 5.30 a.m. (and returned westerwards at 01.05). We would be met by a yawning driver and taken to Settignano where we bathed, breakfasted and awaited to be summoned to the Royal Presence. After lunch B.B. and I would have one of those hair-raising drives with Parry, the ancient English chauffeur. Mounting the rough road through the woods of pine and cypress and olive, Parry woud head straight for every stone, every boulder in our way, dipping dangerously over the lip of the road, grazing tree-boles, flattening patches of wayside scrub until at last we reached a sort of rocky plateau on to which he skidded, fetching up with a bump against an outcrop of obliging rock. I opened my eyes, stopped praying and out we got, B.B. as spry as a chicken, admiring the view over to distant Florence. Thence we would begin our descent on foot down the goat paths winding through the sharp-smelling trees, B.B. waving his walking stick, as dapper and nimble as any twenty-year-old. Every so often he would pause, whether to deliver himself of the classic amorous passage (for which he was celebrated) or to gain breath, I never could decide, and finally we would reach the point in the road where the redoubtable charioteer Parry awaited us, the car wheels precariously over the rim. I would direct B.B. who at ninety-one weighed about 100 lbs (and myself about 112) to the inner side and climb in hoping that our additional weight would not topple the car over the fatal fall towards which Parry had parked it. And so swerving and swinging, jerking and bumping we would go back to a delicious lunch at I Tatti and lots of gossip.

Now in the summer of 1958 we were returning to familiar surroundings but this time with unsuspected consequences. Taking a morning walk, Y noticed a charming farmhouse nearby, and with his usual insouciance opened the gate, walked through the vegetable field, knocked on the door, demanded to know all about it and was greeted amiably by the caretaker and his wife. I, having been soaked since childhood with Keep off the Grass, Trespassers shall be Prosecuted, Beware of Dog, Bull and Danger, kept pulling at Y's coat and expostulating. Despite my protests, a long and interesting parley ensued. At last, red-faced and relieved, I dragged Y back to I Tatti where at lunch he asked B.B. who owned the farm?

'I do,' said B.B.

'I would like to bring the family there.'

'Oh! gather ye B.B. while ye may!' cried B.B. in delight. The fattore was summoned, all arrangements made à la Yehudi within one hour including plans to install a telephone (alias Y.M.'s life line), and a list of possible schools for Jeremy.

Three months later Schwester Marie and I packed up the chalet in Gstaad and departed with twelve pieces of luggage by train for our new GHQ, Jeremy receiving a tremendous send-off at the station by a dozen or more envious school pals from Chalet Flora. We arrived in Florence at dawn as usual battered and exhausted, and drove straight to our farmhouse which was called Il Villino, there to be given that particularly Italian kind of welcome – a mixture of warmth, love and chatter – by Teresa and Antonio. After we had helped drag our trunks and cases up to the bedrooms and removed some of the grime peculiar to a night in a wagon-lit (compounded of mustiness, lurking dirt from hidden corners, stale cigarette-stink adhering to hairy blankets and that horrible wash in faintly slimy water, all of which seems to cling doggedly), we ran, Jeremy and I, across the road to say good morning to Nicky and B.B., both very excited that we had at last arrived. B.B. was 'receiving' in bed in his pale-blue crocheted shawl, fresh and cool as only very small babies and very old people who are cared for by others can be. 'So you *have* gathered your B.B.' he said. 'I'm so happy darling.' Nicky, as pretty and sparkling as elderly women used to be before they lifted their faces into parchment masks, handed me a cable from Yehudi: GAVE BEST EVER ELGAR WILLIAM STEINBERG EXCELLENT HOPE NEW HOME WELCOMING AND JERE-MA HAPPY PRAY MY DARLING FINDS SOME REST AND EATS MUCH PASTA HUGS LOVE TO NICKY & BB SIGNED PUDL

Light-hearted, loving and successful, thought I, and turned my attention to kindly Hannah Kiehl, the German lady in charge of the Library, who had already got the name of a piano shop written down for me and the telephone number of Signora Nardi, the best piano teacher, together with name and address of the local Italian village school in Settignano. 'Rest and eat lots of pasta?' Highly unlikely. To work at once, despite pouring rain and icy wind. That night I dined with Nicky, B.B. and his sister Bessie with lots of laughter and a rare sense of joy shared all round and then to bed where for once I slept like a dead log.

The next few days were filled with that ceaseless activity and problem-solving inseparable from setting up house: battling with the Customs to extract our larger pieces of luggage, running from shop to shop to furnish the Villino with a decent stove, radiators, waste-paper baskets, coffee percolators, toaster et al. I found the enchanting Signora Nardi delighted with Jeremy's playing and arranged for Jeremy to go there twice a week. Signor Bucci from Settignano school was more than willing to enrol Jeremy. Schwester Marie, worried about Jeremy's tonsils, had asked Hannah Kiehl to make an appointment with Florence's king of paediatricians, Il Dottore Cocchi; the trunks were finally released as harmless and got stuck in the doorway. In the midst of all this a message from I Tatti: 'Please to come il Signor Menuhin on telephone.'

I staggered across, glad to have returned from our marathon first day's efforts only to be asked by Y why I had not yet managed to find an English tutor for Jeremy? I lost my temper which is hopeless in B.B.'s telephone booth, where the slightest movement causes the light to go off and a cacophony of pans from the adjoining kitchen convinces one that Italian chefs throw or juggle or toss saucepans round the stoves for exercise. Mustering what calm I could, I bade Y a loving goodbye, hit my head on the wall, finally found the door, slopped my way up the fields to our Villino and collapsed with fatigue and smothered fury on my bed. All I needed to complete the day was the sight a quarter of an hour later of Schwester Marie returning from a short walk with Jeremy with blood streaming down his face from having run into a stone wall.

At tea next day I found poor Nicky very worried. B.B. had flatly refused to sign the contract drawn up by the fattore and Yehudi for monthly payments, saying:

'I could never take a penny from him.'

I promised her that instead we would completely refurbish the Villino, at which, somewhat cheered, she said:

'I *do* wish I could convince B.B. that he is *not* a rich man!'

Lorry-loads of stuff began to arrive and by the end of three or four days we had moved from the fifteenth into more or less the twentieth century. Triumphantly Schwester Marie installed the new gramophone in the sitting-room (which just about managed to contain the baby grand, the sofa, two armchairs and a table). There was an ominous growl, a huge explosion and the gramophone burst into flames. Instant hysterics from Teresa and great help with buckets of water and expletives from Antonio. Charred remains removed. Myself only too relieved it was not the charred remains of Schwester Marie. One more problem remained to be solved: the Settignano school didn't work out for Jeremy (he knew no Italian). So instead I found a charming intelligent woman, Miss Burbridge, who ran a small school for English and American children and also taught them Italian.

At last all basics had been seen to and some kind of 'home' established. And such a change for me: Florence (albeit several miles away), I Tatti and B.B. and Nicky and some conversation of interest and wit. Colour and warmth and beauty and liveliness to fill up the still rare gaps between work and duties, but all made lighter, illuminated by Latin incandescence and loving company.

All this time as the Villino gradually took shape, Y had been roaming round Europe giving concerts in Spain, France and Germany. Now, in one of his sporadic darts home, he returned for one night to celebrate my birthday. Before leaving the next morning he proposed that I should join him on a short Italian tour, insisting that I could jump on his train during its five-minute stop in Florence. And so a few days later he hauled me and Marcel Gazelle aboard and off we raced to Naples.

This was a typical Italian tour: no-one to greet us on arrival (nor incidentally to ensure we had even arrived or whether Y would indeed be playing a recital at the San Carlo Opera House). If there be to me a nadir of settings for piano and violin, it is just such an one. The huge house stuffed to bursting and there on the frontmost part of the wide stage looking sheepish and lost a grand piano and stool (very dusty too). I had a seat halfway back in the stalls of the arena just below the first tier boxes. Out onto the stage, looking like a conjuror and his assistant, came Y and Marcel to a roar of applause and plunged into the first of their three sonatas. The applause was quelled by the first chord and downbow, but not, oh most certainly not, the chatter from the boxes around, largely occupied by plump Neapolitan ladies. A sort of *perpetuum mobile* accompanied the entire work followed by frenzied clapping at the close. Whether for what they had listened to or for the pleasure of a musical accompaniment to their gossip I was in no position to tell. Came the second sonata, and if anything, an increased crescendo in the general gossip. To my delight a handsome, middle-aged man just ahead of me and obviously outraged called out 'Silenzio!' The ladies returned the outrage reinforced by shocked surprise and continued their prattle all the way through.

During the interval, Y was quite unperturbed, saying he loved the Italian vocabulary; Marcel merely laughed. At that point a strange man appeared carrying an enormous portfolio, the first sign we had had of any local manager. I returned to my seat. During the last sonata the chatter was sporadic; either they had run out of topics or breath, or maybe they felt they should at last listen to what they had paid (largely) to hear. Nonetheless the rustle of talk swept like the wind through parched corn across the huge house from side to side. My hero in front continued his furious 'Silenzios!' to continued looks of cold disregard. At last the awful ordeal ended to screams and shouts and whistles of delight. I scrambled out, anxious to thank in my shrunken Italian the one man who had tried to teach the Neapolitan boxholders manners; 'Please not to thank me, Madame,' said he in a strong German accent. 'It was an absolute disgrace.' Disappointed, I introduced myself and took that worthy Herr Dr Burckhardt round to see Yehudi.

From Naples we managed a quick outing to Ischia to see Sue and

Willam Walton, hiring the only launch crazy enough to take us across a sea which rose and fell like heaving porridge. We made it, soaked through, my nice new red Jaeger coat ruined, found a taxi, drove to their villa only to find it deserted. Sadly, cold and wet and shaken, we left a little note under the door and had just turned out of the drive when we saw them both coming out of yet another of Sue's marvellously built and decorated houses (five by then). Screeches of Argentine joy from Sue, rumbles of Sitwellese pleasure from Will, and we were hauled off to a friend's house for lunch. The journey back was even more terrifying. In the dark we missed by a hair's breadth a large unlighted smugglers' skiff and all but capsized.

The next concert at Genoa was marked by the same total lack of contact we had experienced in Naples, even to the point of not being informed as to the management's final choice of programme. Marcel told Y to have a good rest while he went to practise at the theatre where he would try to fathom what they were expected to play, ringing back so that Y could practise the same work. After an hour or so I went down to the concierge. Indeed there was a message for the Maestro, it was in French. I unfolded it: 'On joue SRANK', it stated simply. So Yehudi practised the César Franck sonata, we went to the theatre, the Genoese audience behaved beautifully (shades of Paganini?) and I noticed again what had struck me the preceding night: thin little Marcel's behind had swollen to an extraordinary steatopygous shape *after* the interval. Why ever? I soon found out. The ever-invisible local agents waited till a good two-thirds of the concert had been honourably delivered and then arrived as had that strange man at the San Carlo with the fee which judging by the vast bulge in Marcel's tails pocket, came in bills of one lira denomination.

Occasionally there were days stolen from the tour to return to the Villino. The new stove was still not installed but a new cook, Settimia, found by Schwester Marie, was, for Teresa had too much farmwork to look after us regularly. It *would* happen of course that my sister Griselda and her husband Louis Kentner, both high-tone gourmets and she an excellent cook, were in Florence and coming up to lunch. I'd ordered saddle of lamb, tiny 'piselli' those exquisite, hardly born Italian peas, sautéd potatoes and some pudding like crème brûlée or œufs à la neige. I can't remember exactly. Little did I know that a disaster was in the making. After waiting an eternity I went to the kitchen to find Settimia in a rage,

Schwester Marie near tears. Settimia had never had to deal with a wood-burning contraption straight out of the Cinquecento, she yelled, with the result that the lamb was, after an hour and a half tepidly glistening. Teresa, screaming 'Ma, stupida, you should have lighted it after breakfast' added nothing to leaven the general atmosphere of frustrated drama. Schwester Marie said she was sure it would be ready in another twenty minutes. I returned to my guests. Both looked rather hungry and declined another drink. The talk hung in loops and whorls like sagging string. At last lunch was anounced and we trooped into the little dining-room. Uncertainly Settimia placed a big ceramic dish before Y. It held a large shiny piece of lamb swimming in a great deal of blood. Griselda averted her face. Y sprang into action before this ghastly sacrifice; wielding a carving knife and fork (with which he is no virtuoso under the best of circumstances) he plunged it into the glutinous mass. The knife promptly bounced back, rejected by the meek lamb. Undeterred, Y returned to the attack and managed to dig the tip of the knife into the impermeable skin. With all the strength of his bow arm he hacked away, landing with a triumphant cry of joy several slabs of blood-red blubber on to each plate. Lou accepted his with typical Hungarian sarcasm, Griselda with the barely veiled distaste of one who knows how to feed her guests. I was slowly (far too slowly) dying. A big dish of the tiny peas appeared to cries of acclaim and delight from Y who ladled large spoonfuls on to each plate; he appeared as deaf to the rattle they made as to the fact that an inordinate amount of them bounced on to the floor.

Griselda, ever the perfect lady, picked away at her slice, I tried to spear a few of the blood-stained peas on to my fork, failed, shovelled them into my mouth (and all but broke my teeth: marbles, one and all); Yehudi, chewing away at the revolting slab he had somehow managed to cut, incoherently declared it delicious with his mouth full. It was almost with relief that I heard Louis's sarcastic Hungarian voice saying 'I can't eat this stuff, Yehudi', pushing his plate away with revulsion. Miserably, I explained the circumstances. Schwester Marie had bolted into the kitchen with the rest of the lump of bleeding meat and shoved it back into the oven – the piselli were irredeemable. Meanwhile a selection of breads and cheeses replaced the disaster course with a slight lifting of the guests' mood. After all, mozarella, ricotta and mascarponi wrapped in vine leaves and full of fresh walnuts are hardly to be dismissed as fodder and I dawdled over mine, praying that the lamb reach a presentable state as soon as possible, talking distractedly the while of cabbages (raw?) and kings (deposed) without much encouragement. At last the lamb returned fit to eat. Lou, graciously accepted some as did Jeremy (both carnivore). Griselda declared herself to be off her feed and Y, to cap the grisly meal, cut himself a large slice and insisted it was nowhere near so good as it had been in its primeval state. Somehow, solaced by Italian coffee and fruit, we parted company on a happier, less strained note. Griselda and Lou, anyway, gained by it; rumour has it that they dined off the story for weeks after.

That evening Yehudi, Cassado and Kentner played for B.B. the Beethoven Archduke Trio. Only Alda Anrep, Nicky's witty sister, and Nicky were allowed to attend. B.B. was very Archduke himself and not over-generous with what he considered to be benefits exclusive to himself and therefore of special value. I was sad, for Hannah Kiehl had been of inestimable service to us and without Iris Origo we might never have met Berenson. I was all the more disappointed in him because I had boldly asked if I might invite them and had been crisply refused. How infinitely depressing it is when you hold someone in admiration, respect and affection to watch them shrink in a hundred such petty ways before your averted eyes.

In December came the gathering of all the children for Christmas at the Villino. Schwester Marie goes up to see her parents and brings Mita back from Hermannsberg, Zamira flies in from London. We are all madly busy making Christmas presents, Mita a beautiful cardboard castle with turrets and castellations and towers and little wax figures for Jeremy, Schwester Marie and I five golden crowns. Meanwhile, she, Teresa and Settimia prepare a buffet supper in the dining room to follow a lovely session of string quartets played by Yehudi, Cassado and a violist and violinist he had brought from Florence, all crammed into the tiny salotto. What with the four musicians, three children, James Pope-Hennessy, Alda Anrep and the familiar cortège by which Y was inevitably trailed, to say nothing of Schwester Marie and myself sitting in the fireplace, it was as warmly different and full of joyous appreciation as the cold and kingly musical performance chez B.B. was not. Next day 'our' Christmas. Two suits of armour marked Sir Mittahad and Sir Jiminot, all of us wearing our gold crowns, presents, a tree and once more the rare precious being together for a handful of days.

Afterwards we drove up to the Origos' beautiful house 'La Foce' in the Tuscan hills and there Iris gave us all a second Christmas. Her lovely daughter Benedetta accompanied Y in a Diabelli piece and Jeremy reluctantly played a short composition of a friend of Signora Nardi's stopping the applause with a 'not a good pieth at all' coldly. A wonderful three days walking through the huge terrain (sixty-seven farms in all), conversation which at its best means discussion plus gossip plus argument tempered by wit and warmth with Antonio and Iris, and fond farewells clutching a bottle of the most perfect olive oil I have ever tasted.

Thence the family returned to I Tatti only to disperse again. We were becoming increasingly like a tide swept apart by currents. Zamira's took her back to London, Mita's to Germany. Schwester Marie and Jeremy alone remained in Florence while Y and I caught that cruel 12.59 p.m. to Paris falling into our familiar wagon-lits too tired even to celebrate the last minutes of the dying year 1958.

But already our new Italian base had lightened my spirits. After the pink balloon of California and the kindly asepticism of a Swiss hillside, Florence did bring warmth and colour, character and that kind of reality that I had been longing for, something to underpin the ceaseless travel, the juggling with growing children, now spaced in various schools all over Europe. It diminished the exhaustion that our peripatetic life demanded. There was a source from which to draw at last, to replenish the psyche and the body. The little Villino sitting in its pines and arbutus looked across to the grandeur of I Tatti in which the tiny B.B., ever smaller and whiter, sat enthroned – that King of Florence to whom poets and painters and writers, most of the intellectual and cultural world came, together with the floral-hatted ladies from America fawning upon their monarch. There was movement of the mind away from the train tickets and tattered trunks of our everlasting travel to conversation, exchange of ideas and the loud arguments of the Italian or Italianated opinionates thumping and gesticulating, expostulating and exploding with that enviable self-confidence they all shared in their own particular ideas (and in no one else's).

Florence itself as a city, I had never much liked. Those menacing gun-metal grey stone buildings seemed like closed eyelids, basilisk and somehow unsettling. Even the great square with its breath-stopping David discomfited me. It was the beautiful conquering boy gazing at the dead Goliath, from the height of a courageous spiritual faith, now almost lost. I would hurry through the Galeria, alien and draughty to the river and the Ponte Vecchio and the smaller world of shopkeepers and vendors and noise, or to the smells and cackle of the market, averting my head from those slabs full of tiny dead birds, lying in heaps with their hundreds of miniscule claws upraised in protest, to the glorious cheese-counters, there to fill my basket with ricotta, mozarella and that exquisite mascarpone. As for pasta, our Teresa made her very own, especially when all the children were at home and could watch her nimble fingers rolling and slapping, cutting and twisting into little cappeletti the fine soft dough.

Much of the spring and summer of that year we spent at the Villino and it was always a healing of body and spirit to return there from some trip abroad. I particularly remember one occasion after we had survived an appalling sea-crossing from Cyprus to Naples, taking the train back to Florence through the early Italian spring, pink with almond blossom and budding vines, silvered with olives, looking like a Renaissance tap-estry but for the missing unicorns. The scenery restored our battered nerves while the longing to reach home and the children effaced all physical fatigue. The excitement of regaining Mita, taller and handsome, and picking Jeremy up at Signora Nardi's where he had been having his piano lesson, also bigger and bouncing and full of tales of new pieces for Y to hear, made me forget my giddiness and wobbly legs long enough to unpack our usual eight pieces, dine joyously with the boys and fall into bed. Even when I was found to be suffering from danger-ously low blood pressure soon after our return, the pleasure of being back at the Villino did not desert me. To be ordered to rest was bliss and so I did, filling the time reading *Pickwick* with Mita and listening to the chamber music rising through the floor from the room below.

And so the spring advanced into summer, the woods filled with arbutus blossom and tough little flowers clung to the rocky soil. The time for the singing of birds had come together with the peasants' hungry guns and I walked warily through the trees with Jeremy as the crack and pop of their nasty fire-arms brought minute sparrows and all manner of tiny flying things greedily to the ground. The Villino filled with music many an evening, Gaspar bringing carfuls of players to join in a Mendelssohn octet or Brahms sextet, playing elbow to elbow half in the fireplace, the rest of us squatting in corners or squeezed in the stone passage on cushions till midnight, Jeremy in transports turning pages for piano works and jotting down very weird compositions in his pyjamas at one in the morning on his bed. B.B. revived with the sun and although my blood pressure still remained obstinately low, the whole atmosphere – of Settimia and Teresa yelling at each other below, of Florentine gossip brought in by Alda's guests ringing round her dining room like a peal of cracked bells – was life-enhancing. The children dressed up for Y's birthday – only marred by his insistence that Schwester Marie's glorious classical chocolate cake be made with one of his newest horrible organic substances (called 'cocomerde' or 'Grottochoc') that contained no such sins as sugar or cocoa-bean but pure health-giving substitutes. The revolting cake, of course, turned out like a huge cow-pat reducing the children and Schwester Marie to angry tears as they finally abandoned the attempt to make forty-three tiny candles stay upright in the sticky mess. At such moments Y withdraws to some unattainable metaphysical 'safe-house' of his own and I am left to blow sundry noses and wipe eyes and suggest roasting potatoes on the wood-fire for dinner and doing jigsaw puzzles while we wait.

As the autumn approached that short golden time drew to a close, Zamira and Yehudi departed for London leaving the boys and me to walk and talk and read *Tin-Tin* every evening. I had one lovely lunch at I Tatti, though B.B.'s growing deafness irritated him more and more. When the party broke up, he caught my hand and begged me to stay a little so that in the comparative stillness he could hear more clearly.

The packing up of most of our things – I was soon to follow Y to London and then to America for the winter tour – held a Chekhovian note for it bespoke a sadness to come that had not yet arrived. Over everything hung the shadow of B.B.'s inevitable passing. Knowing I was unlikely to see him alive again, I nevertheless perversely fought the finality of every sock and shoe and jacket I put in the cases in the hopeless dream that I could perhaps leave some behind for the coming spring. With leaden hands and a switched-off heart I disciplined myself to clear away everything that was Y's and mine. Going to bed on those last evenings at the Villino I used to look down upon that strange and rather ugly villa, even the origin of whose name could not be traced, and imagine B.B., white beard, white face against white pillows, exhausted after the hour-long ceremony of preparing him for his narrow bed, faded blue eyes closed, beautiful thin hands crossed over each other on the lace-edged sheet; and I would wonder what little spark of illumination would stay his slipping over the living side of that almost invisible edge into the dark of which, in the stillness of his position, he already presented the image?

That whole shifting of our hard-working and repetitive lives to Italy had been like moving from the shade into the sun for me and I was grateful to B.B. for every moment of it, especially for giving me a sense, for however short a time, of being myself and not simply part of Yehudi.

Next morning I called in at ten, the car packed, Mita waiting in it on our way to the station. Feeling certain by now I would never see B.B. again, I begged Nicky if I might kiss him goodbye. She flatly refused, muttering something about his not being fully ready yet to 'receive'. I might I suppose have pleaded with her to go and ask him, I might even not have held back the tears, I might have argued gently with her – I was not asking very much. But I sensed an anguish in her, she who had been so utterly loving and loyal to him and who had put up with so many of his *Schwärmereien*; now perhaps she wanted the small time left with him to be entirely her own. I kissed her goodbye and went away desolate.

A couple of weeks later Schwester Marie and Jeremy returned by train to I Tatti while we embarked on the Queen Elizabeth for America. On arrival in New York I rang Nicky. My premonition had been right: B.B. was dead.

That was not quite the end of our time at the Villino. Once or twice during the American winter tour we telephoned I Tatti to talk to Nicky, Jeremy and Schwester Marie. From Nicky we heard that the telephone which the fattore had promised would be installed 'pronto pronto' in the Villino in July 1958 on that exciting evening when Y and B.B. had settled the details of our move, had now at last arrived: still not working, however. Telephoning I Tatti from some distant American town, I would picture Jeremy and Schwester Marie running through the field of artichokes after the maid who would have summoned them, crossing the unpaved road and racing up the hill to the gates, through those and the big open house door, along the carpeted passage and finally, winded, round the little corner where B.B.'s collection of hats and overcoats still hung and into that cavern that contained the one and only telephone in the villa. Jeremy would squeal with delight reporting on a Mozart sonata he had been working on with Signora Nardi. It was so difficult to hang up, to have left part of one's heart so far away and to visualize again that lovely corner, the valley of Settignano, B.B. buried and Nicky desolate.

Returning to Europe on the Queen Elizabeth I was stunned to open the Ship's News one day at breakfast and read of the sudden death of my dear step-father, Cecil Harcourt. The shock of the loss (he was only sixty-seven), so totally unexpected and so brutally learned, made me understand even more deeply Nicky's devastation without B.B.. So when we arrived at I Tatti for a two-week sojourn, I suggested that she might like Schwester Marie and Jeremy to stay on at the Villino until the spring when her loneliness might be less heavy to bear. Nicky was very grateful and I meanwhile made the most of my short stay there with Jeremy, playing and reading and walking, listening to his real progress musically. Already he was able to read a Mozart sonata with his father with perfect ease, adding a composition or two of his own.

And so the day came when inevitably for our final departure: 3 March 1960 and everyone, including ourselves, was in tears. For me it was an epoch whose comparative shortness was not in ratio to its value nor to its significance. To this day I have retained the memory of those eighteen months, of the quickened pulse that was Italy, of the life and talk and company of I Tatti and of the beauty of the surrounding Tuscan landscape. I place it with care in that space in my inner self I had been so afraid of losing forever.

# ❧12❧

# *Roots*

The Villino had been an idyllic interlude which had borne fruit in Yehudi's organically controlled mind. It had made him aware of the peace and security and therefore the need of a real home; had at last given him the taste of and for it. I had been told by Domini Crosfield that one of the beautiful houses in The Grove adjoining her Highgate mansion was up for sale: No. 2, owned by Adrianne Allen, the actress, and her husband Bill Whitney. Y himself on arriving in London had taken Zamira and Mita up to Edinburgh for his Festival concerts and had begged me to stay behind so that I could go and look at the house. I not only had the gift of two unfamiliar relatively idle days at Claridge's but the excitement of knowing that Y was really serious about finding a house – a home at last and that in my beloved Great Wen, London.

That first evening away he rang and immediately asked whether I had been to see the house. Knowing all along that he would ring, I had indeed dug myself out of my warm comfortable bed in a room free from all telephone calls (except from Y), free too from all those squeals and slides of violin practice and rattled all the way up to the highest point in London where the house had stood with its five corresponding neighbours since 1682, surrounded by gardens behind and an avenue of limes before. Adrianne showed me round. It was a dream; way over to the south-west lay Hampstead Heath and Kenwood; in between, binding the two into pure countryside, Witanhurst, the Crosfield twenty acres where we had so often stayed. Lively, witty, hyper-competent Adrianne pointed out that it offered all the advantages of the country and the town (after living there nearly a quarter of a century I have decided it offered all the disadvantages of both). Not gifted with clairvoyance and struck by its undeniable beauty, I thanked her, congratulated her on the warmth and style with which she had decorated it and duly rattled back to the hotel (why *do* English cabs *rattle* in such an extraordinary epileptic way?). No sooner back than had come that call. Y ever-impatient over new ideas. 'Exquisite, my love,' I said, 'but' firmly, 'far too expensive.' Whereupon he rings up Bill Whitney and makes an appointment to see it on return with first refusal to buy, unbeknownst to me. But nothing was decided because we were off again.

Not long after that first visit to Highgate, Y bought me a beautiful Queen Anne desk which further convinced me that he really did want to live in London. I would never have insisted upon it – merely pointing out to Y in one of those rare moments when the last manager, BBC man, promising violinist or destitute Balkan had finally left, that with the fortune he had spent on hotels and hired chalets and with the children growing unsteadily from place to place like torn-up shrubs, we should seriously consider a home. Even if he could only imagine it as a GHQ at this moment, it would be both economically more sensible and psychologically of enormous importance to the children. Meanwhile we had actually seen one other house, but the deal had fallen through. Nevertheless Y still maintained that London was the only place he could dream of living in, so I hugged him, stored my Queen Anne desk and added yet another to my long list of (mainly unanswered) prayers.

For once however, the call was to be heard. Returning one day across the Channel to Dover I went to buy *Homes and Gardens* at the paper stall and there found six pages and an article on No. 2 The Grove, ravishing garden, Adrianne Whitney, Anna and Daniel Massey (her children by Raymond Massey) and all, everything so lovely, so cosy and so settled, that I passed it over to Y and said; 'What do you think after all?' He answered 'I'll take it.' So as soon as we reached London we went up to No.2, found it was still on the market and bought it.

One of the consequences of deciding to move to London was that Mita would have to leave Hermannsberg because it would hardly be right for him to be the only child living abroad. So after a sad farewell to our friends at Salem, I searched around for an English prep school, eventually settling on Stone House which fortunately possessed a very human head master in Mr Richardson. From there Mita was destined to go to Eton where I met his prospective house-master, David Wild, a patient kindly man who would need a great deal of both those qualities should Mita pass his exams.

If buying No. 2 had been a comparatively simple exercise, preparing it for us to move in presented a variety of disparate problems. Despite the generous help of Adrianne Whitney, I had the unenviable task of arranging the whole house in my head without seeing it empty of its own pretty style. And often this task had to be carried out wherever Y's concert schedule took us. One day I would be filling my school exercise book with drawings for the house on a boat somewhere between Athens and Cyprus, while on another I would be projecting my imagination from the quiet countryside of Tuscany.

Nevertheless, I was somewhat daunted when Y, who never does things either in halves or one at a time, told me he had decided to build our own chalet in Gstaad and would I like to look over the designs that the architects, Herr und Frau Lanzrein, had just sent, and begin to conceive its outward and inward character? I recollect muttering dazedly that I was only a quarter way to working out the furnishings of the Highgate house and then halted. After all I'd brought it on myself but had not counted on Y's genius for multiplication: either no sound would strike in his inmost thoughts or seven notes to a chord – nothing in between.

I will return to the Gstaad chalet later – for the moment back to No. 2: one evening Adrianne invited me to the theatre and then brought me back to supper in the Garden Room of the very house she would soon hand over to us. What did I feel? I cannot say, for that ghastly inbuilt habit of refusing to look into my own deeper feelings should they rock the boat, making its compulsory way towards an irreversible direction, was going at full speed ahead. Whatever my real thoughts, I had to accustom myself to the unavoidable process of getting the house ready by fits and starts. As I continued to tour with Y I could only collect lamps from here, there and everywhere and count and list my father's furniture, long lying awaiting its release in the Pantechnicon, when Y's schedule brought us to London for a handful of days. This created such a jungle of problems that the idiocy of trying to plot ahead too arbitrarily would be tantamount to accepting a challenge to conquer Hampton Court maze in five minutes flat. So I continued to draw in my exercise book, to list, to buy what would obviously be missing and to take note of what had to be done. At night I would lie awake trying to empty each room of its present furniture and design my own placings. Fruitless exercise, for it was a gay, bright theatrical house with a very strong personality and every time I tried to replace Adrianne's white and violet-covered *guéridon* bearing a large vase of silk carnations with my grandfather's Chippendale Pembroke, holding a frog-mug and a Chelsea Falstaff, I came to a dead stop. How the devil would I get my mother's rosewood Bechstein into the drawing room where Adrianne's white baby grand stood? No hope. Stop thinking and accept the helpful advice she offered of upholsterers, gardeners and local shops. Meanwhile remove myself to Domini Crosfield's at the corner of the Grove and be grateful that my daily haul of bedding and linen, pots and pans, whirlers, curlers, blenders and binders and all such mystifying kitchen equipment could be left in the vast subterranean caves of Witanhurst.

Y as usual was so busy that he saw little of our slowly emerging future home. But I did manage defiantly to find one afternoon when, together with Miras, I took him to No. 2 where the hospitable Adrianne, still installed, gave us all, accompanied by Puffin Asquith, drinks in the garden. 1958 was a year blessed with week after week of sun and unclouded skies, and as we swung in her garden seat, bemused by the smell and sight of the summer flowers, surrounded by the freshness of May-green trees, my heart and mind soared in anticipation of life to come in Highgate. Having no crystal ball to aid me, I could not know that it would be the first and last time we were ever to experience the *dolce far niente* of Whitney No. 2, and that our long term of possession would not yield such a benison to Menuhin No. 2. Not one Bloody Mary to mingle with the bumble bees beneath the magnolia ever occurred again.

However, we did occasionally enjoy brief excursions elsewhere which deepened Yehudi's love of England and English ways. One such was a visit to Xandra Trevor-Roper's charming Oxford house. Xandra's kindness and concern as well as her deep love and knowledge of music had made her one of the few close friends upon whom I could always count in my jagged, disoriented life. It was there that we met Albi Rosenthal, the antiquarian music book collector and his wife Maud, also to become valued friends. Rachel and David Cecil came to dinner, reviving memories of my ballet days when he would give me delicious teas after the matinée at the 'George', agreeing and disagreeing over books and people and dropping buttered toast on the suspicious carpet that looked as though it had long ingested all manner of food. After dinner we strolled through Christchurch Meadows in the light of a runcible moon, increasing Y's enchantment with his adopted country. The following evening at the Vice Chancellor's dinner we met Isaiah and Aline Berlin. To meet Isaiah is what the Americans so graphically describe as 'an experience'; to meet Aline is to meet a very beautiful and intelligent Frenchwoman and therefore for me part of my Gallic soul. Isaiah with his marvellous seventeenth-century face: a Russian (Lithuanian to be exact) Alexander Pope with all the wit and speed of mind but without the acrid edge, exuding a warmth which to me was a smoke screen for the sudden statements that emitted from him like sparks from a quietly smouldering fire, never extinct, making his company such joy. He and Yehudi discovered they were distant cousins both descended directly from Rabbi Schneersohn, the founder in the eighteenth century of Chassidism, a branch of Orthodox Judaism from which sprang most of the music and the cantor's songs, a flowering of the stern stem to which it belonged.

Back in London I returned to the Witanhurst basement to disentangle the contents of the twelve large packing cases from the Pantechnicon. In between I was coursing up and down crossing items from my interminable list at Messrs John Lewis, Selfridges, Peter Jones, et al. while trying out new chauffeurs to replace my darling old Leach who had recently died, having been with us ever since our wedding, that grey October day nearly twelve years before. One such morning I opened the great front door of that most imposing neo-Georgian pile of Domini's – the twenty indoor servants of pre-war days now reduced to a tiny gathering of Greeks who were sacked for one misdemeanour or another with monotonous regularity. This shrunken Hellenic horde being totally unreliable and mostly half a mile away in another part of the edifice, I had not bothered to wait for the bell to toll twenty times, opened the front door myself and found myself looking straight into a row of buttons. Bewildered, I followed them upwards and discovered that they were topped at 6 foot 2 inches by a very pleasant female face. 'Reporting for duty, Madam,' said the voice above the rest of the stout frame, 'I am Hope MacBride.' And so 'Mrs McB.' became part of the family for the next thirteen years, running, fetching, carrying – a willing and good natured soul if ever there were one, and at that particular moment for me a gift from the gods, helping me to gather and deposit the vast amount of clutter that was at last to be my furnished No. 2.

The next objective was to find a secretary for Y. To fulfil his demand's I calculated that the right female would need to be equipped with at least two or three languages, a working knowledge of music, a university degree or two, the ability to sit for hours while he dictated at any time of the day and night without falling off her chair or fainting in coils on the floor; she would have to be conversant with the geography of most of the world with the exception of Ultima Thule, capable of deciphering the handwriting on those odd sheets of paper on which he scrawled his most recent brilliant idea (a calligraphy more resembling Sanskrit than any known Roman alphabet), to have a pleasant appearance and no halitosis. A tall order by any standards. Not surprisingly at first I drew a blank from the queue of applicants who filed to my door. But then one day on our return from an expedition to Brussels we were met at the station by the impresario and Yehudi's manager, Ian Hunter, accompanied by a very neat young woman whom he had brought along for me to interview. Her name was Mrs Wiggington. At Ian's office I told her what would be required of her, were she to be foolish enough to accept the job. Perhaps my dark-ringed eyes and tousled hair wove a circle round us thrice for I certainly offered no honeydew nor looked as though I drank the milk of paradise. Smiling sympathetically, she produced some fifty letters she had picked up from the house, confessed to a love of music, a good grip of three languages to which I could have added a charming, calm face, a gentle humour and a balanced temper. All of which led to one conclusion: I hired her.

Meanwhile the process of collecting continued. A dash to Stone House to see if Mita were still there or had swum away in dudgeon led to a chance windfall. I took him to one of those typical British hotels, standing huge and lonely dominating the sea on one side and a bleary golf course on the other. The food was just slightly better than school meals. At one of the only occupied tables in that vast dining-room, I saw Francis Egerton. 'Aha,' I said to myself, 'the director of Mallett's, the grandest antique furniture shop in London, is not here for the Irish stew.' Going over to his table where he sat with a very distinguished and scholarly man, I greeted him.

'Diana!' he said in his gentle courtly way, 'What *are* you doing here?'

Pointing at the small schoolboy gazing at his cabinet pudding with disgust, I replied: 'More to the point, Francis, what are *you* doing in this godforsaken dump? Now don't pretend it's the view, the food or the golf.' Trapped, he smiled at me and said that well yes, there were some excellent bits of furniture here and there sprinkled among the Cinque Ports. And, good friend that he was, he scribbled down some names in nearby Sandwich. Mita and I had a lovely afternoon in those winding salt-smelling streets and, thanks to Francis, five beautiful inlaid Dutch chairs, three black and gold Regency, a chaise-longue on which Prinny could never have frolicked, so narrow and delicate it is, a mahogany fire-stool and a Spode jug have been gracing No. 2 The Grove ever since and all bought for the incredible sum of £93.15s.

And so the months passed by with the pieces gradually falling into place without it ever looking as though the job would be finally completed. Too often No. 2 had to take second place to festivals, concerts and sorties abroad. At last as autumn approached Y examined the schedule and graciouly offered me exactly ten days to get the house ready for occupation. It was September 2 and Y was playing at Montreux. I crept out of the concert halfway through and began that awful train-boat-train journey to London. Never mind, this would be our first real home and although I knew the effort and lack of time was quite terrifying, I still loved challenges in those days, and no oily smells or smutty sheets or rattling wheels or rolling seas could diminish nor reduce my ardour.

Mrs McB. met me at Victoria and we sped up that Everest of West Hill, Highgate and opened the door of No. 2. This was the first time I had ever been able to see it empty and I walked from room to room wondering whether the scruffy little drawings in my exercise book would prove partially or even entirely unpractical. I rang the 'Pantechnicon' and told them to send up the family furniture Griselda had so generously shared out. For the next week from early morning till well after dark, staying so conveniently at Witanhurst and, with the help of every available hand, we split open cases, washed china, laid rugs and moaned over the usual wrong orders arriving with sickening regularity from most of the shops. A local electrician named (and directly descended from) Dick Whittington beavered about changing all the electric points to 15 amps. A lovely pair of men made the whole house smell sweet while they cleaned and waxed the panelling which covered all the ground floor, the staircase and bedrooms. Another temperamental but very gifted man was slowly driven mad by me covering sheet after sheet of cardboard while I shouted 'No, more green! No, more brown! No, more ochre!' till at last practically in tears he snivelled; 'You're DREADFUL' with a full hiss like an enraged gander. I said 'Got it!' 'It' was a lovely amber I wanted for the walls of Yehudi's north-eastern facing dressing-room and which would now look warm and glowing in any and every light.

Luckily my measurements and my eye had not let me down too

unmercifully and the house began to look as I had imagined it: a real *country* house built on the highest spot in all London and still surrounded by open land, by trees and lawns and heath. The curtains arrived and were hung exactly as I wanted: no satin or silk – lovely French Boussac cotton framing the big squares of the seventeenth-century windows for all the upstairs rooms, and damasked dark green material especially woven as a gift to me by that irreplaceable textile genius Miki Sekers. Day in, day out we worked. The invaluable Millie (who had been Adrianne Whitney's housekeeper and was, unknown to either of us at the time, to stay on in No. 2 for the following twenty-three years) brought in extra friends to help with various tasks. Meanwhile I was still dashing off to the Portobello Road for small touches I noticed missing amongst my lumber (a pair of 'oriental' regency candlesticks for £6, a patchwork footstool for £2, a hearth-stool for £4). Fifty mainly ghastly family portraits arrived (most of which still line the garage walls facing inwards). Books, hundreds and hundreds. Filthy hands, filthy face, broken fingernails. Agony when it seemed that one of the two tallboys would not make the turn of the stairs. Domini's dear old chef arriving with food for me. Mrs McB. and I (washed as far as our wrists) ate in ten minutes and went on as I ticked off piece after piece, changed the position of a bureau-bookcase, shut my eyes while Steinway wangled Mama's Bechstein into the library by a hair's breadth.

But oh joy! came the eighth day when, aching all over, I could walk in and see a *house*, go from room to room, mistily remembering the William and Mary wing-chairs, the tub chair, the Chippendale sofa with its supple simple line, the Chinese Chippendale table (supposedly Mrs Siddon's theatre dressing-table) all redolent of Mulberry House, all of them dormant, waiting since it was bombed in 1940, and now looking very much at home and ready to receive.

On the ninth day Millie and I made up the beds, put out the soap and towels, checked the hangers in the cupboards and she went off on holiday. The sun was only just sinking over behind Kenwood as I went out into the garden; the trees of Hampstead Heath and the faraway Surrey hills were touched with bronze, the air cool and the light rosy-blue. Chrysanthemums flopped their heavy heads, dahlias red and purple, the first Michaelmas daisies were coming out and the crab-apple tree was aflame at the end of the lawn. Tired and contented I looked back at the house, its corner half-hidden by a huge ilex tree, the windows streaming their light palely on to a not yet quite twilight. Tomorrow I would put flowers in all the rooms, tomorrow Yehudi and the boys and Schwester Marie and the two Italian maids would arrive from Florence, Zamira from her stay in the Bahamas. I closed and locked the old front door. I did not want to sleep there till Y came.

The following day at 4.15 p.m. the party from Florence poured out of the car accompanied by two taxis bearing twenty-seven pieces of luggage. It was a wonderful moment for me – like good reviews after a successful first night. I took them from room to room explaining what small alterations and additions would have to be done later. Yehudi hugged me with joy, the boys ran up and down the stairs exploring everything. Zamira arrived, looking much changed, chic and very sophisticated. Chef brought over, unasked, some delicious soup. Our two Italian maids cooked the rest of the dinner and we all sat down round my Ipswich colts-foot table at our very first meal in our first real own home.

That evening I could at last savour. Candlelight, all of us squeezed round the table, Italian food, followed by scampering in the darkened garden, a minimum of unpacking and so to bed. I lay awake by Yehudi's side feeling as proud and happy to have reached this stage as though I had climbed on to a plateau where the family could tread surely and permanently. Y of course fell fast aleep as soon as his head hit the pillow, but tired though I was I was too full of past, present and future to close my mind for hours. To have all the things round you, your very own, must be a basic sensation for everyone except the most detached and abstract of beings – and I, after nearly thirteen years of hotels and hired habitations, felt lyrical with joy. If I were never to find a new friend again, here I had most of my past life alive in the furniture, china and pictures that did anchor me to some symbol without in any way dividing me from my most precious of all presences – Yehudi.

And what of Yehudi's other scheme, the building of a chalet in Gstaad to complement our new home in London? That was no passing whim. Already we had chosen a site, found by clever Schwester Marie and far away from the millionaires and the great hotels, far away from that collection of either moribund rich old or vociferous painted young, the one lying about the halls and lounges as though awaiting the Great Reaper, the other defying him by driving at a hundred miles an hour in scarlet lizard-like cars. No, we were well set on the wrong side of the tracks and the view of the whole bowl of the mountain and valley lay around and below. The prospect of building the chalet on this spot thrilled and excited us and before leaving we had left instructions with Frau Lanzrein, the architect, for work to begin as soon as possible.

From then on the demands of No. 2 The Grove and an extended American winter tour had kept me from Gstaad, but back in Europe at the end of 1959 Y had suddenly allowed me another of those ten-day stints in which to furnish the new chalet while sending the boys and Schwester Marie on a skiing holiday. Arriving alone in Gstaad, my fury knew no bounds when I found the same large hole in the ground that we had left last September – the only difference being that it was now filled with snow. I rang Frau Lanzrein and summoned her, together with the local builder, whose thick Schwiezerdütsch restricted his full understanding of my angry accusations, as well as mine of more than half of his mumbled explanations. It was obvious that once we had left in September, he had removed his team to build yet another chalet, so I stamped my après-ski boot, glared full into his red-leather face and told him that if the chalet were not fully built by the end of June, he would be responsible for the cancellation of the Gstaad Festival, for we would not give it unless we were all installed as promised in our own dwelling. Whether it was my mime, worthy of Marcel Marceau, or shreds of my ungrammatical German that penetrated that solid bone head, he insisted that the men would start at once despite the fact that the temperature stood at 10° below zero. Snapping back that I too would suffer exactly the same frostbite, I dragged Frau Lanzrein off, asking her to tell him in their common language that by the day I left, the framework of the chalet must be up, so that I could at least work out the necessary proportion of the rooms.

I spent a miserable day. Now there would be no question of flying to London for twenty-four hours to attend the memorial service for my dear stepfather. I rang his wife Stella who could not have been kinder or more understanding. Nonetheless I felt full of guilt and increasingly lonely. Those past twelve months had seen the going of those very few human-beings I could still count as mostly belonging to me, to me in the past, me in the present: dear old affectionate Leach, B.B. and now Cecil, that devoted, kindly and reliable man. It was as though the moorings of my own self were breaking like a frayed rope, and soon I would be floating out to sea entirely at the will of the current that was Yehudi, this ever recurring tide, rarely bringing his galleon into harbour for long; together always poring over the chart which outlined the journeys ahead, while the shore where had been my few close friends became ever emptier of their welcoming smiles with every landing. There had been no time to develop anyone new of the same character, of that same depth of intimacy, who one knows instinctively will gradually replace the inevitable passing of past loves. Life seemed at one and the same time more and more crowded and emptier and emptier: the snow on the mountains, as I shivered on the balcony, would melt in a month or two and fresh green grass would gradually replace it. My remnant of that inner life which all lonely children create was dissolving too; would, I wondered, the ineluctable disappearance of my own tiny world offer me some fragment of the permanence that the cycle of nature would bring to those vast slopes, or would I have to learn to live without anything of my own?

At least there was always the chalet to distract me from such sombre thoughts. Daily I would travel down to Berne in search of stoves and washing-machines, materials for curtains, covers and carpets. Nothing is more boring than plumbing and I would return to Gstaad my head ringing with the ablutionary virtues of baths, basins and bidets and long never to wash any part of me ever again. But there was good news too: we found a wonderful old chalet in the Simmenthal (famed for its ancient ones), had it delivered to be dismantled and eventually lengthened so that we could fit in the compulsory music-room. This adjunct led to frantic new sketches with Frau Lanzrein for fear that the finished appearance of the chalet might resemble the horror-wooden-villas of the very rich, springing up like toadstools all over valley and hillside. Finally I chose the wood for the interior walls and cupboards. And now my allotted time was up, as at least was the skeleton of the chalet. On the other hand my reputation was way down, depicting me as a heartless virago who forced workmen to build at temperatures of 10° below zero. *Tant pis*, I thought. All I cared about was that they didn't down tools again as soon as I had gone.

Two months later, immediately after our final departure from I Tatti, I returned to the charge of the chalet, this time for a whole fortnight. Finding that the taxi asked exhorbitant prices for driving me down from my little hill-top 'Hotel Neueret' to the station, I would get up at 6 a.m., dress in two jerseys, anorak, boots, ski-pants and woollen cap, and (still at 10° below zero) slip and slide mostly on my tough dancer's behind down to the station, breakfastless. There I would catch the early train to Zweisimmen; cross the narrow platform to the next one of a slightly larger gauge, swing down the beautiful snow-clad Simmenthal (getting a hot coffee at last); wait there on the icy, wide, open platform of Spiez for the big international train to Berne and race through the tunnel and up breathless to the farthest platform just in time to catch the connection to Zürich where I arrived at exactly the moment the shops closed: 12 p.m. Ravenous, I would gobble a sandwich at the 'Möwenpick'. Thus fortified, I would go on my window-shopping expeditions in the old parts of the town, pressing a cold and dribbling nose against the windows and making my eternal notes. By the time I had climbed and descended a dozen cobbled streets the shops had awakened and I would bolt into one or the other, seeing either with delight or disillusionment the noted objects at close quarters (the prices too I met with the same emotions), either deciding on the spot or taking the card of the shop; thence I would hare back to the Bahnhof just in time to catch the 3-something train, which was my last possible connection to Gstaad unless I were to spend the night in a snow-drift. This process I would do every other day or so: the bottom-toboggan slide; the four trains, the one and a quarter hour's shopping and the repeat journey, varied by visits with beagling eye down to the slowly growing chalet where I had made one fast friend in the carpenter of great skill and taste who would work well past his given hours and chase any sluggards.

There remained the garden to plan with Herr Vogel, the king of the horticultural firms of Berne. A weird wintry scene, tramping frozen over the masking snow, pointing out where I wanted trees, shrubs, ground cover, and begging Herr Vogel not to remove the big rock his men had found in the middle of what would, one hoped, be a sort of terrace of grass. Terrified of bringing to this German-Swiss region a touch of Madame de Staël's French-Swiss style, I risked nonetheless a trip to Vevey and there found two shops with charming simple antiques and with no further fear of 'Chalet Coppet' bought Y a lovely eighteenth-century desk, a table, a chair and a hanging bookcase. Slowly, slowly, more and more the snowy vapour rolling round me, I watched the putting up of the tiles on the roof. I began to get more and more impatient, but by the time I had to leave, despite huge strides forward, much remained to be done. Joining Y and Jeremy on the train to Paris, I was cheered by their writing each other melodies on scraps of paper which, passing to each other, they each had to sing.

Comes at last the Final Act. Returning to Gstaad in July I found the chalet still full of carpenters, plasterers and likeminded snails. Oh dear: reluctantly I donned my tarnished brass helmet, cuirass, gloves and with huge spear in hand crashed about breathing fire down scorched necks, howling down telephones hoarsely demanding the upholsterer to bring all curtains up else I would pay only half the bill. I had rung the various shops where I had made my purchases all through the preceding month from Vienna, Montreux and Zürich – and the chalet was now ringed with unopened crates like fungi at the base of an old tree.

By the time I felt I had burned the workmen into a frenzy of work I risked going off to Thun with Frau Lanzrein and there found ravishing lamps made out of old spinning wheels, lanterns and coach lamps, and – as was possible in those days – not *Kitsch*. Supplementing these there were the crates of furniture from California. On a brief stop at Alma during the last American concert tour, I had selected some of the pieces from there (others I had sent to London) for the chalet. These had now arrived and once I had successfully reassured the Customs Officer from Geneva that all the furniture within had been in my possession for two centuries, slowly room by room the wood-shavings could be cleared out, the crates opened and the pieces put in place. With beating heart I found that, with the exception of one beautiful Tyroler piece – a huge cupboard which ended gracing the basement, all was as I had designed it.

Nonetheless it was twice as hard an undertaking as had been No. 2, for the workmen had a habit of returning to fetch something or other they'd forgotten – and we would have to clean up all over again. The basement, painted green, sulked and refused to dry. Most of the Tyroler cupboards and buffets were full of very dead insects and stank of coarse red wine. I spent a whole day scrubbing them in the open air out on the lawn. The gardeners had made a beautiful job of the garden, planks, nails, splinters, shavings all cleared away. I ran up the long flight of stone steps bordered with ground-covering ivy and creeping plants. The trees were still very small, the flower beds had been ransacked by Schwester Marie and when I opened the door the whole chalet smelled of pine-wood and flowers. With everything almost done, I drove to the station to meet Y and Mita.

Mita walked round with his critical eye, but thank goodness, admiringly. Y with his warm and spontaneous heart gave me the second house-maker's hug within twelve months.

So we were twice installed – in London and Gstaad. Two cheers for Diana. When Zamira arrives and, loving the whole house, lights a fire we sit around all five and have a passionate theological discussion about the where, what and why of God till 10 p.m. I cannot think why...? I go to bed; our first night in our new chalet. Y very satisfied. We both fall into a drugged sleep (even I, for it is nearly 1 a.m.) – the delicious deep drifting sleep of contentment and fulfilment. The eighteenth-century front-door bell clangs like doom. I wake with a start. 7.a.m.? Yes indeed it is Mr Iyengar, the yogi guru. No comment. But Mita comes up and reads me bits of *Verse and Worse* in bed and we roll about in delight. Next day we're all winded by balloon-blowing, hanging them on eaves and balconies to celebrate Mita's birthday (as usual in Menuhintime six days late). At last there are signs of moorings – the far-flung family is drawing together, and I begin to feel that through the years of travel our own two homes will now offer us increasing steadiness of heart and mind.

# 🎋13🎋

# *The Upholstered Office*

To what extent did having our own home alter our lives? Nothing reaches the full image of one's hopes; imagination always surpasses the possible and practical. One's capacity to enjoy that which does live up to the early vision is in exact proportion to the power one can summon to support it. So too is the flexibility needed to adjust to the disappointments. This was all the more true given the particular demands of trying to establish just that kind of home best suited to the very unordinariness of Yehudi, his character, his work and his unchangeable way of life.

Without question to live in the most vivid, interesting and human capital in the world was what underpinned the whole scheme, made sense of the choice. As the Good Doctor said, 'When a man is tired of London, he is tired of life'. However, he was not married to a famous violinist whose enthusiasms and interests outspanned any other consideration. As far as Yehudi was concerned, with a settled home in a great city and an excellent secretary his scope knew no bounds. Gradually No. 2 The Grove was to become an upholstered office with a team of helpers and Y a sitting pigeon to be grabbed at to chair, preside or become founder member not only of his own slightly cranky ideas, but of others both worthwhile and peculiar. The constant movement of our lives still continued, admittedly to a lesser extent at first, but then accelerating again after a few years (by which time even Y, exacerbated by the tapping of typewriters on two floors, finally removed the 'Office' to other quarters nearby). Although he loved his house and garden, he used the former to expand in greater comfort and order his multiple ideas, and the latter as an exercise ground for Yoga or jogging.

An example of this was his new-found passion for something called Ergomantics. Nastily, I suggested it must mean 'Therefore Antics' and the 'm' was for euphony.

'Not at all,' he replied with a reproachful stare. 'It means the science of sitting, something I have been trying to put across to orchestras for years.' 'Ah,' I said, 'so that is the reason for the odd collection of very unattractive chairs which keep on arriving at the house where they are scattered variously amongst my so lovingly placed Chippendales and Hepplewhites?'

Ignoring the aesthetic tone of my argument, Y launched into an exposition on the appalling and grisly deformations of the spine, but-tocks, hip-joints et al of the average string-player, scraping away for hour upon hour chained to a schoolroom bentwood. I was forced to agree in the end, but silently wished there were somebody else worrying himself about this anatomical problem. And so the chairs continued to arrive, some looking like part of a collage by Braque, others by Frank Lloyd Wright out of Gordon Russell. Quietly, when he was practising in his new music room, transported by its perfect acoustics, I would steal down and remove them one by one, stacking them in the basement with religious respect and a sly eye. To do him justice, however, I have to admit that not only did he succeed in persuading various orchestral managers to take the matter seriously, but also he found a chair-like object to his own taste.

The foray into Ergomantics was all part of what I soon came to call 'Y's ingathering'. Everything moveable in his crowded curriculum was dragged from its moorings and lugged up Highgate West Hill and into No. 2. The drawing room furniture was regularly dislodged and a drugget laid over the Persian carpets. Often the front door was left agape with cables and icy air pouring through to enable BBC, TTV, ITV, Nord-Ost-West-Süddeutscherrundfunk to pitch their boiling and un-lovely lamps and interview Y on everything from mangoldwurzels as a possible food substance for the starving to music therapy for disturbed animals. In these circumstances I would retire, leaving him with beaming face to offer his ideas in English, French or German, loving it all. When for a few days we were free of these interruptions, there would be the cacophony of Jeremy practising scales in the library below while Yehudi warmed up in his study next door to my writing-table. Simultaneously someone might be running over Bach on the harpsichord in the drawing room before being joined by half a dozen other musicians who would arrive like the Midians to play some piece for some concert sometime soon. I had considered myself impervious to any amount of music, having been brought up in a house with three Bechsteins going at once; but I have to admit I was defeated by a piano playing Mozart in one room, a violinist's noisome practice in another, spiced with a small helping of chamber music in yet a third, all one above the other in discordant layers. An American friend of Y's, hoping to catch a glimpse of us, came for a drink and remarked, 'My God Diana – it's like Grand Central!'

I myself sometimes felt that No. 2 was beginning to take on the air of a dentist's waiting-room in one of those Harley Street houses where several dentists work on each floor and their proprietary victims all huddle together in shared misery over the *Bird's Weekly* or the *Financial Times*. As many as could would be perched round my hall table on all the chairs, a circumjacent batch waiting dolefully in the library, while Y blithely worked off the top of the list in the drawing-room. My vision of a graceful house, occasionally filled with music and good talk, alive and loved for its warmth and beauty seemed to be fading fast. Even as a fine and private place, it lost by a long length to any hotel. For there one could hang up a 'Don't disturb' on the door, switch off the telephone and enjoy a modicum of peace. But here one could not even rely on finishing one's lunch.

As a desperate escape I reverted to my family panacea – satire – and wrote the following not entirely imaginary diary:

A DAY IN THE LIFE OF YEHUDI MOSHEVITCH
6 a.m.   Over the Surrey hills a pale sun struggles through a bank of cloud like a labourer fighting his way out of tangled bedsheets and finally emerging to greet the dawn. All is still in the wan light, nothing stirs, nothing except a few early sparrows and that lone, scarcely discernible figure bouncing in the cold dew, barefoot upon the lawn. With a shudder the sun withdraws into its blanketing clouds and when it appears again the daunting figure has gone. Ah! but only gone indoors for the sun's rays, peering through the top of a window, pick out a pair of wavering feet, and as the light travels downwards it reveals that these are joined to the body in the usual way of such extremities, with the exception that in this particular instance their owner has reversed the generally accepted order of anatomical precedence and has got his head where others prefer their feet.

Lonely upon a peak in London, N6, Yehudi Moshevitch begins his day. Upside down.

6.30 a.m.   Comes the first telephone call – from Moscow, and they have forgotten (or ignored) the time-lag. Repolarizing himself for better hearing, Y. Moshevitch lifts the receiver: David! Good morning! You *can* play at Bath next week? Bravo! The Double-Bach together. Good and let's do the Mozart Concertante too. Do you want to play the viola or the violin part? Never mind, we can make up our minds on the day. Let's do a double Vivaldi too and the Spohr duos and the Bartók ones as well, as encores. Programme very long? In India concerts go on till dawn ... very good for Western audiences ... endurance test, love to Tamara, goodbye.

7 a.m.   Telephone: Aloysius Crumpelstein from Agamemnon, NY. Did Y. Moshevitch recall his invitation for the Bathfest of 196X? To sing his exclusive song cycle from the early Alleghenies settlers? Y.M. Oh! Ah! Of course! You say they are in dialect and mainly of a pornographic nature? Perfectly all right. Chance of the Lord Chamberlain's being conversant with seventeenth-century Hillbilly dialect very slender. Same goes for audience, incidentally. Fascinating programme. See you on the fifteenth. Goodbye, Mr Corkelberg.

7.30 a.m.   Breakfast: Hagebutten tea; Birchermuesli; Echtesjungfrau-bienenhonig; Heiligesparkassebrot. (For translation refer Bircher Clinic, Zurich, Tel. 425262, 10 lines.)

7.32 a.m.   Telephone call from Bathfest Administration, London. George? You feel forty-three soloists too many for the Festival? Nonsense. By the way you'll be glad to hear Oistrakh can come. He rang this morning, and Aloysius Canckelspiel too, so that makes forty-five. Quite all right. Besides, I'll play for nothing. Can't get them all into ten days? Tell you what: I won't appear at all and that'll leave twenty spaces. I'm sure Ian will agree. Goodbye.

7.40 a.m.   Back to cold breakfast.

7.42 to 9.42 a.m.   Telephone calls from Sydney, Hornsey, Montevideo, Asnières and Port Elizabeth.

10 a.m.   Congealed breakfast abandoned for practising.

12 noon   Frantic secretary reinforced by wife put their heads round door. Bathfest Admin. panic. Ian H. on line from Borioboola-Gha (Independent East-West Africa): did Y.M. seriously mean to reliquish his performances of Beethoven, Bach, Bartók, Brahms and Berg in order to accommodate the Ulan Bator Collectives Quartet and the Borstal Boys' Drama Club rendering of the 'Ballad of Reading Gaol'? Now look, Y,

don't do anything till I'm back. I've one more place in the jungle to visit to hear a cannibal tribe playing a xylophone entirely made of missionary bones. Goodbye.

1 p.m. to 2.30 p.m.    Lunch of a raw nature, prolonged by dictation of article to hungry secretary on 'The Ease of Running a Festival'.

3 p.m. to 5 p.m.    Profound slumber on floor cleared for purpose of scores, fan mail, love letters from Germany full of dried flowers, six types of experimental chin-rests, the concert schedule till 1975 and part of a ten-tome treatise on 'La Musique a-t-elle de l'Avenir?' by Achille Andermatt, published in Bagnolles-sur-l'Orme, for which Y.M. has promised a 10,000 word preface for the English edition coming out next month.

5.02 p.m.    Hears five-year-old violinist of Afro-Patagonian parents (sent by Hep).

6.02 p.m.    Says good-bye to five-year-old violinist of Afro-Patagonian parents, having given it a lesson on how to hold the violin and advised it to take up the flute.

6.03 p.m.    Finds six people waiting since 5.05 and sweeps them all into the library together to save time. After ten minutes general conversation, discovers that they are severally: a man with a slipped disc wanting to know about yoga; the Gypsy King from Romford (sent by Hep); a man from ATV waiting to do a piece entitled 'Whither Serialism?'; ditto from BBC Third Programme to tape Gounod's 'Ave Maria' and Tosti's 'Good-bye'; the Minister for Groceries and the Arts to discuss Supermarket Music for Elysium New Town (sent by Hep); and the plumber who has been trying ineffectually to get into the kitchen for the last twenty minutes to mend the hot tap.

6.15 p.m.    Fetches the violin and gets the whole lot done by 6.30 p.m. and then stands on his head.

7.00 p.m.    Descends from head full of new ideas and proceeds to jot down first ten pages of them while answering Ian H. on the telephone: No really can't play for highest fee ever paid for Festival Brasilia, but what about nice charity concert for Sweat and Soil Association at Harringey Stadium instead? Money? Oh, that always turns up. Ring you tomorrow. What you're going into hospital for ulcers for next six weeks? Terribly sorry. Send you my earthworm cure – infallible. Dear George, can't imagine how you got them.

7.30 p.m.    Meets secretary staggering home after ten-hour day. Beamingly signs fifty letters on stairs and dictates forty-four more.

9.00 p.m.   Lets secretary out after advising her to do deep breathing while typing.

9.02 p.m.   Eats dinner of groats and Ghanaian honey (sent by Hep), which has been waiting since 8 p.m.

9.05 p.m.   Practices two Bach solo sonatas, a piece for violin and nose flute by a niece of Sukarno, and a recently unearthed Pièce de concert of Paganini's entitled 'Vesuvio! E vietato fumare'.

11.05 p.m.   Recognizes wife on way to bedroom and decides to call it a day.

11.30 p.m.   Gets into bed and prepares sketches of knee exercises for music-school children to strengthen their octave passages, which get entangled with the galley proofs of a piece entitled 'Ornithological Brothels' (subtitled 'Battery Hens: a Protest'). Falls asleep, smiling.

1.05 a.m.   Wife removes spectacles from Y.M.'s nose and turns out light.


Despite all these hectic comings and goings, there were compensations in having one's own home in London at last. Friends were returning to my life, people like Juliette and Julian Huxley who one day carried us off to see what he considered was one of the most perfect of ephemeral sights in all London: the single white magnolia standing in full bloom on the lip of the sloping lawn at Kenwood. Juliette's flower-like sweet-ness and Julian's huge enthusiasms were marvellously matched and a tonic for us. Gradually those precious exchanges, those touchings of mind and hand I'd missed so much, were coming back.

One day we lunched with John and Diana Murray where John, with admonitory finger wagging, told Y what he described as the 'Awful, disgraceful story of Diana and the bust of Lord Byron': Jock is, of course, the hereditary director of John Murray's, Byron's original pub-lisher. 'I was going to take her to lunch and she met me at Albemarle Street. She was quoting "The Isles of Greece" as mock heroic. So I showed her the big red tin boxes full of the long thick black tresses Byron had sliced off his various Greek mistresses' heads. She was so overwhelmed at this romantic extravagance that before I could stop her, she leapt down the stairs to where Byron's bust stands on the half-landing and wrapping her arms round it planted a scarlet kiss upon his lips. Aghast, I told her I was expecting a very serious group of Greek intellectuals that very afternoon. Diana without much enthusiasm wiped the marble lips with her handkerchief to absolutely no avail. We tried soap (Wright's Coal Tar) and only succeeded in smudging the red into a kind of leer. I had to explain to my visitors that there had been an act of vandalism only that morning and I would of course attend to it the very next day. They looked outraged and the following discussion was distinctly cool. It took six weeks and as many experts to put the bust to rights again!'

Other threads from the past occasionally turned up to form my thinned-out personal life into a pattern of a sort. My father's best friend, Harold Nicolson, was a guest at a birthday party given for Yehudi by the Swiss Ambassador. Harold was the family trustee, but as my mother had been unable to face seeing my father's close friends after he had died so young, I had rarely met him since then. We made a bee-line for each other, and he talked of that father I'd never known. Suddenly bearing down upon the Ambassador's wife, he announced in a commanding voice that so belied his teddy bear face: 'I am going to sit next to Diana at lunch. You can remove Lord Tomnoddy, he is of no consequence I assure you.' A quick shifting of place-cards was made and I had a delicious time of gossip and humour. A few days later he sent me a first edition of *Some People* with the inscription, 'My dear Diana. I have found one at last and here it is from your late guardian, Harold Nicolson'. Sadly he soon became ill and, too slowly, died. I had written him a letter suggesting that his family must be the only one extant for whom it was a distinction to drop one's aitches. He got it too late.

And, of course, apart from reviving past friendships all manner of happpenings occurred at different levels in Y's fifty-storey life. He spoke on 'Monitor' on Indian music; his Indian guru arrived whom he dumped first on Domini Crosfield, then on the good Francis Huxley. Yaltah married the brilliant young American pianist Joël Ryce. I continued to finish off the last touches needed in No. 2, deciding that the basement corridor, dark and dismal, could only be brought alive by turning it into a harem. During my search for Turkish lamps I found one which I sent to the turner's. (It was pitch-black and I was convinced that beneath the layers of dirt lay brass.) I asked the shopowner to tell the turner to put red glass in the empty panels. Two weeks later the telephone rang:

'Is that Mrs Menuhin?' in strong Cockney.

'Yes.'

Him: 'You're right, it is brass and it looks lovely. Do I understand you want *red* glass in it?'

Me: 'Yes.'

Him: 'For a brothel?'

Me: 'Yes.'

One of the happenings I least enjoy remembering belonged to the blue side of my life, the part in which I have to do the unpleasant and embarrassing things which burden an artist of Y's calibre. Around him was the usual satellite of devoted admirers, some worthy and warming, others pushing and an infernal nuisance. Y, being quite incapable of deliberately hurting anybody, was a perfect target or idol for the frustrated woman longing to dump her bundle of repressions upon the most rewarding lap. Such a one was a woman of Nordic extraction who found in Y the epitome of her dreams. Thick and solid as a cladded boiler, adorned with a small, man-cropped head, very intelligent eyes behind large metal glasses, she spoke with one of those childishly bleating voices that arouse a distaste I can hardly hide. As for Y, who tends to shut out all that is superfluous to his central task, I think he merely saw her as a piece of furniture like any other. I, therefore, could only avert my eyes, sigh and listen to the rehearsals she inevitably attended.

One day, however, the last straw fell that shattered my camel's back. Primo: I learned that the orchestra referred to her and a few of her rivals in persistence as 'Yehudi's fan-belt'. Secondo: as Y finished playing she thudded across the hall, opened the violin case he'd laid across the stalls, picked out the rose-pink silk cover I'd made, loosened the ribbons and held it out in a gesture both coy and obscene. As a vestal virgin she was sorely miscast. Something snapped, I ran down the aisle, snatched the cover from her outstretched hands and said icily: 'Miss Blank, my husband is not a retarded child and can perfectly well pack away his own violin, and were that not the case, I would be performing the task for him. But, as I have no intention of making a paralytic fool of him, I would beg you to realize that it would be better if you were to desist.' She looked at me with loathing and turned away.

That however was not the end of the affair. Poor Miss Blank had had a book made of her letters to a friend describing with cloying glue her ecstacy after every concert she attended. This she had given Y in a leather show case copy adorned with an assortment of rather smudgy photographs taken at those moments when Y was either damp with sweat after a concert, tumbling from a train at dawn or snatching forty winks with his mouth open between intervals of rehearsal. When she submitted the book to me, I had thanked her prettily for she had promised that there would be only the three precious copies, i.e. this one, her own, and the lucky correspondent's, so not wanting to squelch her sickening ardour, I agreed that it was a touching tribute and – retching – forged through enough of the text to prove to myself that it was strictly emetic. Imagine my horror when, passing a book shop a little later, I found a whole window display of this abortion, and, worse to follow, opening my *Times Literary Supplement*, an extremely spiteful review suggesting that it was probably a publicity stunt on the part of Menuhin. My rage knew no bounds and I promptly arranged a meeting with Miss Blank at Claridge's, of all places, almost asking for her choice of weapon and seconds. In hidden misery, I arrived and went straight to my very much loved Gibbs (one of the last great concierges of that almost extinct breed).

'Gibbs,' I said, 'I have an awful meeting in the foyer with a woman who has got herself caught up in Mr Menuhin's bicycle wheels. I think she may prove stubborn. Will you get one of your elegant footmen to come in every twenty minutes or so and ask me if there is anything I need?'

Gibbs looked at me with his large, doleful, infinitely wise and experienced eyes and said:

'I understand, Madam, don't worry.'

Miss Blank was already there sitting in the corner, large and formidable as ever and ill-fitting the small French sofa. We exchanged forced greetings and got down to business. After protracted wrangling (the meeting lasted a full hour and a half with no less than five visits from the footman), the beastly woman finally compelled me to say that if she did not withdraw that dreadful and harmful book (*TLS* review waved at her as proof) I would have to sue her (whereupon she produced a slavering review from *Peg's Own* which I flipped into the coffee-cup). Came a whimpering voice:

'May I still attend rehearsals and concerts? . . .'

'Oh, for God's sake, woman,' I said, 'you can stand on your head all during the Beethoven Concerto if you want to – I have neither objection nor power to stop you. Simply the necessity to protect my husband from people like you who, blinded by their own obsessions, imagine they are offering tributes to their idol when they are actually shying coconuts at him.' With that we went out together and I offered her a lift. She accepted and, as we drove off, I said:

'Remember, Miss Blank, this is entirely private and secret. My husband knows nothing of it, and we will both bury it as though it had never happpened.' She agreed. For the following year or two until its value to herself had expired, I wearied of learning of her version of this 'private meeting' which she chose to broadcast far and wide, as heavily embroidered as a Victorian tablecloth, from one capital to another.

Away from these disagreeable encounters there was always the more rewarding experience of watching life grow up round the children: town life with living people of all types and classes, temperaments and problems – not just trees and flowers and the scrubbed buttocks of Swiss cows and hand-picked friends. Jeremy was now at Westminster Under School, where I had sent him after removing him from a school up the road which taught him little other than how to turn his desk upside-down and throw paper-darts at the teachers. Much to the surprise of those who thought it very odd to put that gifted child accustomed to European ways into grey flannel English tutelage, Jeremy loved it. Meanwhile Mita with the aid of a tutor had passed his Common Entrance Examination and scraped into Eton. For the time being he remained at his prep-school, Stone House, where in those comparatively simple first years in London Yehudi could still spare the time to come down, run in the parents' race and congratulate him on being top in English.

I, too, was less tied to the writing-desk and suitcase and could spend more time on other things. I took the boys to the Royal Tournament, a great success even though a storm of Wagnerian proportions all but drowned the exciting rattle of the Royal Horse Artillery as they pounded round the tan. They were quite proud when I told them that that was their great-grandfather's regiment. We even got to Glyndebourne to see *Rosenkavalier* and *Don Giovanni*. For Yehudi it was the first time and he was as excited as the boys. On another occasion we visited my late grandfather's little Tudor house and the Tunbridge Wells 'Pantiles' and rolling common which Griselda and I had inherited as 'Ladies of the Manor of Rusthall' and which would in time pass on to Mita and Jeremy. On the way back, we got a puncture. Y hopped out and was changing the wheel (he is extremely nifty at things mechanic) when a policeman passed. Recognizing Y, empurpled face, black hands and all, he jumped out horrified: 'Doing things like that with *your* hands, Mr Menuhin, good Heavens! Here, hand over.' Y was as pleased as though he'd played three encores, which incidentally he never would.

One day Bernard Miles, who ran the Mermaid Theatre, came to the house and, seeing Mita, now aged twelve, suggested that he should come down to the theatre and audition for *Emil and the Detectives*, the show with which he was starting that season. Terrified of putting Mita through the possible agony of trial and failure, well knowing the pride of his nature, I rejected the proposal out of hand. But then during the night I mulled it over – had I any right to deny him the chance? Was it my own fear of what I would go through if he were summarily shot out on to the pavement after the first audition that prevented me from even telling him of the offer? Next morning I put the proposition to him and after some thought he agreed to give it a try. A very intelligent and attractive young woman, Marjorie Sigley, the co-producer, came up to the house and read over the script with him. She told him to come to the theatre in three weeks' time for the first audition.

Came the day I took Mita there and left him. His face was expressionless when he came out, saying that he had been asked to go back that afternoon. This we did, but still there was no decision. Half-hopefully, half-wearily I drove him home. Some time later he was summoned to the Mermaid again but again without result. And then, just as my nerves were about to crack, he was told that he had won the rôle of 'The Professor', the second lead in the play. Great relief and rejoicings: I had not judged wrong. So far.

And indeed Mita's début on the stage turned out to be a triumph. Anxious though I was on the first night, I could not restrain my delighted pride in his playing the part with a style and timing quite astonishing for a twelve-year-old who had never even recited poetry at school. Next day's papers – that is *The Times* and the *Daily Telegraph* – both gave him high praise, both saying it was invidious to draw out one child from another of the thirteen boys, but they could not resist remarking upon the unusual aplomb, wit and self-possession of Gerard Menuhin's 'Professor'.

During the play's run a bizarre incident occurred which was later related to me by Miss Sigley. Apparently she had been away on holiday for a time but returned unexpectedly one evening to hear screams for help coming from one of the two dressing rooms. Gently she opened the door a crack and looked in. Now the 'Mermaid' was then right on the river as all warehouses were and the windows looked down upon it.

What Miss Sigley saw was eight small boys crowded round the open window, two of them each holding an upturned foot, whose owner was obviously dangling head-first over the flowing water.

'Lemme go! Lemme go!' screamed the unmistakable voice of the boy who played Emil.

'Not till you f...ing well promise to stop f...ing about like a bloody toff, you crummy little bugger.'

Miss Sigley quietly closed the door, shaking with laughter. She recognised Cockney law when she saw it. There was no more trouble and the cast resumed their play as equals.

It was during Mita's involvement with *Emil and the Detectives* that I discovered that I was pregnant again. I was thrilled to the core for I had always wanted three children and five years had gone by since I lost that third baby in California. In my usual way I said nothing to Yehudi for three months. Only when my doctor ordered me to rest after I became exhausted from the ceaseless round of activity at No. 2 did I tell him the news. He was very excited at the prospect and put me to bed. It was 7 p.m. and tomorrow would be Sunday with fewer callers at the house.

The next day I felt odd and weak but determined not to show it as Y had a very important recording to do, the two delicate Beethoven Romances with John Pritchard conducting the Philharmonia. Millie, our housekeeper, was back and taking one look at me refused her Sunday off. I stayed in bed in terrible pain refusing with a kind of mad fierceness to allow myself the truth. Y returned at 1.15. The recording had gone very well. I suppose it was then that I stopped pretending and by the time my doctor came, I was haemorrhaging badly. My kind gynaecologist followed, examined me and said: 'My dear, I'm so sorry, you've jumped the gun.' Everything, it appeared, had gone wrong as well. The ambulance men were incredibly kind and kept opening the slide window and saying 'You all right duck?' or 'What a shame, dear' and carried me into the hospital as though I were glass. Within ten minutes I was whipped off into the operating theatre.

It was a terrible blow for me from which I found it hard to recover, despite the kindness of my sister Griselda who immediately rallied round, the 'perfect foul weather friend', as she calls herself. When I got home I found that darling Yehudi had gone to Mallett's and asked Francis Egerton to find me a chaise-longue. The one both those dear woolgatherers had chosen was the most superb and ravishing gold and white Regency boat-canapé, an object to gaze at and worship, upon which even Madame Récamier would have found it impossible to nap.

What pulled me up was Y's awful sadness. With his Guardian Angel who please God will never desert him, as well as his own sweetness of nature and great gift, he is not trained to the hideous shocks and cruelties of life, and one could see him struggling to regain his true centre, angry that there might have been something he should have done in the past few months when I was so understaffed and he so engrossed in his own life. I pointed out that he did not even know I was pregnant and that his achievements meant everything in the world to me. The cloud behind his eyes lifted a little and the worried, wondering look on his face lessened.

But achievements did come to help lift me from my hidden darkness and him from his unaccustomed shock. One morning, taking Y down to his rehearsal at the Albert Hall, I was troubled by his limp dimness, his almost determined lack of confidence in the coming concert. Nothing I said would blow away the mood. That night I sat in cold fear in my box. Y came out pale and with a strange absent look and proceeded to play like an angel (the Beethoven). Next day's *Daily Telegraph* said: 'Head and shoulders above his rivals'. And I knew the shadow had passed.

Mita's success in *Emil and the Detectives* had been another cheering achievement. So too was Zamira's marriage to the pianist Fou T'song, which we celebrated with a party for 180 people at No. 2. I began to feel that the house had indeed created a certain security to underpin the velocity of Y's life. Not that the Menuhin caravan had ground to a halt: in 1960 it had passed through eighty-eight different towns, given eighty-six concerts, not to mention seventeen recordings. Truth to tell, that was an improvement on previous years.

Alone in the house on New Year's Eve, I opened the casement window in Jeremy's room on the top floor and smelled the icy night air. It had been a beautifully cold crisp day. The massed leafless trees stretched as far as the Surrey hills, the moon was in its first quarter and there were stars opening tiny holes of light all over the invisible sky. No wind. Perfect stillness. A night owl hooted from the ilex. Happy New Year to you too, I said and fell into bed, too tired to stay awake till midnight.

# Russia

One day Yehudi came to me and asked hesitantly whether I would consider our flying again. It had been eight years since the deaths in air crashes of Ginette Neveu and Jacques Thibaud, having deprived France of its leading violinists, had persuaded Y to give up air travel.

During that time we had been unable to go to the more distant countries because sea journeys would have separated us from the children for too long. I agreed to the idea at once. I too, since we had settled in England, had got mightily sick of that camel journey of train-boat-train and was beginning to look longingly at airports as we passed them by on road or rail.

So it was by plane that Yehudi and I, accompanied by Hephzibah, set off for Russia in November 1962. Descending on frost-tipped forests (Y *would* choose November) we landed in Moscow and, after meticulous searchings and gropings, were passed sanitized into a fascinating 'lounge' complete with Turkey carpet (*circa* 1909), red velvet couches and armchairs all adorned with off-white lace antimacassars and the statutory portrait in highly varnished oils of the Reigning Monarch of the People. There our long-time friend Barshai, the violinist and conductor, and Galia, the Intourist girl, were the only deputies to meet us, Galia charming, slender, pretty and dressed in drugget. We drove through miles of nightmarish Grimms' fairy tale forest which gave way to nightmarish square blocks of inhuman dwellings in an ancient huge black car out of which, I speculated, they had just removed the coffin of an Enemy of the Régime. Silence from the Menuhins frère et soeur who thought my humour a shade too black. I was so depressed that I demanded that we go first of all to Red Square to see – through the dirty windows – the Vassily Church. Galia agreed, after which, feeling at least a wisp of the Russian dream in which I had been brought up, we were decanted before a hideous twenty-five storey building squatting like a broody hen before us, which turned out to be our premises. Inside it was a cross between a dilapidated Grand Central Station and a morgue. We dumped the luggage on the nth floor and Galia took us to the shoddy dining-room where neon lights blazed and a band banged out bad jazz while we waited for two hours to be served two courses. Both indifferent. Stacks of stale black bread adorned the tables and were only edible when, having blown away the dust, you broke them into bits and sucked them. Then to bed, so cold that I only removed my hat and shoes, awaking next morning hungry and shivering. No room service, of course, only a cafeteria to which dear Y repaired, returning with two pieces of bread sitting in the saucer of a cup of tepid brown juice representing coffee. Ian Hunter, who was with us, to our delight clutched a pot of Cooper's marmalade which he thumped down on to the break-fast table as though it were the Union Jack. A small island of pleasantness in a country that so far would have made Cannes during the Fête des Fleurs look like Daventry in a drizzle.

In due course Galia arrived and I told her firmly that as we were going overnight to Leningrad (Oh! praise the Lord) when we got back we would stay anywhere from a garage to a brothel, but not, repeat not, in this mausoleum for live people. Poor Galia said she would report. Meanwhile in freezing pre-snow weather we visited the Kremlin. There hugged by the ancient walls and safely protected was 'my' Russia: churches with golden domes like the backdrop of the last act of *Firebird*, icons lovingly restored, iconostases of unbelievable beauty and elegance, all filled with shabby Russians of all ages, also being restored to their ancient faith as they peered at the marvels cap in hand, some of them even furtively crossing themselves. It was very moving and somehow not anachronistic, rather it demonstrated the failure of man totally to destroy what is man. I found the Ouspensky church the most beautiful, all white and gold outside with faded friezes, but unfortunately closed for restoration at the time; the Armoury was a feast of gold and silver, of great coaches and wonderful clothes, the ghost of Peter the Great clearly to be seen in the immensely long faded velvet coat and knee-breeches fit to be worn by a tree, but a slender tree all of six foot six inches - a silver birch perhaps.

Back at the hotel we had the enormous pleasure of finding Natasha and Igor Oistrakh, the violinist son of David, so that the regulation two hours' wait for lunch was at least filled with talk and companionship.

There were only five tables to serve, all of which were ignored by a gaggle of waitresses chatting up the head waiter in one corner, so I imagine the delay must have had something to do with wood-burning stoves in the kitchen; or maybe despite the Great Revolution they had not yet succeeded in obliterating the ghost of Goncharov's 'Oblomov', who took the whole first chapter of that wonderful work to get out of bed. Dinner that evening arrived at the same hectic speed with the same septic food and then we were off to the 'Leningrad Vauxhall' (the latter term was adopted by the Russians to signify 'station' – another touch that somehow delighted me).

On the train we were given very comfortable sleepers with a small table between the beds bearing two plates of rubber biscuits of indeterminate age. At the end of the corridor sat a uniformed figure guarding his bubbling samovar. I suggested some tea. There was an inch of sediment of a russet colour in the bottom but we drank it because it was nice and hot and after all what could be dangerous about swallowing a mixture of coal-dust and gravel? The line was smooth and absolutely straight as had been the road it followed between the two great cities in Peter the Great's day. Strange! Where was the bed light? Ah! at the *foot* of the bed ... so I remade them and we started reading. Suddenly the lights went out. Imagining a fuse, I poked my head through the door to ask the attendant's help. The lights in the passage were dimmed and he was lolling asleep beside the samovar. Of course, I should have realized: Big Father had ordained that travellers should sleep at 11 p.m. All to bed and lights out in the dormitory, boys! Oh! dear Lord, how was I going to bear three and a half weeks in this giant reformatory?

We arrived at Leningrad at 8.15 a.m. and were met by an extremely bossy fellow who treated us like freight. My Russian had long since dissolved into a dozen swear words, Y's was rusty, Hep's (typically) fluent, but Boss was unmoved by her charm. We drove down the Nevsky Prospekt to our Hotel Europe in a side street opposite the white and gold-pillared Philharmonie. In the smoky light we had caught glimpses of long straight streets lined with classic façades. My spirits rose. The hotel was of about the same 'Regency' or 'Directoire' period as the concert hall and had not had a hand put to it as far as one could detect since around 1839. Nor a duster since 1917. No matter: the splintered parquet of our bedroom, the white and gold porcelain stove, walls, chairs , beds – all rose like ghosts of the elegant past to illuminate what had been Russia, Baltic Russia, if you will, but not ever Soviet Russia.

My heart lifted into my eyes as they took in the graceful shabby room and its cracked ceiling of enormous height. I didn't care a damn about the tepid brown water nor the skimpy curtains hanging like shrunken washing from their peeling gold poles; what fascinated me was the Russianized translation of Napoleonic furniture upholstered in faded green plush. The dining-room was identical and breakfast the only dismal Moscow touch. Across in the colonnaded hall Yehudi rehearsed the No. 2 Bartók Concerto (première in Russia) while Hep practised in a veritable drawing room of a dressing room on a golden piano covered with cupids and simpering ladies painted à la Boucher.

Seeing that I was straining at the leash, the good Ian Hunter kidnapped me before Y and Mr Petrov, the conductor, had finished disentangling the Bartók and we walked for three quarters of an hour along the Nevsky Prospekt among the Sunday crowds. The people here were much more shapely and better dressed than the Muscovites and reminiscent in their fine-boned features and carriage of the emigrés who had decorated my life since I was a child in Paris and London. Most wonderful of all we went to the Maryinsky Theatre (renamed Kirov in order to expunge every royal trace) where all my teachers had been trained and made their débuts and danced. A whole part of that transparency that is imagination suddenly became palpable and shifted into the memory to be embalmed forever. It was no longer a sacrosanct dream but a living actuality in blue and gold which not even the shabby audience nor the stodgy academic *Don Quixote* ballet could spoil. I simply held the two apart and recognized that despite that hefty choreography, the dancers still adhered to the style I had seen in Diaghilev's company and the grandeur which somehow shone through the boring *enchaînements* as well as the stupefaction of those windmilling mime passages. The bones of that unique structure survived. That evening I wrote a long letter to my beloved and respected Karsavina in London and dreamed all night of the buried past.

The following day we drove to the Hermitage past classical buildings of greenish-white, ochre, saffron and orange, all beautifully laid out, and there after much searching Galia dug out a bright young woman in charge, Dr Kroll, to whom I gave my letter of introduction. The magic collection of Impressionists put together by Shschukin and Morosov and till now confined to the cellars as 'decadent' by the Soviets were beginning to be dusted and hung up. But most of all I wanted to see the treasures excavated by the recent great Scythian 'dig'. Dr Kroll hesitated. I was horribly afraid I had made an irreparable blunder but it turned out that all she wanted me to do was surrender my bag. This I did, handing it to a large dignified landslide of a woman whom I hardly looked at, so anxious was I to get inside. The big door was unlocked, Aladdin's cave revealed. Wonderfully well arranged against black velvet hangings, a treasury of gold helmets, spears, masks, images, flasks, figures, chains, rings, amulets, shells, knives, plates, daggers, beaten or chased or moulded, all different, most in perfect condition. A feast dug from the earth, though still displayed subterraneously in this cavern above which people dragged themselves through the unlovely and dark lives of the driven herd. I could have spent all day and night there.

When I at last tore myself away something clicked in my mind that had been lying dormant under the shock of seeing that dazzling collection – the woman who had taken my bag whom I had hardly noticed – hadn't she spoken perfect English? Going to pick it up again, I looked at her. Yes, the figure was indeed a landslide but topped by an exquisite small head which betrayed the remains of that famous beauty of the Baltic women such as Thamar Karsavina's. I gave her my ticket and said 'May I ask you how it is you speak such perfect English?' Looking coolly at me she replied: 'My dear, we *all* had English nurses and governesses.' I did so want to talk more, but I realized she had dismissed me. Of course, I reflected, the only class of people with whom they could entrust handbags now would have to be the ci–devant aristos.

After Y had given his concert of Brahms and Bartók we returned to Moscow, this time to a smallish old Victorian hotel, the 'Budapest', near the Bolshoi, full of drab furniture, but at least human. Here we were once again confronted by official dilatoriness. For three days we had tried to get to the Bolshoi Opera, but only a quarter of an hour beforehand had we been told that our tickets were at the box office. I pulled on a dress, rushed to the Conservatoire where Y was rehearsing, captured Hep who was talking on children's crêches, criminals or some such subject and we raced across the road to the theatre to find ourselves ensconced in the front row of that splendid house just as the curtain rose on *Eugene Onegin*. The scenery was very grand and old-fashioned but it was clearly the occasion for the Most Famous Russian Tenor's Genuinely Finally

Final Farewell, and, being about twice too old for the rôle, he had covered his face with fourteen layers of violet powder. From our position in the front row we saw him through a haze of mauve dust which was occasionally dislodged by the highest notes into a cloud that descended upon those nearest to him. He was also very small and stout and wore precarious high heels. His voice, in which there were still some lovely tones, squeezed as it went towards the top, producing a strange buzz like a wasp in a tin. Tatiana was beautiful and I thoroughly enjoyed the whole performance, for greatness lingered there, and a kind of solid simple realism, and the audience was rapt. We ran back in icy rain and argued ourselves to sleep.

It turned out to be no easier to get a permit to watch a ballet class at the Bolshoi school than go to the opera, but Galia eventually managed it for me. I was immediately transported back into the past century: a big old institutional building buzzing inside with scores of bright children of both sexes, all the girls pigtailed, all in uniform and all curtseying or bowing. One cheer for egalitarian society. Bureaucracy at the barre. I was dragged into the administration office and shown huge ballet albums. Saying quietly that I had studied with Karsavina, Egorova and Kschessinskaya, and danced with Massine, Balanchine, Woizikowsky and Lifar (two generations of their greatest stars), a strange silence descended – a compound of fascination and fright, obviously a longing to ask me about them and fear to mention those Tzarist names emanating from the great Maryinsky Ballet Theatre and School. Sad. I had lost some precious minutes and impatiently begged to see a class. Upstairs through endless corridors I was led to a fine, big, light, airy classroom where girls and boys of about fifteen to seventeen were at the *barre* being taught by one of those *danseuses périmées* with spread waists, wrinkled faces and perfect legs and feet. Dull young dancers, alas, showing as yet none of the temperament they should already have developed nor any of the patina that should be endemic in the smallest beginner. To be fair, the main company was in the States on tour, but that still did not excuse such uninspired gyrations in the material supposedly being trained eventually to join them. I left after half an hour and went to Y's rehearsal for that night's concert.

When the evening came we had to bash our way into the Conservatoire hall because there were such crowds around that the police had been called out. Unfortunately they had made no provision for the artists to get through. We sat in our taxi, Y quite unperturbed. The driver apologized for not daring to crash the barricades and the minutes ticked on. I suggested we just get out and try to forge our way in. Maybe, recognizing Yehudi, they would give way? And indeed they did, beaming and calling out his name and Hephzibah's with delight. In the meantime Hep had discovered three of her mother's cousins and it was left to me to get them somehow into the stage box, which entailed my having to crouch on the sharp edge of an ancient gilt chair, feet turned inwards and my knees at waist level. In that acrobatic position it was a feat of devotion to St. Cecilia to enjoy the Beethoven concerto with the Moscow State Orchestra conducted by Svetlanov; but I soon forgot all discomfort, swept along in the electrical current between audience and stage, with Yehudi giving an inspired performance in that welcoming warmth.

Afterwards we had a pleasant supper with Leonid Kogan, one of their greatest violinists, in a block of flats called the 'Musicians' Cooperative'. In this strange emporium lived all the leading pianists, violinists and cellists piled one upon another in horrid proximity like the rolls in layers on bakers' trays. Shunted here and there by 'Goskonzert', (the Soviet Concert Agency) or sometimes ordered to stay and teach in their own town, it was no wonder they leapt at the prospect of touring in the West even though they had to relinquish all their earnings apart from daily pocket money to that same Goskonzert.

Yehudi's burgeoning longing to offer a full musical tuition to the gifted young moved a step further when he was invited to attend the Music Boarding School in Moscow. Aptly enough it was established on exactly the same lines as had been the Tzar's Maryinsky Ballet School, in which the pupils received scholastic and musical tuition under the same roof, a system which Yehudi had long realized was the reason for which the Russians reached the top of nearly all the international competitions. However, the morning we spent there held an undercurrent of anonymity and drill that was disturbing. Dear little monsters aged four or five or six, their pigtails pinned to the crowns of their heads, whipped their way through Chopin and Liszt and all the showier composers with a cool competence that was at once admirable though alarming. Later we heard older boys and girls who had graduated to more serious but still dramatic works showing their paces with a skill and perfection of execution that also left one baffled. Especially perplexing was the weird withholding of all names either of the performer or –

particularly – of the teacher. Any inquiry was automatically ignored. These were gifted and well tooled machines, part of the State's organization and property for home consumption and export. They were not individuals. Hep remained silent, Yehudi obviously more determined than ever to bring to the West his own version of such training.

From Moscow we travelled to Kiev, where only daily doses of the beautiful church, the Sophiski-Sabor, on my morning walks kept me from succumbing to the depression of the hotel with its scummy cataracted windows gummed all round with thick brown paper, the inevitably inedible food and the wasted time, the whole sluggishness like a stopped-up drain that was the behaviour of a society weighted down by bureaucracy and lack of incentive. But a heaven-sent surprise awaited me – whom should I bump into at the lift-doors but Balanchine himself! His ballet company, the New York City Center, was performing here on this, his first return to Russia. 'Dianchik!' and we fall into each other's arms. 'Tonight you come to ballet.' I did and it was ravishing: all those lovely long-limbed American girls and boys, the scenery and choreography and the bewitched audience clad in their sad sack and mud-coloured clothes carried away in an animated fairy tale that moved the heart.

Next day Yehudi and I were taking a walk in the bleak little park near the Sophiski-Sabor. It was empty of everything at that season, dusty dead flower-beds, ragged naked trees, ancient benches. Suddenly a man approached us, and, looking furtively around, said to Y in Russian:

'Excuse me but is that lady with you from the Balanchine Ballet? It has been so wondeful to see all that beauty and line and movement and she looks like a dancer.'

I smiled, delighted for once to be the recipient of a little praise and Y answered:

'She *was* with Balanchine and danced with him, but now she's my wife!'

We smiled at each other and he watched us wistfully till we disappeared down the hill.

The following evening Y insisted upon my escaping the sonatas of César Franck, Bartók and Beethoven and going again to Balanchine's Ballet, escorted by John Martin, the *New York Times* critic. Yes, I could understand the exaltation of the man who had stopped us in the park. The City Ballet was indeed another world of light and line and beauty

– freedom of movement and joy expressed by free young dancers. And yet it was as Russian as was Balanchine himself (Georgian in actual fact). This interpretation of the Russian ballet was in direct descendance from the Maryinsky via Diaghilev. What I had seen in Leningrad's *Don Quixote*, was but the costive remains of the nineteenth century.

At supper afterwards with Balanchine I was saying this to John Martin, who asked me what I felt was the basic reason for the difference. 'The Revolution,' I said, 'in part, but before that Diaghilev and his friends of the avant-garde with their magazine *Novy Mir* had moved far away from the dumpy ballerinas pirouetting like piano-stools. Diaghilev had quarrelled fiercely with Prince Volkonsky, the *intendant*, and finally left with some of the best of the dancers for Paris. Paris was at the height of her creative activity and Diaghilev was a catalyst of genius. What you saw tonight was Balanchine (his last choreographer) carrying this marvellous Russian nucleus even further away from what my generation of Russians called the "Oldy-Poldy-you-know-isn't-it?".' Balanchine smiled and added that when he had arrived in Moscow a few weeks before for the first time since he had left to join Diaghiliev as a very young man he was set upon at the airport by crowds shouting 'George Balanchine, welcome to the home of the classical ballet!' To which he had replied sardonically:

'The home of the *classical* ballet? For God's sake, yours is the home of the *romantic* ballet, if you will, it was Serge Diaghilev who saved the classical ballet by exporting it to Europe!' Wicked George also told us that he had gone to a performance of the Bolshoi Ballet in Moscow. Hardly had he taken his seat before he was surrounded by people asking, 'George Balanchine, what do you think of our great Opera House?'

'*Your* great Opera House?', he had replied snappily. '*Yours?* This was built by the Tzars for people who were more worthy of it than you and were tidy and clean.'

It was the dogged sadness of modern Russia that was so dispiriting, that aspect of the half-buried that called forth in one a curious sympathy together with a longing for more contact than was permitted a foreigner. The concerts and the ballet alone illuminated the atmosphere for a moment like the flame of a lighted match, then all was grey again.

The time came to leave Kiev for Minsk. At the airport we sat in the VIP lounge from 6 to 11 p.m. with the local Philharmonie Manager, singing out of tune snatches of operetta and leafing through the usual joyful, positive, boring propaganda magazines. Outside the sleet rattled down. In the end we had to return to the hotel where we managed to bribe them to let us have our room back. Five lost, unexplained, dank hours.

With the weather still bad the next day, I suggested over our breakfast of tepid coffee and tapestry toast that we travel by train. Answer came there none. I returned abashed to my redeemer Agatha Christie. The morning dragged on like beagling in the mud. Nothing happened except the lights going out. Y practised. I wrote. At noon we were actually put in a bus to the station. Tremendous Mussolini-like grandeur: marble floors, chandeliers and Lenin in bronze blessing all travellers after the manner of St Joseph. I stuck out my tongue at him in impotent rage. Even the irrepressible Hep was low. She had left the Beethoven sonatas music in the Hall the day before and walked all the way back to retrieve them. They were gone. We sat mournfully beneath the joyless chandeliers answering devouring questions about the English royal family no less and about three hours later the train arrived. We had two second-class wooden bunk carriages, four bunks in all. But at least bedding could be got with a little greasing of the paw and we were, oh bliss, getting out of Kiev. Priorities, I decided, were all.

We walked down the corridors stuffed with men, women and children like so much fodder, all of them eating some kind of bits of food. A strong smell of onions and feet hung in the air. Why had they taken their socks off as well as their shoes in this cold? They looked at us with perfectly blank eyes, as inscrutable as the food. Finding some kind of eating-place full of soldiers (privilege) we ate what we could keep down and hastened back. Ah! this was the moment, the place, the exact time for that bottle of champagne we had been given in Leningrad. I unearthed it and we all four had warm swigs from the bottle and, slightly sozzled, rolled ourselves in our blankets, shoes off, socks on and rattled and rolled through the long wet black night.

Y woke as the train stopped in the evening, looked out and discovered it was Gomel, his father's birthplace in Belorussia! He scrawled a cable to him. Galia found a nice girl who was getting off, Y gave her some money and begged her to send it. At 5 a.m. we arrived at Minsk, only three hours late. Two poor souls from the Philharmonie, waiting all that time, bundled us and our luggage into a car and we drove in the dark to a huge ugly cement carton of a hotel where we had quite a decent room, peeled off our clothes, washed and fell into bed at 6 a.m. Aba did get his cable and was delighted.

Minsk was brighter in character, the hotel cheaply modern. With Hep and Galia I made a sortie to try out the local shops, finding some ravishing Russian shirts but only in embroidered pieces and at racket prices. Bought two just the same. Broad avenues like hardened arteries led out of the centre to the remains of the old city, where we saw beautiful baroque and eighteenth-century churches, pink, ochre, saffron and once white buildings, their plaster shredding like dandruff, almost as though they had been left to die as corpses on an abandoned battle-field.

The food was distinctly better, the service cut down to an hour's wait. Obviously the further away from Moscow the easier it was for everyone to breathe and become livelier. We put Hep on the train back to Moscow with a picnic-box in a four-berth sleeper. Apprehensively we left her in the care of one soldier and two naval officers who occupied the other bunks and waved goodbye. Meanwhile Y exhausted himself with concerts and endless conversations with reporters.

Moscow again: back at the Budapest Hep and I decided we had to do something or even she might succumb. It was Sunday. There was a single church open in the suburbs to which Hep and I took a taxi. The people there were spilling out all over the road, some pushing, others squeezing through into the gap they had made. Across the forecourt I could hear faintly that hypnotic Russian church-singing. 'Come, Hep,' I said, 'we *must* get in.'

It took us an hour of slow battering-ram technique to shove our way through the huge open doors beyond which lay an exotic spectacle: people crammed right up to the beautiful gilded iconostasis, against which stood a splendid priest with flowing grey beard in golden crown and robes; lighted lamps hung on golden chains, the fog and smell of incense enveloped all, and beneath, ecstatic and moving and swaying in a sluggish current, was the dark shabbiness of the Believers, lifted for a few minutes above the drab struggle of their lives into the Universal. All ages, young and old, in that golden cavern were bewitched by the chanting, bemused by that most sensuous of smells, jammed together as though they had melted into one vast mass of intangible feeling. Russia, that great country which no régime can quite dominate, no régime can quite extinguish. It took us all of an hour to push our way out again. I had wept, even Hep the unbeliever had been extraordinarily moved. We drove back in silence.

After the usual round of routine engagements we took off on our travels again, this time to Lvov, which was memorable chiefly for providing an example of the spectacular confusion created by Soviet officialdom in planning the movement of foreigners round their country. At Lvov we had been met at the station by six rather imposing men who turned up later at our hotel while Y was out rehearsing, and informed me that he was expected to play in Odessa the following day. When I passed this news on to Galia she turned green and fled, only to come back a little later looking more relaxed because she had found a plane that would indeed get us to Odessa in plenty of time the next morning.

But it is never that easy in Sovietland, the cradle of Catch 22. After half-an-hour's trial and error which comprised the anguish of telephoning another town, Galia got through to Goskonzert in Moscow and told them the plane on which they had blithely booked us had not been on the schedule for at least two months and that it was impossible therefore to play in Odessa and Kichinev (planned for the day after). Goskonzert's reaction was typical. Primo: we must cancel Odessa and get to Kichinev. Secondo: we could after all fly to Odessa the next day by taking a plane from Lvov to Kiev and thence on to Odessa. Inspiring prospect. Galia pointed out desperately that planes were always late and if we missed only one connection to Kiev we would not make Odessa at all. Terzo: Goskonzert rang again and claimed that there *was* a plane to Odessa after all but it would take six hours. I decided we had had ENOUGH. It was quite impossible, I declared, to sit frozen (no heating ever) in an ancient dragonfly without food (always so within Russia) and arrive starved like embalmed corpses and still expect Y to play. Alas! there was only one thing to do: renounce our proposed trip to the Crimea to visit Mammina's birthplace, and play both in Odessa and Kichinev each a day later. Since everybody was pushed around in this country, the concerts too could be shuffled. But what about Hephzibah still in Moscow? All right; she would be dumped like freight on the midnight train and arrive in Lvov the next day. Meanwhile Yehudi had to play while this chaotic changing of schedules continued. Fortunately the small opera house in Lvov (once the Polish Lemberg) was enchanting, the audience extraordinarily soigné if a trifle vocal.

In the end it was the train we took from Lvov, only to find on leaving that there would be no food on the way. The trip to Odessa would last fifteen hours (Russian twenty). Galia jumped out at the first stop and got two rolls and some frankfurters. For once Y felt poorly, having eaten something which disagreed with even *his* ostrich innards so I made up his bed into which he immediately collapsed. A few hours later the train stopped again and a perfect avalanche of people poured off it. The peasants, their legs still bound in linen as in past centuries, reminded me of 'Sacre du Printemps'. Heads wrapped in dirty cloths, their clothing layer upon layer of wrapping, they looked like parcels left in 'Lost and Found'. Galia and I battled our way to the wayside food-stand and found apples and two buns. Reboarded the train just in time. Y fell asleep. He had not eaten for ages. I settled down and nibbled and read until Big Father turned off the lights at 11.30. Sleeping, I half-dreamed of those huddles of muddied cottages, some of them wound in thatch right up to the roof top, and the hordes of human bundles fighting to get on to the train. If, I wondered, Stolypin had succeeded in forming his constitutional government and that sealed train carrying Lenin to the Finland Station had never reached its destination, wouldn't those sad creatures from medieval Russia have closed the gap on the twentieth century?

Trains in Russia are run for the definite purpose of some unknown sadist who spends his entire day working out schedules in total disharmony with any sane person's life, be he office-worker, educationalist or bureaucrat. For no imaginable reason we had left Lvov at a time calculated to decant us at Odessa at the unlovely hour of 5.15 a.m. ... Why? It was still dark and cold and we fell out, stiff, bruised and hungry to be met by a nasty fat specimen in a dressing gown of an overcoat. In statutory fashion his cap was pulled down so that his pointed ears stuck out at each side while his large fleshy hook-nose jutted just beneath its peak like a knocker under the eaves of a neo-Tudor front door. I took an instant dislike to him which was fully reciprocated. He absolutely refused to lift so much as one of our ten cases. Obviously in the infinite strata of a classless society he could not lose whatever precarious level he had clawed his way to by carrying suitcases; not even in the pre-dawn of an empty station. How I longed for a common language with which to belabour him. In the event, Galia, Hep, Y and I had no option but to drag the luggage ourselves to the usual hearse, into which we all piled to be taken to the hotel.

We entered the dark hall lit by one small naked bulb and reeking of a very strong and disagreeable smell. Silence. No. Wrong. A rhythmic snore. Following my nose in the gloom, I found myself confronted by a pair of enormous socks from which the odour emanated. Further research revealed a body asleep on a camp-bed directly facing the front entrance. 'Nasty', the man who had met us at the station, shook the recumbent figure roughly and, with a roof-raising snore, he awoke.

Looking bleary, he shuffled in his revolting socks over to the counter, glanced disparagingly at us, handed out a few keys and was obviously preparing to regain his bed of roses without a thought of helping with the luggage. At the moment I spotted what appeared to be a lift. I advanced. Certainly there was a lift door and a lift shaft, but long ago someone must have pinched the lift itself. In front of me was a beautiful view straight up eight storeys of empty rust. It could, I reflected, have made a good modern painting done in perspective entitled 'Whither?'. Finally I lost my temper and insisted that if neither Hep nor Galia would use their Russian to command Nasty and Socks to help with the luggage, I would knock the two men's heads together. This seemed to galvanize Galia, who got the pair into action and together, all six of us, we staggered up the worn stairs, a bag in each hand.

Now there was, as I had already discovered in Poland, one great drawback in being considered a 'Special Person' behind the Iron Curtain: one was inevitably given the Royal Suite. This, as I said before, meant the only room which had not been modernized. The one small advantage of the Royal Suite was that it was always on the first floor. We unlocked the faded double-doors and beheld the familiar scene. There in the alcove with its huge lumpy bed like a badly ploughed field, we left Yehudi fast asleep.

I was beginning to find Y's flexible optimism rather oppressive. His and Hep's sublime indifference to ugliness of surroundings and discomfort made me ashamed of myself. But then he had, despite his origins, not known or loved 'Russia and all things Russian' as I had. It did not arouse in him the bitter disappointment it did in me. There were no Russian ghosts, vivid and marvellous, amoral and forgiveable, gifted and ghastly and yet so full of vitality and warmth, Byzantine colour and wonder – sheer wonder – in his past. Darling Y, it was sufficient for him to be brought the filthy Caucasian 'Kefir', the fermented mare's milk talked of since childhood by his mother which had long before sunk into his mind as a symbol of Slavic nutrition. When he drank this foul-smelling stuff he felt the same kind of ecstasy stealing over him as would a marooned French sailor experiencing his first taste of champagne after a shipwreck.

At our hotel we again found ourselves ensnarled in the clutches of far-flung bureaucracy. Galia had been trying to get through to Goskonzert in Moscow for a solid hour when Y told her to stop and wrote a curt cable to them saying he could not play in Kichinev. Period. Ah! But he had not calculated that there were no such punctuations in Russia. Soon after some vague voice came over the telephone lines from Kichinev saying it had had no confirmation of any concert, but would nonetheless either send us by private plane or in an excellent car on excellent (?) new roads for the journey was only 165 kilometres. My heart sank. We would have to go to Kichinev after all. Scarcely had we digested this news than we found Galia in floods of tears because she had been telephoned from Yalta (capital of the Crimea) to confirm that we were, as expected, coming *there* to give a concert the next day. Oh God, oh Goskonzert. No, we said, no Yalta, nor any other Crimean town, sadly.

Meanwhile Y and Hep went off to the concert hall in Odessa to warm up before playing, letting me off to wash my gritty hair. On their return from the concert they reported that the audience had been most unusual. Judging by the hordes who came round afterwards, neither to condemn nor to praise but to enquire about fingerings and bowings, they must all have been violinists. Y reminded me that the great teacher, Leopold Auer, had had his pupils here, a legion of them: Heifetz, Milstein, et al. Frightening it must have been - like facing a jury full of judges.

So it was definitely on to Kichinev by car on that highly recommended new road, bumping and lurching through mud clotted to everything like cheap melted chocolate. The rain poured steadily down, streaming off the car mile after mile, the open countryside occasionally interrupted by little huddled groups of stone 'isbahs' hardly constituting villages in their serried ranks; and everywhere the gluey mud, layers upon layers of it. Suddenly I saw the signboard 'Moldavian Republic', just beyond which appeared beautifully carved wooden houses with chalet roofs, Byzantine folk art on doors and gables, and around the windows, pride and style revealed in the bright blue stencillings of the fronts.

'Galia!', I said 'Russiya at last.'

'No Diana, it is the Soviet Republic.'

'Well they've not managed to drag it down, have they? Isn't it beautiful?'

Poor Galia, torn between pride in Russian art and loyalty to the régime.

As with the little houses, so with the concert hall. Romania, as truth to tell it once had been, showed in the dusty gold velvet curtains and all the ladies were dressed in their best silk or satin and there was that sense of occasion that had been missing everywhere else. Y, changing the programme instinctively to the Enesco sonata, was mobbed. Unfortunately, our supper was rendered hideous by a very bad twenty-two piece band which made up in noise what they lacked in skill. But all of a sudden a gypsy fiddler appeared from nowhere and played Romanian gypsy music with an astonishing beauty. The Romanian gypsy's melody and harmony are subtly different from the Hungarian – sadder and deeper, with a savour of the oriental. It was superb and carried Yehudi and Hephzibah back to their childhood in Sinaia and their beloved Enesco.

We were up next morning at 6 a.m. in the freezing dawn, our fingers so stiff with cold that it was difficult to button anything up. This was to be our last flight back to Moscow. Breakfastless, we drove to the airport, which boasted a ridiculous Greek (Doric) portico. That at least was funny. Inside were bundles of human beings wrapped in every imaginable type of cloth, fur hat jammed down to the jawbones, slumped in dejection, judging from what could be seen of their faces. After an hour we were led across miles of wet tarmac to an antediluvian old bird squatting in a huge puddle. An ancient turbo-prop plane fit for a museum. We were shovelled in and sat in the front row, huddled and hungry. The poor old bird took off with a rattle and a shake and as we climbed the cold grew worse and worse.

Back at the Budapest we received a call from outer space – Margot Fonteyn asking whether Jeremy would present the bouquet next Thursday to the Queen Mother at the Gala where she was to dance the adagio from Swan Lake to Y's accompaniment. 'Yes', we said.

After a shopping trip with Galia and tea with the British Ambassador in that gloriously hideous sugar baron's house that is the British Embassy, looking across the river to a Kremlin covered with clean new snow, I was reconciled to the nuisance and the muddles and promised myself to try and remember the real Russia underlying the straitjacket.

Our last day arrived. While Y did his usual round of telephone calls, I packed leaving an assortment of clothes, food, scents and shampoos for dear good frustrated Galia. She embraced me with delight. I felt guilty. Such an easy gesture but I could not give her my freedom. I dragged Y from the telephone for a last glimpse of that stupendous bubble of a church, the Vassily, built for Ivan the Terrible, who was so deeply satisfied with its coloured domes and Byzantine beauty that he blinded the architect to prevent his repeating his masterpiece.

In the afternoon there was one final muddle to seal the lot. Y was practising at the hotel when Galia suddenly arrived, announcing that he was expected at 4 p.m., not 5, at the Conservatoire. Together they rushed off, getting there just in time for Y to play Bach solo sonatas and partitas to the students. By the time I joined him he was fascinating them with the Bartók solo sonata. Next we proceeded to the 'House of Friendship' (one of millionaire Morosoff's old houses) where grateful and kindly speeches in praise of Y and Hep rained down upon their embarrassed heads.

And so at last we left. Our plane, all but empty, rose over the snow-covered trees. It was freezing but the stewardess, looking a cross between a nasty nanny and a piece of drag, declined to give us any coffee. We must wait three hours, she said, and then we would have caviar. I didn't want caviar either then or later. *I wanted my breakfast.* Y and Hep came to the rescue. Realizing that I had shared little of the worship, fulfilment or self-expression with which they had been warmed on our trip but mostly cold and alienation, they battered that bit of drag into digging out a bottle of white wine and some near-hot coffee.

As a perfect last act to the drama, London airport was closed down with pea-soup fog. We waited two hours in Amsterdam, were ladled into a charter plane and decanted at Southend, where we got hold of a crew car to stow our luggage, proceeding to crawl at 10 m.p.h. through total invisibility and cold. It seemed as though Russia were shadowing us like a KGB agent. After six indescribable hours of groping and peering, we were finally home.

Was that, I wondered, a punishment for my ungenerous reaction to Russia? The penalty, perhaps, for allowing myself to criticize the transformation of a life-long dream that had represented all beauty and colour and light for me since my childhood into the stark reality I had witnessed in the last three weeks?

# ❧15❧

# Festivals and Festivities

Of all Yehudi's many musical activities I suppose it was the festivals that I enjoyed the most. They were full of friendship, of wonderful music-making, of variety and of sheer hard work for a cause that was really worth the gigantic effort and, therefore, evoked from all and sundry the best in spirit, heart and behaviour. I would return from the weeks we spent at them cleansed as by nothing else in the long year's spate of travel, towns and tours of the claustrophobia which ineluctably closed in on a life spent mainly trapped inside buildings and every variety of transport. Of course festivals were not without their own complications. The already overcrowded drawing-room at No. 2 was often invaded by additional groups of musicians practising for the coming events. And for all the beauty of its setting in the Bernese Oberland, the Gstaad Festival did rob us of our summer holidays once it got into its stride, expanding all through August. But these were really small hardships compared with the pleasures provided by such occasions.

In the late 1950s and early 1960s it was the Bath Festival more than any other which put back into my life much that for me had been missing. Y had first appeared there in 1955 under the direction of Sir Thomas Beecham. For his last concert that year he played the Viotti Concerto No. 22 with the Royal Philharmonic Orchestra. It went beautifully because Y and Beecham suited each other. It was also broadcast by the BBC and we learned afterwards that as Sir Thomas and Y had swooned a little too much over the slow movement, the BBC, shocked at their running overtime, had seen fit to lop off the last four minutes of the Concerto. In no time at all their telephones were jammed with at least 140 outraged complaints. That was 1955, remember; it would never happen now, probably never did happen again after that outrage.

Four years later Ian Hunter suggested that Yehudi become the Artistic

Director of the Festival and one of the first things Y did was to form an orchestra, which was in time to be called the Menuhin Festival Orchestra. Its concert-master was Robert Masters and under his auspices Y made his first serious attempt at conducting. To begin with he was terrified because there never has been anyone less fond of bossing. I had a hard time persuading him that he was not 'directing' or 'dictating' but simply 'gathering' a group that by its own nature needed a leader.

Y's new role in the Festival took up much of our time and there were frequent meetings at No. 2 to discuss its composition as well as visits to Bath to reconnoitre various sites. When the day itself came we caught the train down to be met by a battery of television cameras. The sight of Bath's elegant silver-grey streets lifted my spirits somewhat as we drove up Lansdown Hill to the hotel. They sank a little when I found we were in the same suite where four years earlier I had been carrying the baby that was to die two months later in faraway San Francisco. No time for irreversible sorrows, however. Y shaved, bathed, dressed and went at once to a press conference attended by most of the London papers and all the local ones. Suddenly I could not bear to be alone with my ghosts any more, and knowing that Y would be busy for another hour at least with television, I walked down the long Bath hill to where I recollected there was a health shop and there stocked us up with all such weeds and groats, seeds and oats as would keep the mote out of Y's eye and the beam on his face. Staggering back up to the hotel carrying two pots of Mexican honey full of genuine bee-stings, added to an enormous loaf purporting to contain whole-grain-stone-ground-husk-filled-grit-milled-gravel-ravelled-drought-sprouted flour or whatever, turned my journey into a pilgrimage. All that was missing was a hairshirt and dried peas in my sandals to earn me three years off purgatory.

Y was practising as I puffed and huffed into the room and dumped the lot on the floor at his feet. I went over and looked out on the beautiful terraces lined with their green trees, the crescents with their aprons of grass, the whole natural bowl filled with the delicate tracery of Bath stone, now a deeper grey in the twilight. 'How lovely!' cried Y. I turned. He was gazing rapt at the health food.

Soon, however, we were both engrossed in the marvellous diversity of the Festival. There was a witty and interesting Symposium on Music at the Guildhall with Yehudi in the chair and Isaiah Berlin, William

Glock and Nicholas Nabokov all arguing inaudibly as the mikes had failed at one end of the hall. Summoning my courage, I suggested the audience move their chairs forward to the platform so that they could hear what was being said. After a moment or two of that outraged silence which is the average English reaction to any show of individuality, they obeyed, enabling them to enjoy the quiet and pithy comments of Glock, the humorous wisdom of Isaiah, the gloriously Russian improvisations and interruptions of Nabokov and Y's clever and skilled manœuvring of the whole discussion. And there were many other *bonnes bouches:* poetry and harp music provided by Peggy Ashcroft and Ossian Ellis; a recital by Ben Britten and Peter Pears hall-marked with their usual beauty and musicality and style; and another of Indian music on the veena by Ali Akhbar Khan, the star player of that complicated instrument. Part of my enjoyment of Ali Akhbar's performance sprang from the bamboozlement of the audience whose classical European tastes were utterly confused by what they were hearing. Bartók's 'Contrasts' with Yehudi, Hephzibah and Reginald Kell, on the other hand, were greeted so rapturously that they had to repeat the whole work. And there were Handel sonatas in a pretty little Regency church with Y and Raymond Leppard. Y kept leap-frogging from one rehearsal to another, conducting his own new orchestra for the first time in public.

I tried to blend all these performances into a gathering of friends by taking out the various musicians after concerts to that then inimitable restaurant 'The Hole in the Wall', run by Perry Smith. Marvellous food and a perfect setting in the vaults of an old building so that what might be dispiriting to a Spanish guitarist, a Hungarian pianist or a French cellist setting out for rehearsal on a breakfast of coffee like liquid fertilizer and bath-mat toast, could be quickly compensated for by a glorious supper lengthened by much jolly conversation. Yehudi was veritably Herculean and he and I loved every moment of it.

True, there were a few antics: an unsavoury moment when Nadia Boulanger's group of four singers marched down the aisle of the Abbey, refusing to rehearse for that night's concert unless they were paid on the spot (they sang and got their money a month later); and the odd hysterics in the vestry thrown by one or other of the star performers who thought they were not being treated as such. As a rule I had little sympathy for them, pointing out that the progenitor of the Festival did not behave like one, so why should they worry about the insecurity of their eminence and anyhow it was time to take their instrument on stage and leave their nonsense behind. But for every would-be prima donna there were musicians of such quality who needed no such fancy antics while in Sir Edwin Leather, our chairman and MP for North Somerset, we were blessed with a marvellous worker who gathered the whole county into the running of the Festival, organizing entertainment in beautiful houses in the neighbourhood and generally keeping us out of trouble or debt.

Over the years the Festival blossomed with a whole range of diverse ideas. On one occasion Yehudi and Maurice Gendron played the adagio from *Swan Lake* for Margot Fonteyn and Rudolf Nureyev. On another he and John Dankworth shared a jazz and classical evening. And it was at one of the Bath Festivals that Y first played with Ravi Shankar, the greatest Indian musician and sitar player and, since our first visit to India, a dear and cherished friend. If I remember correctly, Y invited them, Ravi and his 'team', two or three days before the performance to give himself the chance to work his way into an entirely novel expression of the violin, while continuing to perform almost every night in several other capacities. 'A man for all seasons', as the press called him. Ravi arrived smiling and happy as ever bringing a wonderfully exotic touch to the Bath railway station. There were three or four or maybe five of them in all: Indians have a gift of multiplying and dissolving at the same time, making it quite impossible to decide how many they really and in actual fact comprise. Chatur Lal was there, of course, together with his incomparable tabla (drums), a lovely female and a totally silent drone-player as well as a hanger-on or two whose place in the scheme of things was obviously of imperative but baffling importance. I swept them up in our local car to the Lansdown Grove Hotel, deposited them in their rooms and told Ravi that Y would be with them within an hour or so when he should have finished rehearsing the six Brandenburg concertos.

When Y duly returned great shouts of joy and embracings emanated from one and all. The furniture in our bedroom was swiftly pushed aside, one of Ravi's mute myrmidons spread a glorious carpet on the floor, another lit the incense tapers in their brass-vases and I withdrew to consider how they were to be fed. As the hotel menu – fruit cup, beef rissoles, boiled potatoes and raspberry blancmange – was unlikely to be to their taste I hied me down the hill to the Hole in the Wall and howled for Perry. He appeared, large and comforting, accepted my dilemma with the delight of a born cuisinier and told me to come back in an hour. When I returned I found two huge baskets smelling of Delhi's best, which I proceeded to haul up the hill. There was no other way. The station taxis were having their siesta and Perry's staff was fully occupied serving lunch. So I set forth full of triumph and joy, my spirits only partially lowered by the amount of boiling-hot curry sauce and other spicy dainties leaking steadily through their coverings on to my favourite summer dress. For once the sun shone, the temperature had risen to the high seventies and I must have presented a very odd and strange-smelling spectacle to the passers-by. At last my bowed and aching head and burning eyes espied the begonias rimmed with lobelias which announced the municipally planted bed of the hotel drive. The lift man had gone to his lunch so I had to heave the baskets upstairs myself. I had managed the last few hundred yards up the hill simply because I was wafted thousands of miles away on the magic carpet of Ravi's incense, billowing down amongst the prim and proper and very English buildings. By the time I reached the sitting-room it was over-powering, and, half-fainting and slightly dotty by then, I was beginning to wonder whether the use of incense as a verb, i.e. 'their behaviour *incensed* me', was exactly the reaction we were going to receive from those retired service officers and their spouses who composed the main clientele of the hotel.

Banging the door of our room with my knee (the noise of sitar, violin, tabla, drone and voices was overpowering), I succeeded in drawing attention to my arrival. The picture I presented must have held just the right amount of serio-comic. Ravi, Y and Chatur Lal dropped their instruments and rushed towards me roaring with delighted laughter and deploring the sacrifice of both my dress and my strength. They were overcome with joy at Perry's Indian meal which we all ate sitting on the floor to accompaniments of Ravi's better shady stories and jokes. The Indians have a marvellous gift for spontaneous humour which bubbles up from the cauldron that is their warmth of nature – innocent, mischievous and rarely malicious.

When I had cleared up the remains (hardly anything because they had mopped their plates dry with lumps of chapatti), Y and I left the musicians rolled up on the floor in varying positions like parcels at a poste restante and went off for a short nap in our neighbouring bedroom.

The ensuing concert two mornings and many rehearsals later was a matinée and will long remain as one of the oddest in my long and kaleidoscopic life with Yehudi. To begin with he had arranged a very odd programme: in the first half he was to play a Bach solo partita, after the interval would come India in the form of a solo performance by Ravi and Company and as grand Finale the piece Ravi had arranged to include Yehudi (the violin having been adopted by the Indians already some 150 years earlier there was no question of a 'stunt' in this work). After the morning rehearsal in the Guildhall, Y ate his picnic and I left him fast asleep on the boardroom table. My task lay, as usual, in seeing to Y's attire so at the hotel, I collected with care the odd assortment of clothes in which he would shortly appear: afternoon concert suit consisting of striped trousers, double-breasted jacket, cream silk shirt, black and white tie, black silk socks and black shoes for J.S. Bach. Then to follow the geographical progression of the music a pair of navy blue linen trousers and a fine embroidered white Indian shirt given him by Ravi. Desperately counting, it seemed to me that there was nothing missing. The bones were in his shirt-collar, the links in his sleeves and there was an extra undershirt or two were he to get hot.

I returned to the Guildhall just in time to wake him from his accustomed sleep and get him into the Bach outfit. I don't think I have ever seen Y so green-faced. 'Forget about the Raga, darling, and enjoy the Partita,' I said as cheerfully as I could. Y, smiling bleakly, went out on to the stage and threw himself into the partita with a passion I suspected was summoned up to blow away the terrors ahead. Sitting as I always do out front, I was enjoying myself immensely when suddenly towards the end of the great Chaconne, my heart gave an awful leap; his feet! Oh dear Lord, I'd forgotten to think of them. He couldn't shuffle on in silk socks alone; I should have brought his black felt bedroom-slippers, but I had not. I felt sick. Huge applause for the Partita did little to comfort me and I hastened round to the dressing-room, which was by now totally transformed. Ravi was in full fig sitting cross-legged on the boardroon table, long-retired councillors and mayors gazing disapprovingly upon him from the walls; Chatur Lal tuned his drums with a small mallet in one corner, the mute and beautiful drone-lady in a ravishing sari plucked vaguely at her instrument. Meanwhile the posse of hangers-on were lighting incense burners or gently nodding their heads from side to side in that particular Indian manner which can mean confirmation, appreciation, salutation, consideration or several other significances all of a companionable nature.

I summoned up my courage and admitted to Y that I had totally forgotten his feet.

'Doesn't matter,' said Ravi, 'he can go on barefoot.'

'Won't that look a bit odd protruding from blue linen trousers? After all, *you've* got jodhpurs on.'

'Never mind – all will be splendid!', said Ravi. Y was pulling the shirt over his head. I looked at his face. It was verdigris. With nerved like knotted ropes I went back to my seat.

Out they trooped: Ravi, handsome, walnut-coloured face, glistening black hair, a Moghul print come alive, carrying his beautiful red-brown sitar; Chatur Lal, like a mischievous monkey, grinning white teeth, and those huge rolling eyes, together with the lovely sari lady and Y, green of face with his mop of corn-coloured hair looking extremely alien like a newborn chicken emerging from the shell of his white shirt. The shouts of delight and waves of anticipation rippling from the audience did not help poor Y at all – it merely rocked him as he palely returned Ravi's encouraging warm smile. They launched – Ravi and Chatur Lal that is – into the Raga while Y, waiting patiently cross-legged on the carpet for his entry, looked like the deaf-mute at a funeral rite. It was a scene such as Y alone could have dreamed up: the Guildhall mahogany, gilt, glass chandeliers, all the coldly graceful panoply of the eighteenth-century bureaucracy disturbed by an ugly platform covered in green cloth and redeemed by Ravi's beautiful but barely visible carpet; the perfumed vapour rising quietly like scented grey plumes from the daïs, the peacock colour of the drone-player with her lovely smooth bent head and long bejewelled fingers, the tabla-player awaiting his turn quite silent yet communicating with Ravi on some inaudible musical beam, giving that head-shake whenever Ravi performed more impossible feats of climbing up and down the myriad strings with the joyful skill that belongs only to the complete master ... and Yehudi, his pale skin looking like an ivory mask, his fair hair lending to the whole scene a weird touch of the mythopoeic.

At last the dread moment came. Chatur Lal had had his turn with Ravi, miraculously beating out complicated rhythms with twenty fingers and the heel of the palm of his hand. Ravi nodded to the ghost on his left. At first Yehudi modestly played his melody and then, gathering spirit and speed from Ravi, let himself go till all three – Ravi, Chatur and Yehudi – were tearing through a conversational trio that carried the audience away until at the end they rose and called for more. Now with colour in his cheeks and a huge sigh of all too audible relief, Yehudi rose with the others, bowed and trouped off the daïs. Time and again the audience recalled them. Yehudi and Ravi embraced hoping that this affectionate gesture would serve as a final farewell. No such hope. The yelling swelled. On they trouped again, Yehudi holding up his hand for silence said: 'I warn you I mayn't be able to do it a second time.' Roars of delight. Down they squatted, cross-legged (I don't mean the dowagers and attendant public) and launched merrily into the piece. I was twisting my hanky into a dirty rag, but Y got through it even better the second time and I returned to breathing rhythmically again.

It was just such mad visionary dotty risks as this that compensated for all those sonatas and concertos from London to East Overshoe, Paris to Vinegar Bend and made life with Menuhin, violinist, so worthwhile.

That night, awake as usual, I thought over the day's content and sought to analyse Yehudi's musical temperament. It somehow seemed as though music entered his bloodstream permeating head, heart and fingers and that there were no gap in that extraordinary union. I felt I was fully justified in my surmisal when immediately after the Festival we travelled by train to Vienna where Y was to give a series of three concerts within three days. One of the works to be performed was Bartók's newly found First Concerto for Violin which, as I have related elsewhere, had been given to Y by the Bartók Trust to play for a year before it entered the public domain. This was to be its première and I had been worrying myself sick because at no time had I heard Y practising it, although on the train I had heard him spend three hours on what was recognizably some Bartók work in the next-door compartment.

When we arrived in Vienna I asked Y if it had indeed been the First Concerto I had heard through the panelling. He nodded and put the music aside to be free to concentrate on the other two preceding concerts. The first night he and Marcel Gazelle gave a recital. The night after he played Bartók's Second Concerto. On the morning of the third day there was at last a rehearsal of the 'new' concerto. And then that night Y went out and played the work *by heart*. And, of course, brought the house down.

No alien thoughts ever seem to intervene to deflect Y's inner harmony. He does not care whether the 'house' is full or empty and can only be put off his stroke if he has not succeeded in drawing into this harmony the orchestra and the conductor, so that they are all equally engaged in what they are saying. His modesty is total. Too much so perhaps, to the extent that at the beginning of our life together it was difficult to convince him that he had a perfect right to ask for a change in tempo if a particularly significant phrase occurred which he could only play as he held it in his heart and heard it in his mind; that in fact it was his duty to protect his own performance from the contortions and distortions of sundry conductors whose self-expression was to them the *sine qua non* of the piece. Fortunately there were few such conductors of any importance and a great many who were either of the same mind as Y or who sensed his integrity and devotion to the work in hand and were all too willing to comply with his wishes: for there are magnificent conductors who are very poor accompanists. It would almost appear that they cannot bear a solo voice that is in some measure not quite as controllable as the body of an orchestra. Or maybe they simply lack the gift of sharing. Y can generally evoke from this type of conductor a little elasticity but not always.

There was the classic time when he was appearing in one of the major German cities, where he had been landed with a totally rigid and un-gifted conductor (long since sunk into deserved oblivion). He had to play both the Mendelssohn and the Tchaikovsky concertos. At rehearsal after the first few bars he realized sadly that this man was not 'a giant of the future', rather 'a midget of the near past'. Y struggled through the rehearsal, trying his utmost to loosen the unmusical fellow from his rigid beat, but to no avail. So when it came to the evening performance his usual optimism gave way to a feeling of gloom, even though he tried to believe that there might lurk in the conductor some tiny spark of musicality that, at the rehearsal, he had somehow failed to ignite.

When the moment for the Mendelssohn concerto arrived, it did not take Y more than the first page or two to realize that he had made no impression whatsoever upon this frozen effigy who was beating away according to the rules of some misguided textbook written in the pre-vious century by a provincial band-master. Summoning all his musician's code with a truly Kiplingesque effort, Y proceeded to do or die and, feeling miserable at the betrayal of that exquisite work, did the best he could with the first movement. The slow movement being elusively lovely, Y and the orchestra were freer to make it sing as it should.

Encouraged, they launched with lighter heart into the finale. It took about eight bars for Y not only to lose all faith but, a rare event, to lose his temper as well. From that moment on he chose to whip through it as he wanted, hoping that a determined attitude might evoke a spark of co-operation in the conductor's stony breast, and they could thus at least offer the public a relatively pleasing version of the concerto. But it was not to be. The human metronome on the podium beside him hacked away in his indomitable style, part of the orchestra following Yehudi, the rest (dazed) the conductor. Yehudi finished with a neat flourish together with the first violins and stood quietly with his violin lowered in front of him and his lips set while the rest of the orchestra tumbled on to a disorderly halt. The final touch of black comedy was added by the audience, some of whom applauded Yehudi as he defiantly finished while the rest followed in disciplined Teuton order only when the conductor laid down his baton.

After a few calls, avoiding Metronome's eyes, Y went back to his dressing-room sunk in despair at the nightmare prospect of the Tchaikovsky to come. In the lonely silence of the interval he carefully thought over the situation. There was absolutely no point in doing battle over the coming work which anyway was so different in style and scoring from the Mendelssohn that it would be relatively easy to bring off at least an heroic interpretation which might obscure the lack of finesse. So he behaved like a perfect little gentleman and was mildly comforted by the obvious fact that Herr Metronome possessed a sense of guilt and this time did, within his poor competence, make valiant efforts to cooperate. They stayed together politely through all three movements of the Tchaikovsky, accepted the audience's vociferous applause with relief and never crossed paths or swords again.

So much for Y's musical temperament. Apart from Bath there were two other festivals which for me provided a beacon of light each year they came round. One was the Gstaad Festival, which owed its existence to Yehudi, the other was Aldeburgh whose high reputation derived exclusively from its progenitors Benjamin Britten and Peter Pears. Y had been invited to play at Aldeburgh for several years running and when the idea of a festival at Gstaad was first mooted, it was Ben and Peter who suggested that they would be happy to give the first concerts as a token of gratitude for Y's contributions at Aldeburgh.

The original suggestion of a Gstaad Festival had in fact come from the Kurdirektor of the town who had approached Y with a courteously determined mien and bewailed the fact that Gstaad enjoyed but a short winter season and that by June and July most of the big hotels closed for lack of clientèle. Wouldn't Herr Menuhin, known for his generosity, alter this financial disaster by giving perhaps just two concerts, say in August, and thus create some summer season? Unable as usual to resist a fresh challenge, Y agreed and so on 4 August 1956 the First Gstaad Festival was inaugurated with a modest but beautiful pair of concerts. We had been joined by Maurice Gendron, the French cellist, at Ben's suggestion and he fitted in perfectly with the musical atmosphere, being at once highly professional and yet not remotely 'commercial'.

The simple little white stone, wood-shingle-spired church of the neighbouring village of Saanen was to be our 'concert hall'. Built in 1603 with charming primitive faded frescoes, it contained an immovable stone font which stood in the way of all grand pianos and made the disposition of the chamber orchestras a very knotty problem. So we dumped flowers in it and pretended it was irreplaceable rather than immovable. I remember they played Telemann and Bach, and Yehudi and Ben the Schubert Fantaisie, Peter two groups of songs and Maurice a Bach solo sonata. The church was crammed and all was heavenly sound and simple peace. The second concert was equally successful with Mozart trios, Peter singing Ben's arrangement of five Donne sonnets, Y playing Bach's D minor Partita with the magnificent Chaconne ringing through the silent church, and some captivating works Ben had found by Bach for voice, harpsichord, cello and violin. Coming out on to the greensward afterwards with a big moon hanging like a lantern above the mountains, the air sharp and cool, was idyllic, and we all went back to eat and talk late into the night.

Soon the Festival was firmly established and each year brought a variety of musical visitors. One memorable evening an hour before the concert Y's tails were nowhere to be found. A wild search all over the small chalet produced nothing. I asked Schwester Marie as I knew she had taken the tails from me after the last concert. Smugly she reported they would be where she always hung them, on the clothes hook of the back balcony. I raced up to look. Again nothing. Running down I told her the bad news crossly. All sign of smugness was wiped off her face. With sinking heart I reminded her that since Y last played it had stormed and poured as it only can during a Swiss summer. She rushed out. There lying in a neighbouring field hundreds of yards away, huddled in a sodden mass was the missing garment looking like something rejected by an alcoholic and totally unwearable. I telephoned all and sundry for a replacement. That night Y appeared in a coat whose tails swept the floor, making him seem like a bewildered penguin.

But perhaps it was Aldeburgh more than either of the other festivals that was the high spot of those years for us. Often we would go down there for rehearsals before the Festival itself began. Oh! the blessed calm and peace of Crag House where Ben and Peter then lived! Music-making, trips to wonderful Suffolk churches such as Blythburgh and Southwold, sitting on the cliff-top at Dunwich catching odd glipses of the drowned church which brought back memories of those seven pagodas all but swallowed by the sea on the East Indian coast at Mahabalipuram. Falling asleep at night to the rhythmic crash of the waves on the shingle beach. Fresh air and talk, lots of it, by the fire if it were a cool night, Ben's quick concise voice, Peter's humorous ecclesiastical drawl. All the cobwebs and pin-pricks of hotel life blown away and dissolved. When Y, at Ben's suggestion, rang the American Embassy to beg them to ask their aeroplanes from the local US aerodrome to fly wide, if fly they must, during the evening concerts, they immediately complied. And there was croquet on the lawn at Red House, then owned by the painter Mary Potter. Ben, my partner, intent on winning; Peter, Yehudi's, slap-happily enjoying himself.

A few days later at the start of the Festival the house party which regularly came together over several years would assemble, one of the nicest house parties I ever belonged to, consisting of Ludwig, Prince of Hessen, with his wife Peg, whom we already knew from Ansbach, and George and Marion Harewood. Added to whom, long-lost friends appeared like ghosts from a past exaggeratedly far away in my mind, musical friends from my mother's Sunday salons and discarded suitors (oh Lord! how could I for a moment have entertained the slimmest thought of marrying Marmaduke?).

One year a small incident occurred to mar those otherwise halycon days. Yehudi, Peter, Ben and I were all sitting in the long fresh grass among the tombs of Blythburgh Church eating a picnic when a *Life Magazine* photographer (actually a very nice man) materialized from behind a couple of gravestones intent upon snapping Y. (The magazine was doing a long piece on his European travels and could be counted upon to sneak up on us at the most uncomfortable moments.) This was one of them and Ben's ire rose like a rocket from the fronds and sent him packing. Poor Y looked miserable – he had not asked for this – he never did nor does seek publicity. How could one explain to Ben and Peter that it followed *him*? A cloud no bigger than a man's hand holding a camera – and yet the destruction of that verdant bliss. We picked up our sandwich papers and went into the cool of the little church, Y and I feeling hang-dog and suddenly involuntarily estranged by that brutal reminder of the broader and necessarily more commercial world to which Y, given the nature of his career, could not help but belong.

Fortunately, the music – Y playing together with those two supreme artists while the sun shone through the clerestory windows – and that special audience Ben and Peter had created, erased that unhappy Press-pistol-shot, and we drove home through Suffolk fields to dinner. Next day we all went to hear Edith Sitwell and Cecil Day-Lewis reading Blake in the village hall. After a very ribald lunch as we sat in the garden, I ventured to ask:

'Dame Edith, do tell me what that particular verse from "The Secrets of the Earth" means? I could never work it out.'

'Dear child,' she said benignly, looking gloriously out of place in her long black dress, swags of amulets, polished hair and poised coif against the flint and brick house, 'I have not the *faintest* idea!'

'But you *sounded* so convincing.'

'Oh, I *am* so glad. I hoped I had . . . .'

Neither the quality of the music nor the special company alone made Aldeburgh so apart. It was the setting also that contributed to the creation of a perfect whole.

I was overcome by the beauty of the surrounding countryside. One day towards the end of June when it was still light I escaped out of the drive and down the country road, past the coppice where sometimes nightingales sang, and on to the shore where the little red brick and half-timbered Moot Hall stood – all alone, a strip of rough grass, a slope of shingles and the North Sea behind it. Suffolk is separate from the rest of England, separate even from the rest of East Anglia. It seems to turn its back on this country and remain as it had been in earlier centuries looking towards Holland across the shallow sea. Even its light is Dutch, with that strange pallid hue, translucent, aqueous, a faint yellow underlying the blue as though the whole sky were illuminated from below, indirectly and secretly. I walked along the straight uncompromising asphalt path that is the only 'esplanade' past huge clumps of wild lupins tugged a little by the evening breeze. The sea slopped in lazy waves throwing brine over the huge pebbles among which those with sharp eyes can detect the amber washed from the ancient forests of North Russia down past Norway to Denmark and across to the Suffolk coast; that coast which was being slowly and inexorably eaten away year by year. Moments such as these revitalized me, symbolizing the whole experience of being at Aldeburgh.

That year the Festival ended with a glorious flourish. A large party of very grand-looking aficionados crammed the somewhat unalluring quarters of the Workmen's Hall near Lowestoft, which had been completely transformed by dozens of kegs and beer barrels. These served as tables on each of which stood, gilded and magnificent, that symbol of money and merriment, champagne, together with plates of delicious canapés, grouped round a small raised and carpeted stage designed for the cabaret. Our party had arrived rather late and the room, lit only by candles, was extremely hot, filled with smartly dressed people and already redolent of fun and jollity. As the heat rose, so did the champagne corks of their own will. One after another like a barrage of rifle-shots they burst high and descended in cascades over the beautiful coiffures and down the elegant bosoms of outraged Dowagers and their companions. Fountains of Heidsieck and Bollinger, Mumm and Veuve Clicqot wasting their bubbles on the desert air. Despite the ruined locks, the soaked décolletées or maybe because of that extra touch of bedraggled fun, the cabaret, a perfectly constructed masque by Peter and a small company who sang Purcell's more bawdy songs, made a sublimely elegant and extravagant finale to that most uplifting of festivals.

# Epilogue

Question asked in an I.Q. test of school children: 'Who or what is Yehudi Menuhin?'

Among the answers were the following delights:

a) He is a world-famous cyclist
b) He is a Chinese emperor
c) It is a kind of Indian food
d) He is the Patron Saint of Music.

So much for the image of Y.M., ingested from countless television appearances in a protean range of rôles and transmuted in young minds' galleries of prominent persons.

Why 'cyclist'? Could that child have been possessed of extra-sensory perception and divined that a man who puts a girdle round the earth in forty minutes nearly every year must be some kind of athlete on wheels?

'Why Chinese emperor'? A muddled memory of eminence and virtuosity coupled with a very strange name?

The child who metamorphosed him into a 'kind of Indian food' came nearest in sheer fact. Yehudi's appearances, standing on his head with his guru in attendance balancing on both hands with his feet in his mouth, adjoined to other such BBC 1, 2, 3 and 4 programmes demonstrating the paramount importance of organic sustenance (better eaten from a horse's nose-bag), would indeed remain in any impressionable young mind welded together in magic harmony.

The 'Patron Saint of Music' I find very touching. Obviously a musical child who had (as I with Diaghilev) made Yehudi his god, benevolent, inspiring and protective.

Fifteen years together had alike created a muddled image in my own mind when at night, too tired to sleep, I tried to analyse our marriage. The Chinese emperor riding a bicycle while chewing Tandoori chicken, wearing a halo composed of shining sharps and flats, was not so very far from the truth. 'A man for all seasons', *The Times* had called him when he played concertos, jazz, chamber music, Indian ragas, conducted his own orchestra and chaired discussions on esoteric subjects for the Bath Festival.

Neville Cardus, the doyen of English critics, once wrote: 'How could Yehudi Menuhin at the age of eighteen or, still more remarkable, at the age of eight, play the violin as though music were his natural form of speech? These are mysteries that we cannot resolve.'

It had always been my unspoken hope that when I abandoned my own life of dancing and acting I might have the great good fortune to harness that energy, that devotion to someone to whom it would be of use. To me love means service in its deepest and highest sense and marriage a sharing of like minds. Whatever the challenges it should fulfil its purpose; however many hardships they would dissolve in the pattern of the whole.

After all I had been trained since early childhood to that self-discipline which is the foundation of all art, the structure which upholds both the creative and the performing artist. What may appear intolerable pressures, harshnesses, a draconian way of life are dissolved in the absolute companionship, the untarnished love burnished by a common vision in terms of achievement, aspiration and fulfilment. Amazingly, in the face of seemingly insuperable difficulties there can emerge a special harmony.

'Affliction is a treasure and scarce any man has enough of it. No man hath affliction enough that is not the matured and ripened by it and made for God by that affliction.' So, in his seventeeth Devotion, Donne gives a cosmic significance to 'affliction', to the darker side of living which, if transmuted by acceptance, becomes brighter and more lasting than itself.

Both Yehudi and I had been born 'trailing clouds of glory', but his were so much greater than mine that they were destined to form a veritable nimbus, durable, a quality of light offered to and recognized by everyone possessed of eyes to see and ears to hear.

'Yehudi Menuhin learnt to put his palette, his beautiful range of colours at the service of his developing mind and musical insights. Only the second-rate remain static.' Neville Cardus again. My task was to create rhythm out of ceaseless travel, to find means to close those ever-recurring gaps with which our frequent absences distanced us from our children, to make an acceptable pattern from a multiple mosaic.

No matter the constant call upon all ones faculties, the effort to keep the equilibrium of an acrobat, to concentrate and remember while always on the move the bewildering amount of enterprises Yehudi's synoptic mind relishes; even though I may on occasion feel like the stoker in the boiler-room keeping the S.S. Menuhin afloat while Y is the captain on the bridge gazing at the inspiring view, I do emerge when my task is done and share the results with him.

Twenty and more years have lengthened this tale and I can repeat with even more conviction that my life with Yehudi has been a celestial one.

# Index